In this new work, Bernd Heine claims that the structure of grammatical categories is predictable to a large extent once we know the range of possible cognitive structures from which they are derived. The author uses as his example the structure of predicative possession, and shows how most of the possessive constructions to be found in the world's languages can be traced back to a small set of basic conceptual patterns. Heine identifies these patterns, and using grammaticalization theory he describes how each affects the word order and morphosyntax of the resulting possessive construction. Illustrating his argument with a wealth of examples, he proposes that grammaticalization theory explains much of the observable typological diversity which characterizes 'have'-constructions in the world's languages.

CAMBRIDGE STUDIES IN LINGUISTICS

General editors: S. R. ANDERSON, J. BRESNAN, B. COMRIE,
W. DRESSLER, C. EWEN, R. HUDDLESTON, R. LASS,
D. LIGHTFOOT, J. LYONS, P. H. MATTHEWS, R. POSNER,
S. ROMAINE, N. V. SMITH, N. VINCENT

Possession

In this series

52 MICHAEL S. ROCHEMONT and PETER W. CULICOVER: English focus constructions and the theory of grammar
53 PHILIP CARR: Linguistic realties: an autonomist metatheory for the generative enterprise
54 EVE SWEETSER: From etymology to pragmatics: metaphorical and cultural aspects of semantic structure
55 REGINA BLASS: Relevance relations in discourse: a study with special reference to Sissala
56 ANDREW CHESTERMAN: On definiteness: a study with special reference to English and Finnish
57 ALLESSANDRA GIORGI and GUISEPPE LONGOBARDI: The syntax of noun phrases: configuration, parameters and empty categories
58 MONIK CHARETTE: Conditions on phonological government
59 M. H. KLAIMAN: Grammatical voice
60 SARAH M. B. FAGAN: The syntax and semantics of middle constructions: a study with special reference to German
61 ANJUM P. SALEEMI: Universal grammar and language learnability
62 STEPHEN R. ANDERSON: A-Morphous morphology
63 LESLEY STIRLING: Switch reference and discourse representation
64 HENK J. VERKUYL: A theory of aspectuality: the interaction between temporal and atemporal structure
65 EVE V. CLARK: The lexicon in acquisition
66 ANTHONY R. WARNER: English auxiliaries: structure and history
67 P. H. MATTHEWS: Grammatical theory in the United States from Bloomfield to Chomsky
68 LJILJANA PROGOVAC: Negative and positive polarity: a binding approach
69 R. M. W. DIXON: Ergativity
70 YAN HUANG: The syntax and pragmatics of anaphora
71 KNUD LAMBRECHT: Information structure and sentence form: Topic, focus, and the mental representations of discourse referents
72 LUIGI BURZIO: Principles of English stress
73 JOHN A. HAWKINS: A performance theory of order and constituency
74 ALICE C. HARRIS and LYLE CAMPBELL: Historical syntax in cross-linguistic perspective
75 LILIANE HAEGEMAN: The syntax of negation
76 PAUL GORRELL: Syntax and parsing
77 GUGLIELMO CINQUE: Italian syntax and universal grammar
78 HENRY SMITH: Restrictiveness in case theory
79 D. ROBERT LADD: Intonational phonology
80 ANDREA MORO: The raising of predicates: predicative noun phrases and the theory of clause structure
81 ROGER LASS: Historical linguistics and language change
82 JOHN M. ANDERSON: A notional theory of syntactic categories
83 BERND HEINE: Possession: cognitive sources, forces and grammaticalization

Supplementary volumes

LILIANE HAEGEMAN: Theory and description in generative syntax: A case study in West Flemish
A. E. BACKHOUSE: The lexical field of taste: A semantic study of Japanese taste terms
NIKOLAUS RITT: Quantity adjustment: Vowel lengthening and shortening in early Middle English

Earlier issues not listed are also available

POSSESSION
Cognitive sources, forces, and grammaticalization

BERND HEINE
Professor of African Studies, University of Cologne

CAMBRIDGE
UNIVERSITY PRESS

CAMBRIDGE UNIVERSITY PRESS
Cambridge, New York, Melbourne, Madrid, Cape Town, Singapore, São Paulo

Cambridge University Press
The Edinburgh Building, Cambridge CB2 2RU, UK

Published in the United States of America by Cambridge University Press, New York

www.cambridge.org
Information on this title: www.cambridge.org/9780521550376

© Cambridge University Press 1997

This publication is in copyright. Subject to statutory exception
and to the provisions of relevant collective licensing agreements,
no reproduction of any part may take place without
the written permission of Cambridge University Press.

First published 1997
This digitally printed first paperback version 2006

A catalogue record for this publication is available from the British Library

Library of Congress Cataloguing in Publication data

Heine, Bernd, 1939–
Possession: cognitive sources, forces, and grammaticalization /
Bernd Heine.
    p. cm. – (Cambridge Studies in Linguistics : 83)
Includes bibliographical references and index.
ISBN 0 521 55037 8
1. Grammar, Comparative and general – Possessives. 2. Cognition.
3. Grammar, Comparative and general – Grammaticalization. I. Title.
II. Series.
P299.P67H45 1997
415–dc20   96-26940 CIP

ISBN-13 978-0-521-55037-6 hardback
ISBN-10 0-521-55037-8 hardback

ISBN-13 978-0-521-02413-6 paperback
ISBN-10 0-521-02413-7 paperback

For Tom Givón

Contents

List of tables and figures		*page* xi
Preface		xiii
Abbreviations		xv
1	**The state**	1
1.1	Introduction	1
1.2	Distinctions	9
1.3	Some possessive notions	33
1.4	Problems	41
2	**The process**	45
2.1	Sources	45
2.2	Grammaticalization	76
2.3	Targets	89
2.4	How to reconstruct schemas	96
2.5	Language-internal variation	104
2.6	Schemas and possessive notions	117
2.7	Further issues	134
3	**On attributive possession**	143
3.1	From source to target	144
3.2	Specification	156
3.3	On 'possessor ascension'	163
3.4	On inalienability	172
3.5	Attributive and predicative possession	183
3.6	Conclusions	186
4	**From possession to aspect**	187
4.1	Parallels	188
4.2	Specifying possession	190

x   *Contents*

4.3	Patterns of shift	195
4.4	Existence, possession, location, and other domains	202
4.5	Conclusions	207
5	**Evaluation**	209
5.1	Alternative approaches	209
5.2	Event schemas	222
5.3	On categories and universals	224
5.4	On explanation	228
5.5	Conclusions	233
	Appendix: A world-wide survey of 'have'-constructions	240
	References	245
	Index of Authors	264
	Index of Languages	267
	Index of Subjects	270

Tables

1.1.	Definiteness vs. indefiniteness in 'have'- and 'belong'-constructions: Typical associations.	30
1.2.	Some prototypical properties of possessive notions.	39
2.1.	A formulaic description of schemas used for the expression of predicative possession.	47
2.2.	Source schemas for 'have'-constructions in 100 languages according to continents.	75
2.3.	Contrastive properties of source schemas for predicative possession.	91
2.4.	Typical correlations between source schemas and 'have'- and 'belong'-constructions.	92
2.5.	The main possessive constructions in Manding and the notions expressed by them.	123
2.6.	The main stages in the development from location to possession in Ewe.	126
2.7.	The main stages in the development from existence to possession in Ewe.	128
2.8.	The main constructions of predicative possession in Ewe and the notions expressed by them.	133
2.9.	Typical participant encoding in 'have'-constructions according to source schema.	135
3.1.	A formulaic description of source schemas used for the expression of attributive possession.	144
3.2.	The distribution of inalienable and alienable nouns in Pima-Papago.	181
5.1.	Correspondences between event schemas and Locker's propositional types.	210
5.2.	Correspondences between event schemas and the classifications proposed by Hengeveld (1992) and Stassen (1995).	213
5.3.	Semantic relationships according to Casagrande and Hale (1967:167).	223

Figures

1.1.	A prototype characterization of possessive notions.	40
2.1.	The Overlap Model.	82
3.1.	A radial network of genitival meanings (based on Nikiforidou 1991).	156

Preface

The claim made in this work is that the structure of grammatical categories is predictable to a large extent once we know the range of possible cognitive structures from which they are derived. This claim is tested here with reference to one example, viz. the structure of predicative possession. It would seem that most of the possessive constructions to be found in the languages of the world can be traced back to a small set of basic conceptual patterns. These patterns are identified in this work and the way each of them affects the word order and morphosyntax of the resulting 'have'-construction is described within the framework of grammaticalization theory (see Heine, Claudi, and Hünnemeyer 1991, Hopper and Traugott 1993, Bybee, Perkins, and Pagliuca 1994 for references). It is argued that much of the typological diversity that characterizes 'have'-constructions in the languages of the world can be explained with reference to the principles of grammaticalization proposed in those works.

The present work has profited greatly from the assistance and co-operation of a number of colleagues. Most of all, my gratitude is due to Ulrike Claudi who, in addition to accompanying my research with constructive criticism, also gave me access to her unpublished paper on 'To have or not to have: on the conceptual base of predicative possession in some African languages' (Claudi 1986), which already contains a number of the basic notions to be discussed below. Furthermore, my gratitude is due to the members of the research team working on grammaticalization at the University of Cologne, in particular to Tom Güldemann, Ingo Heine, Christa Kilian-Hatz, Christa König, Tania Kouteva, Heinz Roberg, and Mathias Schladt, and to my colleagues Leila Behrens, Jürgen Broschart, Claudia Brugman, Joan Bybee, Norbert Cyffer, Karen Ebert, Michele Emanatian, Suzanne Fleischman, Zygmunt Frajzyngier, Orin Gensler, Tom Givón, Paul Hopper, George Lakoff, Frank Lichtenberk, Doris Payne, Mechthild Reh, Hans-Jürgen Sasse, Fritz Serzisko, Leon Stassen, Christel Stolz, Thomas Stolz, Eve Sweetser, Leonard Talmy, Elizabeth

Traugott, and Peter Trudgill for critical comments and advice. I also wish to thank Hassan Adam (Swahili), Kossi Tossou (Ewe), and Mohamed Touré (Bambara) for their patience in providing me with information on their mother tongue, and Hilary Chappell, Ulrike Claudi, Martin Haspelmath, Tania Kouteva, Dirk Otten, Thomas Stolz, and Nigel Vincent for substantive comments on earlier versions of the manuscript on which this book is based.

Finally, I wish to thank the *Volkswagen-Stiftung* (Volkswagen Foundation) for having sponsored my visit to the University of California at Berkeley and Stanford University during the Winter Semester of 1993/4, and to the *Deutsche Forschungsgemeinschaft* for generously sponsoring my research on grammaticalization and the development of grammatical functions.

Abbreviations

A	subject of a transitive or ditransitive verb	EXIST	existential marker
ABL	ablative case	F	feminine gender
ABS	absolute	FOC	focus
ABSOL	absolutive	GEN	genitive marker
ABST	abstract possession	IMP	imperative
ACC	accusative	INAL	inalienable possession
ADP	adposition	IN/A	inanimate alienable possession
AL	alienable	IN/I	inanimate inalienable possession
ALL	allative		
ART	article	INSTR	instrument
ASP	aspect	IPFV	imperfective
ASSOC	associative	KI	kinship term
AUX	auxiliary	LOC	locative
BO	body-part term	M	masculine gender
CAR	carrier	N	noun
CL	noun class	NEU	neuter gender
CLASS	classifier	NF	non-feminine gender
CLFR	classifier	NOM	nominative
CLIT	clitic	NSP	non-specific
COM	comitative	O	object of a transitive verb
COMPL	completive	OBL	oblique case
CONN	connector	P	patientive object
COP	copula	PART	participle
DAT	dative case	PERF	perfect
DEF	marker of definiteness	PERM	permanent possession
DEM	demonstrative	PFV	perfective
DUAL	dual	PHYS	physical possession
EMPH	emphatic	PL	plural
ERG	ergative	POESS	possessive

PRES	present tense	TAM	tense, aspect, and modality
PRS	presentative marker		
PRT	particle	TEMP	temporary possession
Q	question marker	TNS	tense
REC	recipient	TOP	topic
S	subject of an intransitive verb	UNSP	unspecified third-person
		1	first person, class 1
SG	singular	2	second person, class 2
SPCF	specifier	3	third person, class 3
SPEC	specific	4, etc.	class 4, etc.
SU	subject of intransitive verb		

1 *The state*

1.1 Introduction

Possession is a universal domain, that is, any human language can be expected to have conventionalized expressions for it. Nevertheless, when working on the linguistic expression of possession one is likely to be confronted with a number of problems.

One of these problems relates to the cognitive nature of possession. Possession belongs to the kind of concepts that tend to be described as being inherently vague or fuzzy. The English verb *have* has been called 'colorless' (Buck 1949:740) and the possessive concepts expressed by it are said to be indeterminate; *have* has even been described as an 'unsuitable lexical item':

> Take an expression like *a tree has leaves*. In passing we may observe the oddness of this verb *have*, which can appear in a wide variety of contexts, and express a variety of very different relations: *You have a cold, Mary has a sick grandmother, Bill has a good job, Who has the exact time?* and so on. All of these at least share the feature that if you were to take away your cold, Mary's grandmother, or Bill's job, you, Bill, and Mary would still be there intact. But in addition to *a tree has leaves*, we can say *a tree has branches, a tree has roots, a tree has a trunk, a tree has bark*. Take away all the things that a tree 'has', and there is no tree left to 'have' them. (Bickerton 1990:56)

In a similar fashion, possession has occasionally been described as a concept that is neither conceptually nor linguistically basic, or that is not of universal significance. Miller and Johnson-Laird say:

> The ordinary business of life can be conducted without explicit recourse to the conceptual core of possession; people need only grasp the interrelations between having, buying, giving, and so forth. Indeed, many people have only the vaguest notion of the conceptual core. There may be whole societies that do not grasp the core explicitly; it may be embodied in their conventions and forms of social behavior rather than in their mental lexicons. (Miller and Johnson-Laird 1976:558)

Irrespective of how this statement is to be interpreted, I am not aware of any language that would not dispose of some explicit means for expressing, for example, 'This is my wife' or 'I have no food.' But possessive expressions are used for a wide range of experiences and conceptual structures, and some authors therefore claim that linguistic expressions for possession are meaningless, that is, that English items like *have* or *of* are semantically vacuous (cf. Bach 1967). Furthermore, the wide range of meanings expressed by possessive constructions has induced some authors to propose fairly abstract descriptions of possession. For Langacker (1993:8), for example, the various uses of the English genitive have in common that one entity 'is invoked as a reference point for purposes of establishing mental contact with another', and some authors would go so far as to claim that possession simply involves any abstract relation between two entities.

We noted above that the range of meanings expressed by possessive constructions is so wide that referring to all of these meanings as 'possessive' ones would be misleading, and that possessive expressions are likely have other, non-possessive, meanings in addition. For example, there is no doubt that (1a) is an instance of possession, but what about (1b)?

(1)   (a) Liz has a car.
       (b) Liz has a problem.

To take care of cases like (1b), alternative terms such as 'relational', 'associative', etc. have been proposed to refer to concepts that include possession but are not confined to it (cf. Creissels 1979). In a similar vein, Hawkins (1981) claims that possession, at least in English, is merely one particular case of what, following Chomsky (1972), he calls 'intrinsic connection'; whether or not possession obtains, he argues, is determined by context and depends on world knowledge and possibly belief systems.

Nevertheless, even if possessive constructions tend to cover a wide range of relations or associations between two concepts, there are limits. For example, reversing the two participants in (1) would result in a non-sensical sentence: **A car has Liz* is not considered to be an acceptable utterance. Similarly, while *the cat's tail* is acceptable, *the tail's cat* is usually not.

1.1.1   How to deal with possession

In earlier accounts, interest in possession has focussed on how to delimit this domain and to define its status *vis-à-vis* other ontological entities. A number of problems have been highlighted, the main ones being discussed in section 1.4. Among the descriptive concepts that were proposed to deal with possession, 'control' has perhaps most frequently been named, for obvious reasons: prototypical instances of possession imply some kind of control of the possessor over the possessee (see especially Hagège 1993:93ff.). The relevance of the notion becomes debatable in the case of inalienable possession, especially in many cases of kinship relations (e.g. *John's father, John has three uncles*), and in the case of inanimate possessors (e.g. *the windows of this house, This house has ten windows*). Other problems surrounding the use of the term 'control' relate to the fact that it has been associated with at least two different senses. Control is said to involve the ability of the possessor to manipulate the possessee; the question is whether manipulation includes the possibility of discontinuing ownership or not. The phrase *my head* implies control in the former but not in the latter sense: I can manipulate my head in various ways but I cannot normally terminate ownership of it. Accordingly, while some authors argue that body-part possession does not involve control (Chappell and McGregor 1996b), others say it does (cf. Lynch 1973:6; Brugman 1988:229).

Another frequently named property of possession is contiguity of location or spatial proximity between possessor and possessee (Brugman 1988:230; Taylor 1989b:202). As we will see in section 1.3, this property is in fact relevant to canonical instances of possession, but, like control, does not qualify as a definitional criterion.

This does not exhaust the list of concepts that have been proposed to define or characterize possession. One might mention, for example, Langacker's (1987) definition of the relation between the possessor and possessee in terms of a 'sphere of influence', or Brugman's (1988:231ff.) 'schema of interest or involvement'.

Students of law and other people draw a distinction between possession and ownership. This distinction is in fact relevant to the present topic and we will return to it in section 1.3. However, we will not deal with it in any great detail, first, because it appears to be highly culture-specific while our interest is primarily with cross-linguistic regularities. Second, there are a number of quite divergent ways in which this distinction is treated in the relevant literature. For example, while some authors argue that possession and ownership are clearly different things (e.g. Bickerton 1981), others treat the two as being essentially the same (cf. Gentner 1975:212). Rather, we will propose a more detailed classification of possessive notions that serves as a basis for further analysis. 'Possession' will be used as a cover term for all these notions, or any combination thereof.

Another problem concerns the cross-linguistic and cross-cultural significance of the possessive domain. Is it in fact a universal domain, as some argue, or is it culture-specific, that is, does it occur in certain parts of the world but not in others, or did it evolve during certain periods in the history of mankind but not during others?

There is a related problem that has to do with the fact that possession has been widely studied in western societies but much less so in other parts of the world. The implications this fact may have for a theory of possession are considerable. For example, Bach (1967:479) notes that the situation in English, where we have a special verb-like form for 'have', 'is almost pathological' considering the fact that constructions in other languages corresponding to the English 'have'-sentences are notoriously varied. Bach's observation was in fact not new; rather, he was echoing what other authors had claimed earlier (e.g. Locker 1954; Löfstedt 1963).

From such observations it follows that defining possession is perhaps the most crucial problem. For example, should one aim at a definition in terms of linguistic properties? While most linguists will probably answer this question in the affirmative, there are some who are looking for an extra-linguistic definition. Two proposals in this direction are particularly noteworthy. For Seiler (1983:4–7), possession is essentially a conceptual relationship pattern: he defines possession as 'the relationship between a human being and his kinsmen, his body parts, his material belongings, his cultural and intellectual products'. What distinguishes possession from other relational domains such as location, he observes, is that it is bio-cultural. Like location, but unlike valence, it is binary, in that it involves two items, the possessor and the item possessed or, as we will say here, the possessee.

Seiler (1977b) proposes a cross-linguistically relevant distinction between two kinds of semanto-syntactic configurations, which he refers to, respectively, as the 'Agent of an Act'- and the 'Possessor of an Act'-configurations. Compared to the former, the 'Possessor of an Act'- configuration is said to have the following properties (Seiler 1977b:174–9): (i) it is time-stable (ii) it leaves the dichotomy AGENT VS. OBJECT unspecified (iii) this means, for example, that instances of this configuration have properties in common with both active and passive sentences (iv) at the same time, AGENT and POSSESSOR are mutually exclusive entities. The difference between the two configurations is portrayed in the following formulas, where (2a) represents the active and (2b) the passive form of the 'Agent of an Act'-configuration, while (2c) is the 'Possessor of an Act'-configuration (parentheses indicate that the relevant term is marginal).

(2) Three kinds of semanto-syntactic configurations according to Seiler (1977b)
(a) AGENT ACT (OBJECT)
(b) (AGENT) ACT OBJECT
(c) (OBJECT) ACT (POSSESSOR)

That a definition exclusively in terms of linguistic parameters would be inappropriate, is in fact argued for independently by Taylor (1989b:202–3, 1989a:679ff.). He views possession as an *experiential gestalt*, and defines it as a prototypical notion involving a constellation of properties such as the ones listed in (3).

(3) (a) The possessor is a specific human being.
(b) The possessee is a specific concrete thing (usually inanimate), not an abstract.
(c) The relation between the two is an exclusive one, that is, for each possessee there is only one possessor.
(d) The possessor has the right to make use of the possessee; other people can make use of the possessee only with the permission of the possessor.
(e) The relationship of possession is a long-term one, measured in months or years rather than in minutes or hours.
(f) In linguistic discourse, the possessor is presented as a referential entity.

This does not conclude the list of properties that are associated with prototypical instances of possession. Taylor (1989a, 1989b:202) proposes the following properties in addition: the possessor's rights over the possessee are invested in him/her in virtue of a transaction, i.e. through purchase, donation, or inheritance, the possessor is responsible for the possessee, and the two are in close spatial proximity.

It goes without saying that not all instances of possession discussed here exhibit the entire range of these properties. Nevertheless, the more of the properties are present, the more does the expression concerned correspond to the prototypical notion of possession. Canonical instances of possession are characterized by the presence of most, if not all, of the properties listed in (3) and whenever disagreement arises as to whether a given linguistic expression is an instance of possession one may return to this characterization.

Most treatments of the subject do in fact take some highly prototypical instance as a point of departure for understanding and/or defining possession; the reader is referred to Snare (1972) and Miller and Johnson-Laird (1976) for what may be said to be classical examples. But things are more complex: which particular kind of possessive relationship is most 'prototypical' or 'basic' depends on the perspective one adopts and on the conceptual distinctions one decides to consider and ignore, respectively.

1.1.2 The present volume

The objective of this work is to study why possession is expressed the way it is. Thus, our concern is with explanation. The observations to be made are based on findings on grammaticalization, in particular on the following assumptions:

(i) The structure of grammatical categories is predictable to a large extent once we know the range of possible cognitive structures from which they are derived. Underlying this claim there are assumptions of the following kind:
(ii) Grammatical categories can be traced back to semantically concrete source concepts.
(iii) For each grammatical category there is only a small pool of possible source concepts.
(iv) While the choice of sources is determined primarily by universal ways of conceptualization, it is also influenced by other factors, especially by areal forces.

These assumptions are based on research carried out in the course of the last decade within the paradigm of grammaticalization theory; the reader is referred to the relevant works for more details (especially Traugott and Heine 1991a, 1991b; Heine, Claudi, and Hünnemeyer 1991; Hopper and Traugott 1993; Bybee, Perkins, and Pagliuca 1994; Stolz 1991, 1994). We will argue here that most expressions in the languages of the world for what corresponds to 'have'-constructions in English can be described as conforming to the assumptions just made.

The label 'have'-construction to be used throughout this book is suggestive of a Euro-centric perspective according to which verbs meaning 'have' form the or a primary means of expressing possession (Hilary Chappell, p.c.). As we shall see below, a verb corresponding to the notion of a 'have'-verb in many European languages is much less common than one might be inclined to believe.

The book also falls within the scope of what is sometimes referred to as typological universal grammar as developed by Greenberg (1963b; see also 1978a, 1978b), Givón (1979, 1995), Comrie (1981), Mallinson and Blake

(1981), Bybee (1985), Bybee, Perkins, and Pagliuca (1994), Croft (1991), and others. What these works have in common in particular is that they aim at establishing cross-linguistic regularities based on world-wide samples of languages. At the same time, however, the approach used here differs from that tradition in arguing that language structure is derivative of the cognitive forces that gave rise to it and, hence, our concern is primarily with extra-linguistic forces.

From what has just been said it follows that, more than in previous works on typological universal grammar, our concern will be with explanation, more precisely, with external explanation. The main explanatory parameters used are cognition and diachrony.

Cognition involves the acquisition, storage, retrieval, and use of knowledge. We will confine ourselves to one aspect of cognition, namely to the interrelationship between different concepts and the way linguistic expressions used for one of them are extended to also refer to other concepts. We will call the process concerned conceptual transfer. Our task will be to identify and describe salient processes of conceptual transfer relating to the domain of possession and, by doing so, to understand why possessive constructions are formed the way they are.

Conceptual transfer takes place in time and, hence, will be treated as a diachronic notion. Our findings thus are based on hypotheses on diachronic development. This means that the processes that we shall be concerned with can be accounted for with reference to diachronic principles, and that our findings are falsifiable by means of diachronic evidence. This also means that the terminology employed must be in accordance with that conventionally used in works on historical linguistics. Thus, labels such as derivation and reconstruction, even if they are meant primarily to refer to synchronic language use, must not be at variance with the interpretation these terms would receive if used in a strictly diachronic sense.

Thus, the evidence on which our hypotheses rest are linguistic on the one hand, and diachronic on the other. The methodology employed is simple. Suppose we discover that there is a linguistic form somewhere in Latin America, eastern Asia, or Europe which simultaneously denotes possession and verbal aspect; then we are led to conclude that the former is historically prior. The evidence for such a conclusion is twofold. First, it is based on attested cases of diachronic change; we know, for example, that the English construction exemplified in (4a) preceded constructions of the type (4b) in time. Second, it is based on generalizations on grammaticalization, according to which a linguistic item, like English *have*, that combines the functions of both a main verb and an auxiliary, was first used in its former capacity before its use was extended to express auxiliary functions (see especially Heine 1993; Bybee, Perkins, and Pagliuca 1994).

(4)   (a) He has a car.
        (b) He has left.

The relationship between structures like (4a) and (4b) can be described and accounted for in a principled way, as has been done in standard works on grammaticalization. Since we are dealing with a process that either has or has not taken place, such an account is falsifiable. While our goal is to account for synchronic language structure, the findings presented are based on, and hence must be in accordance with, diachronic facts.

One of the key notions proposed is that of event schema, which will be introduced at the beginning of chapter 2. As we shall see there, event schemas are propositional in nature, they relate to ontological domains such as action, location, etc., and they are abstracted from the way we experience our environment and describe our experiences when communicating with other members of our species. There is no evidence to suggest that event schemas are innate structures; what Comrie observes on language universals also applies here: 'innateness remains empty because it is just a name given to the set of language universals, and using this name should not blind us to the fact that a name is not an explanation' (Comrie 1981:24). The relevance of event schemas cannot only be manifested by means of linguistic evidence; as we shall see in chapter 5 (5.2), essentially the same kind of notion has been identified in anthropological works. Furthermore, we will distinguish between source schemas, that is, event schemas providing the structural templates of transfer, and target schemas, which describe the outcome of transfer.

The book is based mainly on the analysis of published sources on the language of possession. Accordingly, the data presented are accessible via the references provided. In addition, data elicited from field research carried out by the author on African languages, most of all on Ewe and Manding, and from a quantitative survey, have been utilized. The latter survey was carried out specifically to ascertain that the description presented is in accordance with the linguistic facts to be found across genetic and areal boundaries.

The work is divided into five chapters. In this introductory chapter 1, seven salient possessive notions are distinguished. These notions serve as a basis for cross-linguistic comparisons, to be carried out in subsequent chapters. In 1.4, a catalogue of questions that have been raised in previous works on possession is presented.

Chapter 2 forms the heart of the book, and it is considerably longer than the remaining chapters. In this chapter, a catalogue of event schemas that commonly serve as structural templates for the expression of possession is identified. In section 2.2, some effects of the process leading from event schema to possessive construction are discussed. The semantic structure of possessive constructions is examined in 2.3 on the basis of the notions proposed in chapter 1. In 2.5 and 2.6, the conceptual skeleton presented in 2.1 is put into perspective by relating the schemas and possessive notions to language development and language structure.

The book is based essentially on the analysis of predicative possession, more specifically of 'have'-constructions. Nevertheless, chapter 3 is devoted to some issues relating to the grammaticalization of the main patterns of attributive possession. As will be argued there, the same kind of schemas that can be held responsible for the growth of predicative possession can also be held responsible for attributive possession.

While possession is analysed with reference to the forces that give rise to its expression, chapter 4 illustrates that possession may itself be the source for even more abstract concepts, the example looked at being verbal aspect. The relevance of the approach adopted in this book is the topic of the final chapter 5, by relating the present framework to alternative approaches and views. In section 5.4, an attempt is made to answer the questions raised in the introductory chapter (1.4). The main findings made in the course of the book are briefly summarized and some conclusions drawn in the final section 5.5.

1.2   Distinctions

A wide range of classifications have been proposed to account for the various manifestations of possession. One of them is based on conceptual properties of either the possessor or the possessee, or both. With regard to the former one could distinguish, for example, between human possessors (e.g. *I have a house*) and non-human possessors (*This house has two bedrooms*); with regard to the possessee, a distinction between concrete possession (*I have two cats*), social possession (*I have two sisters*), and abstract possession (*I have no time*) could be made. Miller and Johnson-Laird (1976) distinguish between three kinds of possession, which are (a) inherent, (b) accidental, and (c) physical possession. The way these three differ from one another can be demonstrated with the following English example volunteered by them (1976:565): (a) *He owns an umbrella*, (b) *but she's borrowed it*, (c) *though she doesn't have it with her*. As we will see below, the use of the term 'inherent' is at variance with the way the term is used by other authors.

1.2.1   Alienable vs. inalienable and other distinctions

A particularly widespread distinction to be observed in the languages of the world concerns what is commonly referred to as that between inalienable and alienable possession. A wealth of alternative terminologies and characterizations have been proposed. The inalienable category has also been called, for example, 'intimate', 'inherent', 'inseparable', or even 'abnormal', while the alienable categories have been labelled 'non-intimate', 'accidental', 'acquired', 'transferable', or 'normal' (cf. Voeltz 1976; Ultan 1978; Seiler 1983; Nichols 1988, 1992:116ff.; Chappell and McGregor 1996b). Nevertheless we will use the traditional labels even if they are not adequate in every respect.

All evidence that has become available so far suggests that whenever there is a language having a grammatical distinction between an inalienable and an alienable category, then the former is a closed class, that is, its membership is limited, while the latter category is an open class (Nichols 1988:562; see 3.4 below).

Superficially, the distinction is a straightforward one: Items that cannot normally be separated from their owners are inalienable, while all others are alienable. Thus, items belonging to any of the following conceptual domains are likely to be treated as inalienable:

(a)   Kinship roles.
(b)   Body-parts.
(c)   Relational spatial concepts, like 'top', 'bottom', 'interior', etc.
(d)   Parts of other items, like 'branch', 'handle', etc.
(e)   Physical and mental states, like 'strength', 'fear', etc. (cf. Lichtenberk 1985:105).
(f)   Nominalizations, where the 'possessee' is a verbal noun, for example 'his singing', 'the planting of bananas'.

In addition, there are a number of individual concepts in a given language that may also be treated inalienably, such as 'name', 'voice', 'smell', 'shadow', 'footprint', 'property', 'home', etc.

Based on Lévy-Bruhl's (1914) pioneering description of inalienability,

1.2 Distinctions

Chappell and McGregor (1996b) propose the following four kinds of relationship that tend to be associated with inalienability: (a) a close biological or social bond between two people (e.g. kin); (b) integral relationship (e.g. body-parts and other parts of a whole); (c) inherent relationship (e.g. spatial relations); (d) essential for one's livelihood or survival.

Several attempts were made to develop alienability scales or hierarchies that would determine which of the domains just mentioned are most likely to be treated, respectively, as inalienable or alienable within a given language or across languages (Seiler 1983:13; Haiman 1985a:130). Nichols (1992:572) proposes the following implicational hierarchy for the semantic membership of inalienable classes: (i) kin terms and/or body-parts; (ii) part-whole and/or spatial relations; and (iii) culturally basic possessed items (e.g. arrows, domestic animals). She observes, for example, that if a language includes nouns other than kin terms and body-parts among its 'inalienables', usually it includes both kin terms and body-parts as well. At the same time, however, Nichols (1988, 1992) points out that

> inalienable possession is not primarily a semantic distinction but the automatic consequence of the closer formal bonding that results in head-marked possession: inalienables typically include kin terms, part/wholes and/or body-parts, nouns which are most likely to occur possessed in discourse, and the formal marking of inalienability simply grammaticalizes that possession. (Nichols 1992:121–2)

A similar view has also been voiced by Chappell and McGregor (1989, 1996b): these authors conclude that none of the attempts discussed above was really successful. For example, the way the three core domains (a) kinship, (b) body-parts, and (c) spatial relations are treated in the languages of the world differs to such an extent that it would be futile to look for a universal hierarchy. There are languages like Paamese or Tinrin, that treat all three, (a), (b), and (c), as inalienable, while in many Australian languages (b) but not (a) is inalienable, in Ewe and other languages again, (a) and (c) but not (b) are inalienable, and in most Athabaskan languages, just (a) and (b) are treated as inalienable.

The way inalienability is defined in a given case or in a given language is largely dependent on culture-specific conventions. In some languages, concepts like 'neighbour', 'house', 'bed,' 'fire', 'clothes', or 'spear' belong to the inalienable category, while in other languages they do not. Languages do in fact differ considerably with regard to where the boundary between inalienably and alienably possessed items is located. Saker, a language of New Guinea, has a consistent alienable/inalienable marking on attributive possession, where the inalienable category consists of kinship terms, body-parts, and relational nouns including parts of the whole, while all other nouns are alienable, yet the nouns for 'husband', 'wife', and 'child' also belong to the alienable category (Z'graggen 1965:124). In Fijian, 'wife' is constructed inalienably, while in the closely related Melanesian language Lenakel, this item receives the alienable morphology (Lynch 1973:15).

That it is ultimately possible on the basis of culture-specific knowledge to understand why a given noun is treated as alienable or inalienable has been claimed by Crowley with reference to Paamese, a language spoken on Paama Island in the Republic of Vanuatu (Crowley 1996; cf. Chappell and McGregor 1996b). In this language, the inalienable category is made up of consanguineal kin, inseparable body-parts including internal organs essential to life, personal representation, body products that are exuded through normal bodily functions or are permanently associated with a person, as well as some nouns for part–whole relations, imprints, spatial orientation, and 'best food'.

Perhaps the clearest way of marking the alienability distinction is by encoding each of the two with a different morphology. This happens in many languages worldwide, at least within the noun phrase. Almost invariably, when this is the case, the inalienable category is not formally marked, that is, it has zero expression, while the alienable category receives some formal marking (cf. Svorou 1993:198ff.). Thus, in the following example, there is no possessive marking when the noun is used inalienably, as in (5a), while the same noun is associated with the marker *ge-* when used alienably, as in (5b). Not infrequently, there are other morphosyntactic distinctions in addition, such as differences in the order of meaningful elements, as in (5): (5a) presents the inalienable use where the possessor follows the possessee, and (5b) the alienable form showing the reverse order. Chappell and McGregor (1989, 1996b) found many languages where nouns with overlapping inalienable and alienable uses are a common feature. For an attempt to explain distinctions like that in (5), see Claudi and Heine (1989).

(5)   Aroma (Melanesian, Oceanic; Lynch 1973:6)

    (a) rauparaupa-ku
        picture-   my
        'a picture of me'
    (b) ge-   ku rauparaupa
        POSS-my picture
        'a picture in my possession'

The linguistic evidence that has become available in the course of the last decades suggests that the distinction inalienable vs. alienable is a salient one across cultures. Nevertheless, its occurrence appears to be constrained by certain linguistic factors. Thus, it has been argued on the basis of cross-linguistic comparisons that the distinction is a common one in certain types of languages, such as stative-active languages or languages characterized by the use of head-marked possession but uncommon in other kinds of languages (Nichols 1992:121ff.).

The observations made above might suggest that the distinction is confined to the structure of noun phrases. As we will see below, it is also relevant to the structure of clauses in general and to predicative possession in particular. One way of marking the distinction is by means of a clausal syntax. The 'mechanisms' perhaps most frequently employed have been described as 'possessor deletion' and 'possessor ascension'; the latter has also been referred to as 'possessor raising' or 'possessor promotion'. Both mechanisms are quite widespread in the languages of the world (see 3.3 below); we can illustrate them with the following examples from Haya. (6) is an instance of possessor deletion: As (6a) shows, the possessor is not encoded if the possessee is inalienable, but it has to be encoded if the possessee is alienable, as in (6b). If, nevertheless, no possessor is encoded in the case of alienable nouns, as in (6c), then there is no possessor or the possessor is not specified.

(6) Haya (Bantu, Niger-Congo; Hyman 1977:100)
    (a) n-k-óógy' émikôno
        I-k-wash   hands
        'I washed my hands.' (Lit.: 'I washed hands.')
    (b) n-k-óógy' émótoká yange
        I-k-wash   car   my
        'I washed my car.'
    (c) n-k-óógy' émótoka
        I- k-wash   car
        'I washed the/a car.'

Possessor ascension is said to come in when, by affecting the possessee, one is also affecting the possessor (cf. Hyman 1977:107). The Haya noun *ómukôno* 'hand, arm' is treated as inalienable and, hence, it triggers possessor ascension, as in (7a). *énkoni* 'stick', however, is alienable and possessor ascension, as in (7b), is therefore not possible; rather, alienable possessees encode the possessor as a possessive modifier, as in (7c).

(7) Haya (Bantu, Niger-Congo; Hyman 1977:101)
    (a) n-ka-hénd' ómwáán' ómukôno
        I-ka-break   child   arm
        'I broke the child's arm.' (Lit.: 'I broke the child the arm.')

(b) *n-ka-hénd' ómwáán' énkoni
    I-ka-break child   stick
    (Lit.: 'I broke the child the stick.')
(c) n-ka-hénd' énkoni y' ómwáana
    I-ka-break stick of child
    'I broke the stick of the child.'

Note that (7a) represents only one type of possessor ascension; concerning other types, see Blake (1984:438), Chappell and McGregor (1996b; see 3.3 below). The significance of possessor ascension can be illustrated with the following examples from German.

(8)   German
    (a) Mein Hund hat Karls   Knie geleckt.
        my   dog has of.Karl knee licked
        'My dog licked Karl's knee.'
    (b) Mein Hund hat Karl   das Knie geleckt.
        my   dog has to.Karl the knee licked
        'My dog licked "to Karl" the knee.'
    (c) Mein Hund hat Karl am   Knie geleckt.
        my   dog has Karl at.the knee licked
        'My dog licked Karl on his knee.'

Apart from differences in their semantics and pragmatics, which we will not be concerned with here, the three sentences in (8) differ in the fact that the possessor (*Karl*) is encoded as a genitival modifier in (8a) and as a dative adjunct in (8b), while in (8c) the possessee (*Knie*), functioning as a kind of restrictive specifier of the possessor, is presented as a locative adjunct. In the tradition from which the possessor ascension terminology is derived, the structure exemplified in (8a) would be regarded as basic while (8b) and (8c) represent common types of ascension in that the possessor is promoted or raised from non-argument status in (8a) to argument status in (8b) and (8c), being encoded as an indirect object in (8b) and a direct object in (8c).

The theoretical framework from which ascension and related terms are derived is not ours: There is no conclusive evidence to suggest that (8a) represents less basic a structure than either (8b) or (8c). We will return to this subject in chapter 3 (3.3).

Another way of marking possessive categories like inalienable, alienable, etc., is by means of morphology, as is the case perhaps most clearly in the possessive classifier systems of Oceanic languages. Generalizations that have been proposed on these systems include the following (Lichtenberk 1985:106, 185; see also Lichtenberk 1983):

1.2 Distinctions 15

(i) If a language has only one possessive classifier then the only function of the classifier is to mark the possession as alienable.

(ii) If a language has two possessive classifiers then these consist of an Alimentary and a General one.

(iii) If a language has three possessive classifiers, the categories distinguished are Food, Drink, and General.

(iv) If a language has a fourth possessive classifier in addition then the category expressed by it is Valued Possession.

Possessive classifier systems have a number of properties that are reminiscent of gender systems, an observation that has been made time and again by students of Oceanic languages (see Lichtenberk 1985:125). First, both involve a semantically motivated classification of the nouns of the language concerned. Second, presence of agreement, which is usually considered to be a necessary criterion for the presence of a gender system (cf. Corbett 1991:105), can be said to be present as well in the case of the inalienable/alienable distinction, in that the relationship between the possessive morphosyntax and the two classes of nouns may be interpreted, at least in some languages, as a kind of agreement. If one were to follow some classical definitions proposed for gender systems one would in fact be led to conclude that the distinction is suggestive of a gender distinction. Hockett (1958:231), for example, defines genders as 'classes of nouns reflected in the behavior of associated words', and this definition would seem to also take care of the inalienable/alienable distinction. Third, as in the case of gender systems, the most common type of classification is a binary one (Lichtenberk 1985:105). Fourth, like many gender systems, possessive classifier systems, at least quite a number of them, do have a relatively fixed class membership, and in some languages membership is largely unpredictable on semantic grounds. Lichtenberk (1985:125-6), for example, observes that in Houailou, an Oceanic language, some kinship terms are treated as inalienables while others are treated as alienables, and that there is no way to predict on semantic grounds which type of construction a given noun requires. Indeed, such a situation is not unlike that found in some gender languages.

That an approach to possession in terms of categorization systems such as gender is inappropriate has been argued for by a number of linguists, perhaps most strongly by Lynch (1973) and Pawley (1973; but see also Lichtenberk 1983, 1985). These linguists point out, for example, that a classification of nouns on the basis of lexical features does not account for the way these nouns are actually used. Further, Pawley (1973:167) notes that in Oceanic languages we are dealing 'with a system which marks several kinds of possessive relationships, and which allows a noun to occur as head with as many different kinds of possessive markers as makes sense to the speakers of the language' (see also Lichtenberk 1983). The noun *maqo* 'mango' in the Bau language, for example, may occur with three different possessive classifiers, as can be seen in example (9).

(9) Bau (Oceanic, Austronesian; Pawley 1973:168)
na   ke- na maqo
ART POSS-his mango
'his mango for eating (i.e. green mango)'

na   me- na maqo
ART POSS-his mango
'his mango for sucking (i.e. ripe, juicy mango)'

na   no- na maqo
ART POSS-his mango
'his mango (as property, e.g., which he is selling)'

There are other observations in addition that would seem to militate against treating possessive classifier systems as gender systems. Thus, the conceptual basis of classification is one that has to do primarily with use and/or usability of the item classified, rather than with perceptual distinctions relating to gender, animacy, number, etc. Rather than masculine vs. feminine, or animate vs. inanimate, the most salient grammatical distinction characteristic of possessive classifier systems is one between an alimentary and a general classifier (Lichtenberk 1985:185). Furthermore, assuming that morphosyntactic agreement is a definitional property of all three grammatical classification systems sketched above, one may say that agreement in possessive classifier systems is confined to, or crucially involves, agreement between a possessor and a possessee. Finally, agreement in possessive classifier systems is normally confined to the noun phrase, while gender agreement tends to affect a number of different syntactic constituents.

With these few remarks we do not attempt to do justice to this general issue here; rather the question of whether and/or how possessive classifier systems are related to gender would require a more detailed treatment, and such a treatment should also consider other kinds of nominal classification. The whole problem may be viewed differently depending on the language one is dealing with or the theoretical orientation one adopts; for the purposes of the present work it is largely immaterial.

1.2.2 Further issues

There are a number of problems that the issues just looked at raise. One problem, that we hinted at above, concerns the question of whether inalienability is a lexical feature, that is, whether lexicographical descriptions should include a distinction according to which nouns are marked as having either the feature [+alienable] or [−alienable] (cf. Nichols 1988:574), or, alternatively, whether the distinction can be described and accounted for only with reference to the syntactic and/or semantic relation obtaining between possessor and possessee (cf. Lynch 1973). Diem (1986:229–30), for example, argues that an approach in terms of nominal features is of doubtful value and that our concern should be with relations rather than with nouns. He presents the following example. In German, as in many other languages, possessors figuring in attributive constructions are 'promoted' to the rank of (Dative) object participants if they are associated with inalienable possessees; we mentioned this phenomenon in 1.2.1 under the label of possessor ascension. Thus, (10a) presents an instance of attributive possession involving alienable possession. Once, however, the possessee is inalienable, as in (10b), then the possessor must be presented as a Dative participant rather than as a nominal modifier.

(10) German
    (a) Ich wasche mein Auto.
        I wash my car
        'I wash my car.'
    (b) Ich wasche mir die Hände.
        I wash to.me the hands
        'I wash my hands.'

Typical instances of inalienable nouns in German would be body-part terms. The noun *Hose* 'pants' would normally be considered to be alienable, yet there are contrastive sets such as the following:

(11) German
    (a) Ich zerriß meine Hose.
        I tore my pants
        'I tore my pants.'
    (b) Ich zerriß mir die Hose.
        I tore to.me the pants
        'I tore my pants.'

The difference between (11a) and (11b) is that in the latter, typically, I am wearing the pants while this is not necessarily the case in (11a). That *Hose* 'pants' is treated as 'inalienable' in (11b) though not in (11a), Diem (1986:230) argues, has nothing to do with the lexical features of this noun; rather it is due to the particular *relation* obtaining between possessor and possessee. Thus, both (10a) and (11a) are treated by him as instances of alienable relations, while (10b) and (11b) are suggestive of inalienable relations. As we shall see in chapter 3, however, using pants or other pieces of clothing as an example may not be sufficient to prove the case in point; clothes are frequently ambiguous *vis-à-vis* inalienability (3.3). Thus, Tsunoda has the following to say:

> 'Clothing' refers to clothes, spectacles, ties, hats, shoes and earrings worn and attached to the body. According to the usual classification, they are alienable possessees. Nonetheless, they are physically (and probably psychologically as well) very close to the possessor, and they are almost body parts – since they are worn and attached to one's body. However, they are of the 'other possessee' type when they are not worn but are kept, say in a wardrobe. (Tsunoda 1996:578)

A number of tests have been devised to distinguish between inalienable and alienable nouns or relations, but, unfortunately, these tests do not all yield the same taxonomy. 'Possessor ascension' of the type just illustrated for German may be helpful to define body-parts plus a few other items as 'inalienable', but not necessarily kinship entities. If instead of the verb *zerreißen* 'tear', a verb like *wegnehmen* 'take away' were chosen, then kinship terms would qualify as "inalienable" while body-parts could not normally be used as possessees. Much the same applies to other tests that have been proposed. Kimball (1973:263ff.), for example, observes that, in English, inalienably possessed nouns have no existence independent of their possessor and, hence, are not pronominalizable by definite pronouns, while alienably possessed nouns are, as can be seen in (12). Still, even this test takes care of a limited set of items only, and that set does not seem to correspond to anything that one would be inclined to associate with a cross-linguistic notion of inalienability.

(12)   English (Kimball 1973:263)
      (a) *There was space in the manger, but now it's in the kitchen.
      (b) There was a cow in the meadow, but now it's in the barn.

Another issue, which has found even more scholarly attention, concerns the relative magnitude and syntactic relevance of the inalienable/alienable distinction in linguistic description. Some authors (e.g. Bendix 1966; Fillmore 1968; Lynch 1973) have argued that expressions for inalienable possession differ fundamentally in their syntactic structure from alienable possession – to the extent that the two have to be allocated to different underlying structures. Lynch (1973:10), for example, claims that alienable constructions differ from inalienable ones in containing an element of control by the possessor over the possessee and he decides that the former have an underlying abstract verb (have) in their syntactic structure that is absent in the case of inalienable constructions; we have mentioned in the preceding section (1.1) some of the problems associated with the notion control.

For many authors, the inalienable/alienable distinction is in fact a fundamental one, one which is treated as cross-linguistically and/or cross-culturally relevant. However, this view is not shared by all students of this general subject-matter. Lyons (1968a:301), for example, suggests that, rather than with inalienability, we may be dealing with a manifestation of what he calls the contingent vs. necessary distinction: contingent states are seen as temporarily (or contingently) associated with particular persons and objects, while necessary states are permanently (or necessarily) associated with particular persons and objects. Lyons argues that if the possessee is contingently associated with the possessor, it is marked in Chinese, the languages of the Siouan family, as well as other languages, as alienable, whereas it is unmarked or marked as inalienable if it is necessarily associated with the possessor.

Voeltz claims that inalienability is not a cross-linguistically relevant category, while part–whole relationship is (see also Herslund 1996). The evidence he presents includes the following. The fact that English body-part nouns, like *cheek*, are inalienable is suggested by the acceptability of (13a), while (13b) is not acceptable since *chair* is alienable. There is general agreement that kinship terms belong to the inalienable category, yet (13c) is not acceptable either. Voeltz (1976:265) argues that if we adopt the notion of *part–whole relationship*, rather than that of inalienability, we would be able to predict that (13a) is grammatical where (13b) and (13c) are not.

(13) English
    (a)   I touched John on the/his cheek.   Cf. I touched John's cheek.
    (b)   *I touched John on the/his chair.   I touched John's chair.
    (c)   *I touched John on the/his sister.   I touched John's sister.

While the proposal made by Voeltz accounts very well for the body of data looked at by him, it does not do so if one is concerned with a wider range of morphosyntactic structures across languages. In most languages having a morphologically distinct inalienable category, an account in terms of part–whole relationship is doomed to failure. This is perhaps most obvious in the case of kinship terms (e.g. 'John's father'), which tend to be treated as inalienable yet which cannot be described meaningfully in terms of wholes and their parts. Furthermore, Chappell and McGregor (1989) found out, on the basis of a larger sample of possessive constructions, that inalienability does not correlate significantly with part–whole relationship in that many concepts that tend to be associated with inalienability are not necessarily of the part–whole type. They note, for example:

> clearly footprints, souls and clothing are not parts of a person in the normal sense of that word, and on the other hand, in many languages (e.g. Nyulnyul), terms for hair and fingernails are not treated as inalienables, even though they are physically parts of the body. (Chappell and McGregor 1989:28)

In a similar way as Voeltz, Fox (1981:323) proposes to discard the notion of inalienability, since it 'is neither necessary nor sufficient to explain the syntactic phenomena observed'. Instead, she argues, *physical contiguity* is a more appropriate concept to account for the syntactic relationship between body-parts and their possessors.

The range of conceptual and/or linguistic variation that the inalienable/alienable distinction exhibits is in fact considerable, and a number of alternative taxonomic contrasts have been pointed out. Rather than between inalienable and alienable categories, for example, the distinction may be one between what Lébikaza (1991) calls intrinsic and non-intrinsic possession and what, following Seiler (1983:13), we will refer to, respectively, as *necessary* and *optional* relationship. Note, however, that Seiler's use of the term 'necessary' is not entirely the same as that of Lyons (1968a; see above).

A necessarily possessed item is one that is found obligatorily on any conceivable possessor, while not every possessor requires an optionally possessed item. Necessary possession is associated with terms for ascending kinship notions such as 'mother', 'grandmother', etc., but not, for example, with descending ones like 'daughter', 'grandchild', etc. (Seiler 1983:13). For example, everybody has (or had) a mother, a grandfather, or a nose (=necessary possession), but not everybody has a son or a niece (=optional possession). That the distinction is a cross-linguistically relevant one is suggested by evidence from a couple of genetically and areally unrelated languages. In the Muslim Arabic dialect of Fez, for example, the distinction is morphosyntactically relevant, as is suggested by the following examples:

(14)   Muslim Arabic, Fez dialect (Diem 1986:278)
     (a) 'ndu   dar   kbira.
         at:him house big
         'He has a big house.'

(b) 'ndu   bnt   mzyana.
      'He has a pretty daughter.'
  (c) 'ndu   ḥa   kbir.
      'He has an elder brother.'
  (d) *'ndu   ras   kbir.
      'He has a big head.'
  (e) *'ndu   bba   mšhur.
      'He has a famous father.'

The 'have'-construction exemplified in (14) is generally used except when possessee and possessor are either in a body-part (part–whole) or in an ascending kinship relationship, hence, when necessary possession is involved. Thus, (14d) and (14e), which are suggestive of necessary possession, are not felicitous utterances (Diem 1986:277–8). Similarly, in Kabiye, there is a 'have'-construction which is confined to optional possession. Thus, whereas (15a) is a possible utterance, (15b) is not.

(15)   Kabiye (Gur, Niger-Congo; Lébikaza 1991:92–3)
        (a) mɛ-wɛ-ná   pɪya
            I be with children
            'I have children.'

        (b) *mɛ-wɛ-ná   neze
            I be with grandmother
            *'I have a grandmother.'

Since predicative expressions involving necessary possession (e.g. *I have a father*) usually do not convey much information, if any at all, people are reluctant to use them, except in a transferred sense, and grammarians tend to describe such expressions as being 'ungrammatical'.

Our distinction between necessary and optional possession closely resembles that between 'everyone-type' and 'not everyone-type' inalienable possession proposed by Tsunoda (1996:618–19) for Japanese. Tsunoda is, however, confined to the domain of the human body and its parts. The main reason for adopting Seiler's rather than Lébikaza's nomenclature for the necessary vs. optional distinction can be seen in the fact that the term 'intrinsic', or 'intrinsic connection' for that matter, was used earlier (Chomsky 1972; Bowers 1975; Jackendoff 1977) for a number of different though related kinds of possessive relationship (see Hawkins 1981:248ff.). For Bowers (1975:346–7), for example, an intrinsic connection exists between an inanimate object and any of its properties, as for example in the case of English *the table's width* or *the building's height*.

As we noted above, prototypical instances of possession involve human possessors, and, less typically, non-human animate possessors. But there may also be inanimate possessors, and in such cases we will talk of inanimate possession. Here again, it may be useful to distinguish between alienable and inalienable inanimate possession, where the former concerns separable and the latter inseparable possessees. As in the case of human possession, what is treated as 'separable' and 'inseparable', respectively, differs greatly from one culture to another and from one context to another. On the whole, however, the distinction is both notionally and morphosyntactically obvious. For example, a bed is likely to be treated as an alienable and a door as an inalienable part of a room, and this distinction tends to be reflected in the respective linguistic expressions. We will return to this distinction in section 1.3.

Another noteworthy framework is proposed by Chappell and McGregor (1989): in addition to the canonical dichotomy alienable vs inalienable, they propose a third construction type which they simply call *classification*. With this term they describe a phenomenon 'whereby the dependent nominal indicates the type of entity that is being referred to by the head noun' (Chappell and McGregor 1989:28), its main characteristics being:

(a) 'Classification' is described by Chappell and McGregor (1989:28) as 'the embodiment of the type-token relation within the nominal phrase'.

(b) Typically, its formal expression is that of apposition, that is, of simple juxtaposition where the head follows the dependent, as in (16a). An exception is found in Amele, which has the order head – dependent instead, as exemplified in (16b).

(16) (a) Maisin (Oceanic, Austronesian; Chappell and McGregor 1989:29)
taru foyang
dog tail
'dog's tail'
(b) Amele (Trans-New Guinea, Indo-Pacific; Chappell & McGregor 1989:29)
na ahul
tree coconut
'coconut tree'

(c) Both the head and its dependent (also called the 'classifier' by Chappell and McGregor 1989:29) *must* be nouns, while in genitive and inalienable constructions, the dependent may be discharged by a pronominal.

(d) There is only one referential noun, viz. the head, while the dependent is not referential; it specifies the class or type to which the head noun belongs.

1.2 Distinctions 23

(e) No material may come between the classifying and the head noun to further modify the head noun.
(f) Classification constructions express such relations as generic-specific, function-form, use-item, status-holder, slot-filler, and rôle-occupant.

To what extent classification constructions should be treated as belonging to the domain of possession is not an issue that will concern us here. We will, however, return to this construction type in chapter 3 when dealing with specification (3.2).

The above catalogue of distinctions does not conclude the list of situation types expressed by possessive constructions; one might add, for example, a grammatical distinction made in the Cariban language Makushi between present and former possession. Furthermore, one could mention notions such as contact, direction, result, claim, or quality, etc. as being relevant for understanding possessive constructions in some languages (cf. Boeder 1980; Seiler 1988:96–7). These notions are based on semantic distinctions to be observed across languages, but they certainly do not exhaust the range of conceptual discontinuities to be observed in the languages of the world. In Tswana, a South African Bantu language, for example, there is a morphological contrast between communal and individual possession. The former relates to possession by the people constituting a local unit larger than the family and is expressed by the element *-ga-*, while the latter is unmarked (Cole 1955:162ff.), for example:

(17) Tswana (Bantu, Niger-Congo; Cole 1955:164)
bana ba-ga-êno
'your children' (=of your place, village, etc.)
bana b-êno
'your children' (=of your family)

Mention should also be made of what Pawley (1973) calls 'passive' or 'subordinate' possession, expressing actions where the possessor is the patient, the target, or the involuntary experiencer and has no control over the possessee, for example:

(18) Standard Fijian (Oceanic, Austronesian; Lichtenberk 1985:106)
na   ke   -na itukutuku
ART CLASS-his rope
'his rope, i.e. the rope to be used on him, such as for binding him or strangling him'

Capell (1949:172–3) makes a related distinction between 'transitive' and 'intransitive actions', which he finds, for example, in Maori. Furthermore, one might mention the distinction between direct and descriptive (attributive) possession/possessives, commonly made in South African Bantu linguistics but notionally present also in many other languages (Doke 1930; Cole 1955). Whereas the former concerns 'canonical' kinds of possession or ownership, the latter relates to possessive constructions where the 'possessor' denotes quality-like concepts involving properties such as use, content, type, material, etc.

Also, the distinction found in Melanesian languages between possession of an item that is intended for immediate consumption and one that is not is worth noting. In Mangap-Mbula, for example, expressions involving the former have *ko-* as a Recipient (REC) marker, as in (19a), while the latter use *le-* instead, as in (19b).

(19)   Mangap-Mbula (Austronesian; Bugenhagen 1986:150–1)
    (a) n-   u   ko- m   pin   sa   (i-   mbot)?
        GIVEN-2.SG   REC-2.SG   banana   any   3.SG-stay
        'Do you have any bananas (to eat)?'

    (b) n-   io   le- ng   pin   be   ang-rai.
        GIVEN-1.SG   REC-1.SG   banana   IRR   1.SG-sell
        'I have bananas to sell.'

In some Melanesian languages, even more refined conceptual distinctions are made. Lynch (1973:1–5) observes that in Aroma, Suau, Lenakel, and Fijian, adnominal possession is characterized by a morphological distinction alienable vs. inalienable, and that Aroma and Suau furthermore classify alienable nouns morphologically into neutral and edible ones, the latter referring to items that are to be eaten, drunk, or otherwise taken into the mouth. Fijian distinguishes morphologically between edible and drinkable items in addition, and, in Lenakel, the alienable category is divided into four subtypes, which are neuter, edible, drinkable, and plantable (cf. 1.2.1).

The languages of Australia and the Pacific appear to be particularly rich in conceptual taxonomies relating to possession. In Mota, six categories are distinguished:

(a)   Inseparable, e.g. 'my hand', 'my father',
(b)   Undefined, e.g. 'my axe',
(c)   Food, e.g. 'my banana (to eat)',
(d)   Drink, e.g. 'my water (to drink)',
(e)   Valuables, e.g. 'my pig', and
(f)   Activities, e.g. 'my work' (Capell 1949:176–7).

Other languages in this general area, however, have even more refined possessive distinctions marked by means of dozens of classifying particles. Possessive classifier languages are not confined to the languages of this area. Many more types exist in the Americas; concerning an example from an African language, see Pasch (1985).

Note also that possession in West Greenlandic Eskimo is associated with a proliferation of derivational affixes, e.g. *gig* 'have a good', *giig* 'have mutually', *lug* 'have a bad', *kit* 'have little/a small', or *tu* 'have much/a big' (Fortescue 1984:171). Such distinctions may be relevant beyond the regions where they evolved; they are suggestive of ways in which human conceptualization proceeds and becomes conventionalized in language. They will, however, not be looked at in the following chapters, first, because they are culturally and/or areally restricted, and, second, because they are of minor importance to the central topic of this work, which is the canonical constructions used for predicative possession and how they can be explained.

In a number of works, doubts have been raised as to whether possession indeed constitutes an independent domain of human conceptualization, or whether it might not be described more profitably with reference to some other domain or domains. Thus, it has been argued that possession can be regarded as a special case of location, for example as an instance of typically animate location (cf. Lyons 1967; Clark 1978). We will not adopt such a position here; rather we will assume that possession is essentially independent of location (but see below). In an utterance like *Our house has four windows on its front side*, the phrase *on its front side* is taken as an instance of location and *has four windows* as an instance of possession, albeit of inanimate possession. To extend the use of the term 'location' to the latter phrase would amount to using this term in such a wide sense that it becomes essentially vacuous. There is, however, no doubt that possession, while being a domain of its own, nevertheless is linked to some other cognitive domains including location, and this relationship will be the main concern of chapter 4.

1.2.3 Attributive vs. predicative possession

Another issue concerns the classification of possession into two main types of linguistic constructions. All languages we are familiar with have a morphosyntactic distinction between what is variously called attributive, nominal, or adnominal possession on the one hand (e.g. *my credit card*), and predicative or verbal possession on the other (*I have a credit card*). Both kinds of possession typically concern a relation between two nominals or between two thing-like items (cf. Seiler 1988:95), and both can be described with reference to a set of prototypical properties as proposed by Taylor (1989b:202–3); we have discussed these properties briefly above (1.1.1).

But there are also differences. An impression of the semantic complexity obtaining between attributive and predicative possession in English may be conveyed by the following examples:

> 'Tom's face' is uniquely Tom's; 'Tom has Bill's face' can only be understood to assert similarity. 'Tom's father' identifies a definite person to whom Tom stands in a particular kin relation; 'Tom has Bill's father' would not be used to mean that Tom and Bill are brothers. Moreover, Tom's face's expression is Tom's expression and Tom's location's location is Tom's location, but Tom's hat's color is not Tom's color and Tom's father's father is not Tom's father. (Miller & Johnson-Laird 1976:562)

For some authors, predicative and attributive possession are different not only in form, but also in meaning. Bugenhagen (1986:129) claims that the two can be distinguished in the following way (his dative–recipient relationship corresponds to our predicative and his genitive relationship to our attributive possession): (a) the possessee has been located in proximity to the possessor for a minimal length of time in the case of predicative, but for an enduring length of time in the case of attributive possession; (b) the possessor is a locative goal of the possessee in the case of the former, but a location in the latter case; (c) the possessor has minimal control over the possessee in the former, but full control in the latter case.

No evaluation of characterizations like this one is attempted here. Perhaps a more obvious way of distinguishing the two would be with reference to their respective presuppositional content; for example, possession is likely to be presupposed in expressions of the kind *my credit card*, but asserted in *I have a credit card*. For the purposes of the present work it may suffice to note that the two kinds of morphosyntactic structures represent different encoding patterns and that this difference is likely to be reflected in some way or other in their respective meanings or range of senses expressed by them. Note that in some languages further presuppositional distinctions can be made by reversing the order of possessor and possessee in attributive possessive constructions. In Turkana, for example, the possessor follows the possessee, as in (20a), but if the possessor is known or presented as a background referent, then pronominal possessors precede, as in (20b).

(20) Turkana (Eastern Nilotic, Nilo-Saharan; Dimmendaal 1993:4)
    (a) a-bɛrʊ` kɛŋ`
        F-wife 3.SG.POSS
        'his wife'
    (b) a-kɛė- bɛrʊ`
        F-3.SG.POSS-wife
        'his wife'

Predicative and attributive possession usually involve entirely different construction types. But this is not necessarily so. In English, a kind of comitative pattern involving the preposition *with* may be used to encode attribute possession (e.g. *the man with a red nose*) and predicative possession (*She is with child*). In Acoma, a Keresan language of New Mexico, there is a 'possessive prefix' *qa-* that may be verbal or nominal: it denotes predicative (active) possession in verbal themes, but in nominal themes its function is attributive (Ultan 1978:14–15).

Biermann (1985:15–16) discusses three possessive constructions in Hungarian of which two, exemplified by (21a) and (21b), are attributive and one, (21c), is predicative. Nevertheless, she observes that, in some way, (21b) has more in common with (21c) than with (21a): (21b) and (21c) not only share the use of the Dative (DAT) suffix on the possessor noun phrase, but also the fact that the order in which the possessor and the possessee are presented can be reversed, the word order in (21a), on the other hand, is invariable. Furthermore, when the possessor noun phrase is plural, there may be number agreement between the possessor and the possessee noun phrases in (21b) and (21c), whereas number agreement is ruled out in (21a).

(21) Hungarian (Biermann 1985:15)
    (a) a férfi-ak ház- a
        the man-PL house-3.SG
        'the men's house'

    (b) a férfi-ak- nak ... a ház- a/ -uk
        the man-PL-DAT the house-3.SG/-3.PL
        'the men's house'

    (c) a férfi-ak- nak van ház- a/ -uk
        the man-PL-DAT is house-3.SG/-3.PL
        'the men have a house'

It may thus happen that predicative and attributive possession are built on both the same conceptual structure and the same linguistic form. It may, however, equally well be that both are built on the same conceptual structure even though the linguistic forms are different. In Ewe, a West African

Niger-Congo language, for example, both the 'have'-construction *le – así* (Lit.: 'be in one's hand') and the attributive possessive marker *pé* 'of' have a locative source, the latter being derived from the obsolete nominal *pé 'place'. Thus, both can be described with reference to a metaphorical formula somehow like (22). Nevertheless, the linguistic forms employed for encoding this formula are strikingly different.

(22)   Y is at X's place > Y is in X's possession

A similar example is found in Luiseño (Steele 1977). The structure of the 'have'-construction in this language is illustrated in (23a), and that of attributive possession in (23b).

(23)   Luiseño (Steele 1977)
    (a) noo=p   nopaa?aš   ?awq
        I   CLIT   my:brother   is
        'I have a brother.'

    (b) xwaan up   poyo?   hunwuti   ?ariq
        John   CLIT   his:mother   bear:object   is:kicking
        'John's mother is kicking the bear.'

What (23a) and (23b) have in common in particular is, first, that both the possessor and the possessee are encoded as sentence subjects, where the possessor precedes the possessee and in addition appears as a pronominal modifier of the possessee, and, second, that both constructions have a clitic *up* (shortened to *=p* in (23a) after the possessor noun phrase). The major difference between the two is that the clitic *up* may follow the possessee in (23b) but not in (23a).

A special relationship between attributive and predicative possession appears to exist in languages of the Caddoan and Iroquoian families, which

> deprive kin terms of the possibility of displaying an alienability opposition, in that those nouns obligatorily take clausal rather than phrasal possession: one says, roughly, 'she is mother to me' rather than 'my mother'. (Nichols 1988:578)

The relationship between the two kinds of possession has been of central concern in some works written in the tradition of generative grammar. A general theme associated with this tradition is that predicative possession is basic/underived or underlying and that attributive possession is derivative, that is, that the latter is derived from the former by means of a specific set of rules. One thread of reasoning underlying this thesis is that the two are semantically similar and that attributive possession is highly general in meaning while predicative possession is more specific. It therefore seems plausible that a phrase like *my house* may derive from a large number of underlying sentences such as *I own the house, I live in the house, I rented the house, I built the house*, etc. Lynch (1973:9ff.) argues that in attributive possession in Melanesian languages like Aroma, Suau, Lenakel, and Fijian, the lexical features of the possessee are far less important than the nature of the relationship between the possessor and the possessee, more specifically the intentions of the former towards the latter. Since in addition he finds some morphological similarities between the two kinds of constructions, he decides that *all* possessive constructions in these languages are derived from an underlying sentence of the form Possessee [relate to] Possessor, where '[relate to]' is an abstract verb establishing possessive relations.

Depending on the purpose the grammatical analysis concerned is supposed to serve, a procedure like the one adopted by Lynch and others may be justified. An approach that allows one to reduce two different constructions to one is more economic than one that does not. If one aims at explaining language structure, however, then that procedure may not be very helpful. For example, *contra* Lynch (1973:13), or Watkins (1967:2196), constructions used for attributive possession are in most cases not historically derived from 'have'-constructions. The whole issue is, however, a complex one and we will have to return to it in chapter 3 (3.1, 3.5).

1.2.4 'Have'-constructions vs. 'belong'-constructions

Among the many different ways of expressing predicative possession in a given language, 'have'-constructions are likely to provide the most salient pattern. What characterizes this pattern, for example, in English, is that the possessor appears as the clausal subject or topic and the possessee as an object or complement. There is a second pattern in addition in which the possessee is encoded as the clausal subject and/or topic and the possessor as the complement or as an oblique constituent. We will call the pattern the 'belong'-construction. The two constructions are illustrated with the following English examples:

(24)   (a) Peter has a car.   'Have'-construction
       (b) The car is Peter's. *or* The car belongs to Peter.   'Belong'-construction

A number of descriptive devices have been employed to distinguish the two kinds of construction. In 'have'-constructions, it is argued, there is 'emphasis' on the possessor, or the possessor is 'paramount,' while in

Table 1.1. *Definiteness vs. indefiniteness in 'have'- and 'belong'-constructions: Typical associations*

	'Have'-constructions		'Belong'-constructions	
	Possessor	Possessee	Possessor	Possessee
Definite	+	−	+/−	+
Indefinite	−	+	+/−	+/−

'belong'-constructions it is the possessee that receives 'emphasis' or is 'paramount' (Watkins 1967:2194). Seiler (1983:61) characterizes the two as follows: In 'have'-constructions, the possessor is the point of departure wherefrom we move on to the possessee, while in 'belong'-constructions Seiler sees a movement from the possessee as the point of departure on to the possessor. 'Movement' in this case must not be understood as a syntactic device, since syntactic relations, including word order characteristics, are not a reliable tool for deciding between 'have'- and 'belong'-constructions: as we will see in chapter 2, many 'have'-constructions in the languages of the world involve the constituent order possessee–possessor rather than the reverse. Rather, we will treat the distinction between the two kinds of construction as being pragmatically motivated. One exponent of this distinction is its association with discourse-pragmatic reference: as Clasen (1981) notes, the possessee is typically indefinite in the case of German 'have'-constructions (involving the verb *haben* 'have') but definite in the case of 'belong'-constructions (involving the verb *gehören* 'belong to'). The possessor, on the other hand, is likely to be definite in both kinds of construction, although it may also be indefinite in the case of 'belong'-constructions. This asymmetric situation is summarized in Table 1.1.

Perhaps a classical way of distinguishing between the two kinds of construction can be found in Nama (Khoekhoe), where the distinction is associated with voice: active sentences have the subject/topic as a possessor and are 'have'-sentences, as in (25a), while passive sentences have the possessee as the subject/topic and correspond to the notion of 'belong'-constructions, as in (25b).

(25)   Nama (Khoekhoe, Khoisan; Heinz Roberg, p.c.)
    (a) kxoe. p   ke   'auto.sa   'uu   hââ.
        person.M TOP car. F   take PERF
    'The man has a car.'

(b) 'auto.s ke   kxoe. pi 'uu- he   hââ.
    car. F   TOP   person.M take-PASS PERF
    'The car belongs to the man.'

According to Leon Stassen (p.c.) the distinction may also be expressed simply by reversing the case functions concerned. Thus, he says that there are languages where a construction *X is with Y* has the conventionalized meaning 'X has Y' while *Y is with X* means 'Y belongs to X'.

Presence of indefinite possessees in fact appears to be a salient property of 'have'-constructions. In many languages, 'have'-constructions require the possessee to be indefinite, otherwise the construction concerned will not necessarily have a possessive meaning. In Diyari, a Pama-Nyungan language of Australia, for example, the verb *ŋama-* 'to sit, stay' is used with the transitivizing suffix *-lka-* to indicate that the object is to be understood as accompanying the subject. The derived stem *ŋama-lka-* has been lexicalized as a verb of possession 'to have', provided the transitive object, which encodes the possessee, is indefinite (Austin 1981:146).

Even if they are encoded as clausal subjects and have some specifying morphology on them, possessee noun phrases in 'have'-constructions may not normally be definite. In Hungarian, for example, the possessee noun phrase is formally the subject and agrees with the possessor in person (optionally also in number), yet it may not have definite reference. Biermann (1985:87) observes that in examples like (26), the possessee noun *votká-ja* may be specific but not definite; if, nevertheless, it is definite, a meaning other than a possessive one emerges, as in (26b).

(26)   Hungarian (Biermann 1985:94)
        (a) Péter-nek van votká- ja.
            Peter-DAT is vodka-3.SG
            'Peter has vodka.'
        (b) Péter-nek van a   votká- ja.
            Peter-DAT is the vodka-3.SG
            'The vodka is (meant) for Peter.'

As we will see in section 1.3, however, there are different notions of possession and not all of them share this correlation with indefinite possessees.

'Belong'-constructions differ from 'have'-constructions in that they tend to be associated only with one possessive notion or, to use Taylor's (1989b:205) characterization, they permit 'only limited extension from the prototype'. Taylor notes, for example, that, compared to the English genitive construction in *John's car*, the corresponding 'belong'-construction *This car is John's* is not open to similar multifarious interpretations:

The expression invokes a relation of true possession, or possibly a relation which is very close to true possession (e.g. authorized usage, as sanctioned by an agreement with a car-hire company). Accordingly, NP's N expressions which invoke a relation which is rather distant from the possession prototype do not permit predicative genitive rewordings: *This rival is Mary's, *This door is the car's, *This invasion was Poland's, *These arrests are yesterday's. (Taylor 1989b:205)

We will return to this issue below (see especially 5.3).

The main concern of this work is with 'have'-constructions. Nevertheless, we will also look at 'belong'-constructions, in particular since the conceptual structures and the linguistic forms employed for their expression may be the same. Thus, in the following two examples, Latin and French employ essentially the same morphosyntactic form and, as we will attempt to demonstrate in chapter 2, the same conceptual source, to express possession, yet the Latin example (27) is suggestive of a 'have'-construction, while French (28) provides an instance of a 'belong'-construction.

(27)   Latin
       mihi   est liber.
       DAT.me   is   book
       'I have a book.'

(28)   French
       Le livre est à   moi.
       the book is DAT me
       'The book belongs to me.'

In a number of works, the distinction is said to correlate with that between possession and ownership: 'have'-constructions, it is argued, express possession, and 'belong'-constructions ownership (cf. Watkins 1967; Bickerton 1981). Such a correlation can in fact frequently be observed; nevertheless it is misleading. While 'belong'-constructions usually have ownership as their primary or even their only meaning, 'have'-constructions tend to express a wider range of possessive notions *including* ownership (see below). The situation in English is characteristic of that to be found in quite a number of other languages in this respect. The utterance *The car belongs to Liz* can be said to have ownership as its primary meaning, while *Liz has a car* has a number of different senses, including that of ownership: depending on the context in which it is used, it may mean that Liz has borrowed or rented a car, or that she has a car to take her somewhere, even if she is neither the owner nor the holder, nor the driver, but simply a passenger in that car, etc. But the utterance can also mean that Liz is the owner. To conclude, the distinction possession vs. ownership is inadequate as a means of defining the difference between 'have'- and 'belong'-constructions (cf. 5.3 below).

The distinction between the two kinds of construction is an elementary one; all languages known to us have conventionalized means for expressing it, and it can be reconstructed back to the earliest stages of Indo-European (Watkins 1967).

1.3   Some possessive notions

In his treatment of possession in Proto-Oceanic, Andrew Pawley (1973:153) cites *Webster's Third* as his authority for defining possession. According to that authority, possession is 'the act or condition of having in or taking in one's control or holding at one's disposal', 'actual physical control or occupancy of property', and, more briefly, simply 'something owned, occupied or controlled.' Pawley decides: 'I will use the term "possessive construction" here loosely', and he is well advised to do so: there are a number of notions contained in this definitional statement, such as 'control', 'disposal', 'occupancy', etc., that do not necessarily mean the same, and the reader may wonder which of them is more relevant for understanding what possession is about. Is it the particular constellation that makes up the concept of possession? Is it the range of possible contributing concepts? Or is it the contextually defined manifestation of these notions that makes up 'possession'?

Some of the notions referred to in *Webster's Third* do in fact capture salient properties of what is commonly thought to be associated with the domain of possession. The complexity of this subject was illustrated in section 1.1, where a number of views were summarized regarding the conceptual and linguistic nature of possession. Langacker (1994; 1995) distinguishes 18 different kinds of relationship expressed by the English genitive, but he adds that only 3 are prototypical, namely ownership, kinship, and part/whole relationships. It does not become entirely clear how prototypicality is to be defined in this case and why it is exactly these 3, rather than any of the other 15 relationships, that are prototypical. Looking at a wider range of languages it would seem that there is a catalogue of possessive notions that tend to be distinguished in some way or other and that might be relevant for a cross-cultural understanding of possession. These notions are (abbreviated labels are added in parentheses):

Physical possession (PHYS) This notion, which has also been referred to as momentary possession (Johnson and Miller-Laird 1976:565), is said to be present when the possessor and the possessee are physically associated with one another at reference time, as can be assumed to be the case we have in (29) below.

(29)   I want to fill in this form; do you have a pen?

Temporary possession (TEMP) Alternative terms that have been used for this notion are accidental possession or temporary control (Johnson and Miller-Laird 1976:565). According to this notion, the possessor can dispose of the possessee for a limited time but s/he cannot claim ownership to it, as in (30).

(30)   I have a car that I use to go to the office but it belongs to Judy.

Permanent possession (PERM) Johnson and Miller-Laird (1976:565) call this inherent possession. The possessee is the property of the possessor, and typically the possessor has a legal title to the possessee, as can be assumed to be the case in (31).

(31)   Judy has a car but I use it all the time.

Permanent possession may be said to correspond most closely to the legal notion of ownership as used in western societies; it includes, for example, property in the sense of what Blackstone had defined in his *Commentaries on the Laws of England* of 1765 as 'that sole and despotic dominion which one man claims and exercises over the external things of the world, in total exclusion of the right of any other individual in the universe'.

Inalienable possession (INAL) The possessee is conceived of typically as being inseparable from the possessor, e.g., as a body-part or as a relative, as in (32).

(32)   I have blue eyes/two sisters.

Abstract possession (ABST) In this kind of possession, the possessee is a concept that is not visible or tangible, like a disease, a feeling, or some other psychological state, for example:

(33)   He has no time/no mercy.

Abstract possession may be said to be also present when the meaning of the proposition concerned is actually the contrary to possession, as in *I have a missing tooth*.

Inanimate inalienable possession (IN/I) This notion, which is frequently referred to as part–whole relationship, differs from INAL in that the possessor is inanimate, and the possessee and the possessor are conceived of as being inseparable, as in (34).

(34)   That tree has few branches.
       My study has three windows.

Inanimate alienable possession (IN/A) The possessor is inanimate and the possessee is separable from the possessor, as in (35).

(35)   That tree has crows on it.
       My study has a lot of useless books in it.

We noted in section 1.2 that there exists a strong correlation between 'have'-constructions and the presence of indefinite possessees, to the effect that, in many languages, 'have'-constructions assume meanings other than possessive ones unless associated with indefinite possessees. Such a correlation does in fact apply to a number of the notions discussed here, for example to permanent possession; but it does not necessarily apply to either physical or temporary possession. In fact, in many languages it is possible to turn an expression whose readings include that of permanent possession (e.g. *Judy has a car*) into one denoting physical or temporary possession once a definite possessee is used instead of an indefinite one (cf. *Judy has the car*).

In English, all seven notions may be expressed somehow by using the item *have*, or else by genitive constructions (see below), which means that these constructions are inherently 'vague'. An English sentence such as *I have your book but I have it at home*, for example, is suggestive of three different possessive notions: the first *I have* of temporary possession, the second *I have* of physical possession, and *your book* of permanent possession. In other languages, different expressions may be required for different possessive notions. In Manding, as we will see in more detail below (section 2.6.1), physical possession is encoded typically by the *kùn*-construction, as in (36a), while the *fɛ̀*-construction may be used for example for permanent possession, as in (36b), and the *la*-construction does not express any of these notions but is the only one used for abstract possession, as illustrated in (36c).

(36) Manding (Mande, Niger-Congo; Bird 1972; Kastenholz 1988; Mohamed Touré, p.c.)
    (a) wari ` bɛ Baba kùn.
        money the be.at Baba head
        'Baba has the money (on him).'

    (b) wari ` bɛ Baba fɛ̀.
        money the be.at Baba at
        'Baba has (=owns) the money.'

    (c) minnɔgɔ bɛ ù la.
        thirst be.at their at
        'They have thirst (=are thirsty).'

One may wonder why all these examples should be subsumed under the label 'possession'. One might argue that examples such as (34) and (35) are not suggestive of possession, rather that they can be analyzed more profitably with reference to other conceptual domains, as has in fact been done (see chapters 4, 5.1). The main reason for treating them all as possessive notions is that in many languages they are expressed in the same way as prototypical instances of possession, as we will see in the following chapters. Furthermore, one might ask what justification there may be for dividing the domain of possession (assuming that it constitutes a domain of its own) into seven more or less separate conceptual entities, referred to as 'possessive notions'. Again, the reader is referred to cross-linguistic evidence to be presented below that suggests that this division reflects a significant pattern of encoding discourse.

Linguistic forms whose meaning includes any combination of these notions are referred to as possessive constructions in the remainder of this work. These are not the only concepts expressed by possessive constructions, and some alternative concepts are discussed in detail in the following chapters (see especially chapter 4). Nevertheless, the seven notions sketched above appear to be the ones most frequently associated with possessive morphologies.

We have illustrated the various possessive notions with examples involving predicative possession. But the same notions are also distinguished in expressions for attributive possession, as can be seen in (37).

(37)   PHYS: Steward, *my glass* is empty, can you bring me another beer?
       TEMP: You can't have *my car* because it belongs to my wife.

PERM: *My car* had an accident, I have to buy a new one.
INAL: *My father, my eyes.*
ABST: *My flu, my thoughts.*
IN/I: *The ceiling of this room.*
IN/A: *The chairs from this room.*

The inalienable notion combines two rather diverse conceptual groupings: body-part and kinship terms. There would be reasons to allocate the two to different notions, especially since in a number of languages they differ in their morphosyntax. For example, in English they behave differently, in that a construction as exemplified in (38) is possible if body-parts are involved, as in (38a), but not necessarily when kinship (38b) or other terms (38c) are involved (Brugman 1988:65).

(38) (a) He has a missing finger.
    (b) ?He has a missing daughter.
    (c) ?He has a missing $5 bill.

We also noted above that, according to Langacker (1994:44; 1995), possession has three prototypes of roughly equal status, which are ownership (e.g. *my shirt*), body-part or part–whole (*that woman's face*), and kinship relations (*Sheila's daughter*). What this observation would seem to suggest is that the distinction between the two kinds of inalienable possession is a salient one; Langacker adds that the three prototypes have an experiential basis, 'deriving from certain types of experience that are so ubiquitous and cognitively salient that they can reasonably be called *conceptual archetypes*' (Langacker 1994:44). That the two also behave cross-linguistically differently is suggested by the observations made by Chappell and McGregor (1996b), alluded to in the previous section. Nevertheless, we will treat body-part and kinship relations here as belonging to the same general possessive notion since the structural similarities to be observed between them outnumber the dissimilarities.

One may also wonder what justification there is to extend the notion of inalienability to 'inanimate possession', as we do by proposing a category IN/I: are phrases like *the legs of this child* and *the legs of this table* really suggestive of the same general category? Note that there are languages where possession appears to be treated as being confined to the domain of human beings. O'Connor (1992:259–60), for example, remarks that in Northern Pomo, a Hokan language of northern California, the marking of possession 'does not extend metaphorically to the domain of inanimate objects, such as is found in English'. She adds that whenever the genitive construction of Northern Pomo involves both an inanimate head and an inanimate modifier it may only denote 'a spatial or conventional association', but not a possessive one.

It would seem that there is no a priori answer to the question just raised. One may say, for example, as has in fact frequently been done, that 'inanimate possession' has to do with part–whole relations and, as such, should be grouped together with those instances of human possession that also entail a partonomic relationship. This would mean that the two English phrases just mentioned are in the same category, while a phrase like *the brother of this child* belongs in another category since it is not suggestive of a part–whole relationship. While our decision to extend the notion of inalienability from human to inanimate possession is arbitrary to some extent, it can be justified on account of a number of structural similarities obtaining between the two. For example, possessor ascension, which was briefly discussed in Section 1.2, applies in much the same way to both human and inanimate possession in many different languages (Voeltz 1976). As we saw in the preceding section (1.2), however, it is advisable to treat inalienability and part–whole relationship essentially as different notions.

The difference between the notions PHYS, TEMP, PERM, IN/A, and, to some extent, ABST on the one hand, and INAL and IN/I on the other, can be described as one between acquired and ascribed possession. 'Permanent possession' is used as a substitute for Miller and Johnson-Laird's term 'inherent possession', especially since the latter is likely to be confused with 'inalienable possession,' and some authors do in fact use the two as synonyms or near-synonyms (cf. Hopper 1972:126). For Seiler (1983; 1988:81), for example, 'inherent possession' is used as a technical term for much of what other authors would subsume under inalienable possession: Seiler calls a possessee inherent if it contains 'some indication of a possessor' and he cites kinship relations, body-parts and relational spatial concepts as typical instances of inherent possessees. Concerning a more extended use of 'inherent' possession or relation, see Bendix (1966:45ff.).

Possession, and distinctions between different kinds of possessive notions, have been described with reference to various parameters, such as control and time. We noted above (1.2) that according to Bugenhagen (1986:128), possession is located at the intersection of the last two parameters, i.e., that it can be described with reference to the extent of control the possessor has over the possessee on the one hand, and the length of time during which the possessee is located in proximity to the possessor on the

1.3 Some possessive notions

Table 1.2. *Some prototypical properties of possessive notions*

	PHYS	TEMP	PERM	INAL	ABST	IN/I	IN/A
I	+	+	+	+	+	−	−
II	+	+	+	+	−	+	+
III	+	+	+	+/−	−	−	−
IV	+	+	+	+/−	+	+	+
V	−	−	+	+	+/−	+	−

other. These parameters are relevant ones indeed. The distinction between the notions PHYS, TEMP, and PERM, for example, crucially involves time, since these notions normally relate, respectively, to momentary, temporary, and unlimited temporal situations. Furthermore, the difference between PERM and INAL, or between IN/A and IN/I can, at least in many cases, be described as one reflecting a difference in the relative length of time the possessee is expected to be associated with the possessor. Similarly, the control parameter may be helpful to characterize many instances of PHYS, TEMP, and PERM or, depending on how one defines 'control' (see 1.2 above), to set these notions off from most other instances of possessive expressions. On the whole, however, neither time nor control, nor an interaction of the two, would seem to be sufficient to understand or describe possession.

On the basis of the parameters indicated above, the seven possessive notions can be characterized with reference to the following properties, which are included in Taylor's (1989b:202–3) list of prototypical properties (see 1.1.1 above):

I	The possessor is a human being.
II	The possessee is a concrete item.
III	The possessor has the right to make use of the possessee.
IV	Possessor and possessee are in spatial proximity.
V	Possession has no conceivable temporal limit.

The way these properties correlate with the various possessive notions can be seen in Table 1.2. Note that these properties are understood to be prototypical in nature, that is, they are characteristic of canonical instances but not necessarily of all instances of the possessive notion concerned.

What the distribution of properties in Table 1.2 would seem to suggest is that the various possessive notions differ greatly with regard to their relative

40 The state

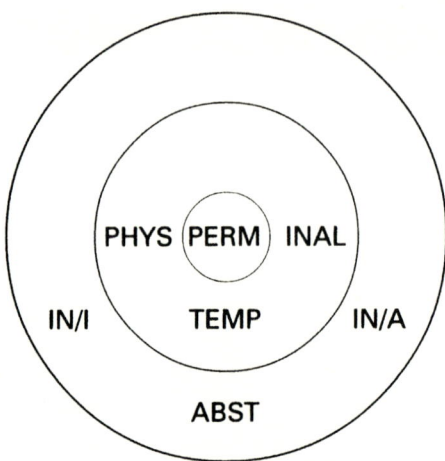

Figure 1.1 A prototype characterization of possessive notions.

degree of prototypicality. At one end there is permanent possession, which correlates positively with all five properties; at the other end, we find inanimate alienable possession, which has only two of the properties distinguished above. In terms of the relative number of properties, one may say that permanent possession is most central to the prototype, that is, it exhibits a maximal degree of prototypicality, physical, temporary, and inalienable possession a reduced degree, and abstract and inanimate possession a minimal degree of prototypicality. This threefold classification is represented graphically in Figure 1.1.

That permanent possession is in fact suggestive of the highest degree of prototypicality can also be derived from other observations. Taylor (1989b:204) notes that, while a possessive expression may be usable for various contents, in certain contexts it is the most prototypical notion, that is, permanent possession, that will surface:

> The interrogative *whose car?* is not a request to the hearer to name some person who stands in some indeterminate relation to the car; the expression is a request to name the possessor (in the prototypical, or close to prototypical sense) of the car. The possession relation is likewise invoked by contrastive uses of possessive expressions, of the kind *not John's photograph, Max's photograph*. Finally consider the following scenario. Someone lends me his car, which I then smash. In approaching a passerby for assistance, I could quite well say *I've just smashed my car*, meaning by *my car* no more than 'the car I was driving'. But it would be highly imprudent of me to report the incident to the friend who had lent me the

car with the sentence *I've just smashed my car*. In such a context, the central, prototypical meaning of the possessive construction would very strongly come to the fore. (Taylor 1989b:205)

Note furthermore that according to Nikiforidou (1991:159–60), the only clearly productive meaning of genitives is what she refers to as 'possessive uses', which largely corresponds to our notion of permanent possession.

1.4 Problems

In the course of the past decades a number of quasi-universal claims have been made on the behaviour of predicative possession, such as the following (cf. Claudi 1986:4):

(a) The clausal subject usually presents the possessee (Clark 1978:102, 113; Ultan 1978:34).

(b) The possessor is usually encoded either in the clausal object or in some locative-based constituent (Ultan 1978:34).

(c) In spite of (a) and (b), the possessor precedes the possessee in the majority of languages. Clark (1978:101–2) attributes this to the preference for animate nominals to precede inanimate ones within a sentence (see 2.5.3, 2.7 below).

(d) In many, and perhaps in all, languages, existential and possessive constructions are related to locatives or, to cite a slightly different perspective, possession belongs to the same general category as location. There are, however, a number of more specific views regarding the relationship between location and possession, such as the following:

   (i) Possessive constructions are locational constructions. This view is held by Clark (1978:89), who argues that the possessor in constructions like *Tom has a book* and *The book is Tom's* 'is simply an animate place'.

   (ii) Possessive constructions are included in locational constructions. Lyons (1977:474), for example, says that it can be argued 'that so-called possessive expressions are to be regarded as a subclass of locatives'.

   (iii) Possessive constructions are derived from locative constructions, where the notion 'derived' is not further specified. This is the position maintained by Lyons (1967), where it remains unclear whether he is concerned with diachronic or synchronic derivation, or with both. In a later paper (1968b), however, he argued that there should be some correlation between synchronic, diachronic, and ontogenetic derivation (cf. Clark 1978:90).

(iv) Possessive constructions are historically derived from locative constructions.

Many of these claims are of doubtful value. For example, we are not aware of any substantial evidence that would support hypotheses (i) or (ii). There are at least two reasons for keeping possessive constructions on the one hand, and existential and locative constructions on the other, apart. First, the two show a different morphosyntactic behaviour; Clark (1978:97–8) observes, for example, that, unlike existential and locative constructions, possessive constructions do not show regular word order alternations depending on the definiteness of the possessed constituent. Second, and more importantly, they are simply different in meaning and speakers usually are aware of this difference.

The preceding discussion may have shown that there are a number of questions that need to be answered for a better understanding of what 'possession' stands for, such as the following:

(a) Why do expressions for predicative possession frequently resemble expressions for identification, description, existence, equation, and/or location?

(b) Why do 'have'-constructions frequently involve verbs having what Seiler (1988:94) calls a 'marginal status', exhibiting for example systematic paradigmatic gaps in the inflectional and derivational morphology they are associated with? And why do so many languages employ 'non-verbal' expressions for 'have'-constructions (Welmers 1973:308ff.)?

(c) Why does predicative possession exhibit such a large variety of different encodings in the languages of the world? For example, why is the possessor presented as the subject and the possessee as the complement in some languages or some constructions of a given language, while in other languages or constructions the possessee appears as the subject and the possessor as a complement or oblique case expression?

(d) In connection with (c): how are we to explain the observation made by some authors (cf. Benveniste 1960:121; Clark 1978:102; Ultan 1978:34) that the situation found in European languages is not really typologically significant?

1.4 Problems

(e)   If possessive expressions are to be regarded as a subclass of locatives (cf. Lyons 1977:474), what exactly does that mean?
(f)   Why is the syntax of 'have'-constructions frequently highly idiosyncratic, in that it cannot be reconciled with rules operative elsewhere in the language concerned?
(g)   What is the relationship between 'be' and 'have' in the languages of the world? That the two are 'closely related' has been argued for time and again (see especially Locker 1954; Benveniste 1960; Clark 1978) and needs no further elaboration; suffice it to mention that both receive the same, or at least an etymologically related expression in many languages. Is the notion 'have' conceptually included in that of 'be', as some claim (cf. Locker 1954:500)?

One issue that has found less attention in the works mentioned above concerns the question of why many expressions for predicative possession resemble expressions for other kinds of semantic content and how this fact is to be accounted for. For example, why do the following utterances express clearly different contents even though the linguistic means for encoding them are strikingly similar?

(39)   Ewe (Kwa, Niger-Congo)
    (a) é-   kpɔ́ ga   lá.
         s/he-see money the
         'She found the money.'

    (b) é-   kpɔ́ ga.
         s/he-see money
         'She has money.'

Assuming that (39a) is closer to the literal meaning of the utterance concerned, one might argue that there is a metaphorical relation between (39a) and (39b), whereby the possessive notion of 'having money' is expressed in terms of 'seeing' or 'finding money'.

Finally, one may also wonder whether possession is a lexical or a grammatical concept, i.e., whether it should be treated as being part of the lexicon or of grammar. Questions like these are the subject of the chapters to follow; we will attempt to answer them in chapter 5 (5.4).

As the following discussion will show, possession is a wide field and, naturally, we are not able to do justice to all of its various manifestations. We therefore decided to delimit the subject by concentrating on one area, which is predicative possession. There are a number of reasons for this choice. First, because predicative possession has turned out in preceding discussions to be particularly controversial, second, because both its syntax and the conceptual patterns underlying its use appear to be more complex, and, third, because areas such as attributive possession appear to have already received considerable attention in previous works (see Ultan 1978; Chappell and McGregor 1996a). Our main interest is therefore with constructions of the type *X has/owns Y* or, more narrowly, with the way an English utterance such as *Peter has a car* is most likely to be translated into other languages.

Furthermore, the term 'predicative possession' is used in its narrow sense. Unlike other authors (e.g. Miller and Johnson-Laird (1976:558ff.), we will not treat verbs such as 'elude', 'refuse', or 'rob' as verbs of possession, not even verbs that can be said to imply or include the notion of possession, such as 'give' or 'buy'. A number of stimulating attempts have been made to define clusters of such verbs as 'verbs of possession' (see especially Gentner 1975; Miller & Johnson-Laird 1976). As we will see in chapter 2, the theoretical framework used here differs from that employed by these authors. Finally, we will confine ourselves to the most unmarked forms of possessive constructions. This means that the richness of morphological patterns that predicative possession tends to be associated with across verbal tenses, aspects, positive/negative distinctions, etc. must be largely excluded. Much of what is going to be discussed below, however, is also applicable to alternative forms of expressing possession.

2 The process

2.1 Sources

One basic strategy to deal with our environment is to conceive and express experiences that are less easily accessible or more difficult to understand or describe, in terms of more immediately accessible, clearly delineated experiences (Lakoff and Johnson 1980; Stolz 1991). This strategy entails in particular that complex contents are expressed by means of less complex and more basic contents, and abstract concepts by means of more concrete concepts. Grammatical concepts are fairly abstract: they do not refer to physical objects or kinetic processes, and they are defined primarily with reference to their relative function in discourse.

Research on the genesis of grammatical expressions suggests that such expressions do not emerge *ex nihilo*, rather they are almost invariably derived from concrete concepts; grammatical morphology, for example, develops out of lexical structures (see Traugott and Heine 1991a; 1991b; Heine, Claudi, and Hünnemeyer 1991; Hopper and Traugott 1993; Heine *et al.* 1993; Bybee, Perkins, and Pagliuca 1994 for references). In addition to lexical items, there are also some more complex syntactic patterns; one type, referred to as event schemas, has been discussed in more detail in Heine (1993) and will be a key notion in the present book.

As we will see below, possession is a relatively abstract domain of human conceptualization, and expressions for it are derived from more concrete domains. These domains have to do with basic experiences relating to what one does (Action), where one is (Location), who one is accompanied by (Accompaniment), or what exists (Existence). Thus, event schemas may be said to be based on the stereotypic description of recurrent experiences. There is no evidence to suggest that they belong to the material that is biologically inherited.

The term 'schema', as used here, goes back to Bartlett (1932). Since the 1970s, it has been used in a number of fields such as cognitive psychology, social psychology, anthropology, and linguistics, and it has found a wide range of different applications (see Tannen 1993:14–21 for a more detailed discussion), sometimes being used largely interchangeably with other terms such as 'frame' or 'script'. An event schema has the properties commonly associated with schemas: it summarizes important attributes abstracted from a large number of related events, and it has to do with stereotyped situations that we are constantly confronted with (cf. Sanford 1985; Matlin 1989). The term roughly corresponds on the one hand to what Hengeveld (1992) calls a predication type, and on the other hand to the notion of proposition as used by Langacker (1978:857), who defines it as 'a simple semantic unit consisting of a predicate and associated variables'.

What distinguishes event schemas from simple concepts in particular is that the former are composed of more than one perceptually discontinuous entity. For example, an event schema like 'X EATS Y' typically contains three entities, which are X, EAT, and Y. Simple concepts, on the other hand, consist of no more than one entity, even though they may imply the presence of other entities in addition. An inherently relational concept like EAT, for example, typically implies the presence of an agent (X) and a patient (Y). Event schemas may be distinguished linguistically from simple relational concepts like EAT in that each of the two is associated with different kinds of questions. The question 'What happened?', for example, implies an answer in terms of a propositional statement, that is, of an event schema, while a question like 'What did he do to it?' would be suggestive of an answer in terms of a simple concept like EAT.

A sort of schema that is related to the one introduced by Heine (1993) and adopted here is proposed by Shibatani (1996). For him, schemas function as construals on scenes or situations, and grammatical schemas 'represent conceptual archetypes grounded in the experiential domain'. Shibatani uses schemas for example to account for the relationship between specific and abstract constructions. 'Give'-constructions, for example, are said to function as schemas for benefactive constructions, or transitive prototypes as schemas for applicative constructions.

With regard to possession, we will distinguish eight event schemas that account for the majority of possessive constructions in the languages of the world (cf. Locker 1954; Claudi 1986). That the structure of possessive expressions has to be accounted for in terms of propositional rather than lexical entities is not new; it has been argued for occasionally in previous works (cf. Locker 1954; Claudi 1986; Bybee and Pagliuca 1985:73; see 5.1 below). We will now look at each of these schemas in turn. Note that whenever we use the expression 'Y is derived from X' in the following paragraphs

Table 2.1. *A formulaic description of schemas used for the expression of predicative possession*

Formula	Label of event schema
X takes Y	Action
Y is located at X	Location
X is with Y	Companion
X's Y exists	Genitive
Y exists for/to X	Goal
Y exists from X	Source
As for X, Y exists	Topic
Y is X's (property)	Equation

and chapters, we are referring to a diachronic process, more precisely to a reconstruction according to which X is the historical source of Y.

2.1.1   The Action Schema

According to this schema, the notion predicative possession is conceptually derived from a propositional structure involving an agent, a patient, and some action or activity; the process involved can be characterized as in (1), examples are found under (2). (In these as well as all subsequent examples, the interlinear glosses supplied by the authors cited in parentheses are adopted, unless we had substantial evidence in favour of alternative glosses.)

(1)   X takes Y > X has, owns Y

(2)   Portuguese (Freeze 1992:587)
O   menino tem   fome.
the child   takes/has hunger
'The child is hungry.'

Nama (Central Khoisan, Khoisan; Heinz Roberg, p.c.)
kxoe.   p ke   'auto.sa 'uu hââ.
person.M TOP   car . F   take PERF
'The man has the car.'

This schema is discussed by Heine, Claudi, and Hünnemeyer (1991:116) under the label 'acquisition model'. Givón characterizes the evolution of the Action Schema thus: 'Most commonly, a "have" verb arises out of the semantic bleaching of active possession verbs such as "get", "grab", "seize", "take", "obtain" etc., whereby the sense of "acting to take possession" has been bleached, leaving behind only its *implied result* of "having possession"' (Givón 1984:103; 1993,1:145). Three decades earlier, Locker

(1954:504) had described the process leading from verbs meaning 'hold', 'possess', 'receive', 'find', and 'take' to markers for possession, and he viewed this process as a 'victory of the notion of activity' over other concepts. What Locker subsumed under the label 'the verbal expression of the notion of have' (*l'expression verbale de la notion de l'avoir*) includes mostly instances of the Action Schema.

Instead of 'take,' a number of related action verbs can be employed, such as 'seize,' 'grab,' 'catch,' etc., but also non-dynamic and/or inactive verbs like 'hold', 'carry', 'get', 'find', 'obtain', 'acquire', or 'rule'. Examples of the former were given in (2) above; instances of the Action Schema involving inactive verbs can be found, for example, in creole languages, as in the following examples, where a verb meaning 'get' forms the predicate nucleus. As we will see below, however, it is not only creole languages that have made use of this source.

(3) Hawaiian Creole English (Bickerton 1981:66–67)
get wan wahini shi get wan data
'There is a woman who has a daughter.'

West African Pidgin English (Schneider 1966:103)
dís kíng-boi nów gét kómbi fo gów . . .
'The prince hasn't a friend to go . . .'

In a number of French-based creoles as well as in some varieties of French spoken in Africa, it is the verb *gagner* 'gain, win' that has developed into a 'have'-verb (Creissels 1996:154–5).

Verbs forming the predicate nucleus of the Action Schema are typically transitive. Accordingly, the possessor is encoded as the clausal subject and the possessee as the object/complement. In the following example from the Cushitic language Dullay it is the verb *-sheeg-* 'carry a load on the head or the shoulders' (also: 'carry leaves, be pregnant') that appears to be the source of possession:

(4) Dullay (Eastern Cushitic, Afro-Asiatic; Amborn, Minker & Sasse 1980:106; Claudi 1986)
ló'ó an-sheeg-a
cow I- carry-1.SG.IPFV
'I have a cow.'

The way the extension process is likely to proceed is illustrated with the following example from the Mochi dialect of Chaga by using a three-stage model as described by Heine (1993:48ff.; see 2.2 below). In this dialect, the verb *-waḍa* 'seize, take' in its stative form *-woḍe* has given rise to a possessive expression (Claudi 1986):

(5)   Mochi (Bantu, Niger-Congo; Raum 1909:141, 194; Claudi 1986:10)
        (a) wa-   ndu   wa-   waḍa ma-   fumu
            CL.2-people CL.2-take CL.6-spear
            'The people take (their) spears.'

        (b) wa-   ndu   wa-   woḍe ma-   fumu
            CL.2-people CL.2-   CL.6-spear
            (i) 'The people have taken spears.', (ii) 'The people have spears.'

        (c) wu -   woḍe   makanju   hafoi
            CL.11-   waste   much
            'It (i.e. honey) has much waste.'

The notion 'three-stage model' is a diachronic one. This means, for example, that Stage I must have preceded Stage II in time. (5a) represents the source-only Stage I, (5b) the either-or Stage II characterized by ambiguity between source and target meaning, and (5c) the target-only Stage III, which can be interpreted only with reference to possession.

Instances of Stage II situations, where the construction concerned can be interpreted alternatively with reference to the source and the target meanings, are frequently encountered in the languages of the world; a typical example is found in (6).

(6)   Wolof (West Atlantic, Niger-Congo; Claudi 1986)
        am   na   xaalis
        acquire COMPL:3.SG money
        (i) 'He has acquired money', (ii) 'He has money (=he is rich).'

Contrary to claims that the extension from action/process to possession/state has to do with the 'semantic relation of consequence' (cf. Lyons 1967:393; Creissels 1996:152–3), Claudi (1986:9–12) shows that aspectual distinctions like perfective vs. imperfective need not be involved. She demonstrates, for example, that frequently it is not the perfective, stative, or resultative aspect that leads to the emergence of a possessive schema. Thus, in the Waata dialect of Oromo, it is the imperfective (IPFV) rather than the perfective (PFV) aspect that has given rise to a possession schema, as shown in the following examples.

(7)   Waata (East Cushitic, Afro-Asiatic; Claudi 1986:13)
        (a) ani híntal   qaw- a
            I   girl   seize-IPFV
            'I seize a girl.'

        (b) ani híntal qaw- e
            I   girl   seize-PFV
            'I have seized a girl.'

(c) ani mín   qaw- a
    I   house   seize-IPFV
    'I have a house.'

(d) *ani mín   qaw- e
    I   house   seize-PFV

Claudi (1986:6) also subsumes a schematic structure of the form *Y is in X's hand* under what we are describing here as the Action Schema. We will return to this issue below when discussing the Location Schema.

In quite a number of languages there are lexical items used for the expression of predicative possession whose etymological source is unclear. Not infrequently, such items can be traced back to verbs that commonly figure as a predicate nucleus of instances of the Action Schema. Thus, the 'have'-constructions in the Romance and Germanic languages that are seemingly opaque, can ultimately be derived from the Action Schema, involving verbs such as 'take', 'catch', 'get hold of', 'hold', 'grasp', or 'lift' as a predicate nucleus. The German verb *haben* 'have', for example, still had the sense 'hold' or 'keep' as part of its meaning at the stage of Middle High German; in modern German, this sense has disappeared (Brinkmann 1959:185). However, not all instances of diachronically opaque possessive constructions are necessarily derived from that schema. Contrary to views expressed in earlier writings on the subject, the Action Schema is not among the most frequently employed sources for predicative possession, and many possessive constructions in Asian, American, or African languages that seemingly correspond to 'have'-constructions in European languages are not derived from the Action Schema; we will come back to this issue in chapter 5. Locker (1954:506) provides an example from Siamese to substantiate this observation. In the sentence *juŏn mī ḍā dăm* 'Annamites have black eyes', the item *mī* seemingly acts as a verb meaning 'have', and the construction is suggestive of the Action Schema, yet *mī* is a verb of existence, and Locker translates this sentence as meaning literally 'As for Annamites, there are black eyes.' Rather than being suggestive of the Action Schema, this construction is a straightforward instance of another schema to be considered below, viz. the Topic Schema.

2.1.2   The Location Schema

The extension pattern of this schema can be described with the following formula, where X stands for the possessor, Y for the possessee, and *is at* for a locative copula or a stative verb ('be at', 'stay', 'sit', etc.).

(8)   Y is at X's place > X has, owns Y

In accordance with its source form, the syntactic structure of possessive constructions derived from this schema is such that the possessee is encoded as the subject and the possessor as a locative complement. The following examples illustrate this extension:

(9)   Turkish (Lyons 1968a:395)
Ben-de   kitap var
me- LOC   book existent
'I have a book (on me/with me).'

Fijian (Oceanic, Austronesian; Mosel 1983:16)
e   sega tu   vei   au na   ilavo.
PRED.PRT not stand near me ART money
'I don't have any money.'

Estonian (Lehiste 1969:325)
isal   on   raamat
father.ADESSIVE 3.SG.be book.NOM
'Father has (a) book.'

Modern Irish (Orr 1992:252)
tá leabhar agam
is book   at:me
'I have a book.'

Not infrequently, there is no, or no obligatory, verbal item corresponding to the notion *is at* in formula (8); the following example from Russian illustrates such a situation. As we will see below (5.4), there are essentially two main explanations for this fact.

(10)   Russian (Lyons 1967:394)
U menja kniga
at me   book
'I have a book.'

The Location Schema has two common sub-schemas involving formulas of the following kind:

(11)   (a) Y is at X's home   > X has, owns Y
        (b) Y is at X's body-part > X has, owns Y

Examples of sub-schemas (11a) and (11b) are presented in (12) and (13), respectively.

The body-part employed in (11b) is in most cases 'hand', as in (13a), but it may also be 'head' or 'back' (see Claudi and Heine 1986; Claudi 1986).

52   *The process*

Instead of a body-part, it may be the entire body that serves as the nucleus of the locative phrase, as in (13b).

(12)   So (Kuliak, Nilo-Saharan; Carlin 1993:68)
       mek   Auca eo-   a   kus- in
       NEG.be:at Auca home-LOC skin-PL
       'Auca has no clothes.'

(13)   (a) Kpelle (Mande, Niger-Congo; Westermann 1924:20, 193ff.; see also Welmers 1973:316)
           sɛŋkau   a   n   yee- i.
           money.PL be my hand-LOC
           'I have money.'

       (b) Gisiga (Chadic, Afro-Asiatic; Lukas 1970:37)
           du   'a   vəɗo
           millet at body-my
           'I have millet.'

Example (14) is an instance of possession from Ewe, where (14a) illustrates the source and (14b) the target schema. Note that the target structure is decategorialized to the extent that it may no longer take the locative postposition *me* 'in', as can be seen in (14b); we will deal with this situation in more detail in Chapter 2.7. That the target structure has been entirely conventionalized can be demonstrated for example by (15): while (15a), which has the form of the source structure, is not a felicitous utterance, (15b) is an appropriate instance of the Possession Schema.

(14)   Ewe (Kwa, Niger-Congo; Claudi 1986)
       (a) lã   le é- sí   me.
           meat be his-hand in
           'Meat is in his hand.'

       (b) lã   le é- sí.
           meat be his-hand
           'He has meat.'

(15)   (a) *xɔ   le é- sí   me.
           house be his-hand in

       (b) xɔ   le é -sí.
           house be his-hand
           'He has a house.'

As noted above, Claudi (1986:6) considers constructions of the form (11b) as belonging to what we call here the Action Schema, i.e. as being related to expressions of the kind *X holds Y*. While there is some justification for doing so, we will treat such constructions as instances of the Location Schema, especially in view of their clearly locative morphology. However, this issue would seem to require further consideration.

Bambara has developed four different possessive constructions which are all based on the Location Schema, as can be seen in the following examples:

(16) Manding (Mande, Niger-Congo; Claudi 1986:24–31)
    (a) wari   bɛ   à   fɛ̀.
        money be.at his 'place'
        'He has money (i.e. he is rich).'

    (b) mobili bɛ   à   bolo.
        car   be.at his hand
        'He has a car.'

    (c) wari   bɛ   à   kùn.
        money be.at his head
        'He has money (with him).'

    (d) dɔgɔkɛ   bɛ   à   la.
        younger.brother be.at his at
        'He has a younger brother.'

The four constructions are identical except that they use different complement heads: in (a) and (d) the complement head is etymologically a locative postposition (*fɛ̀* 'at' and *la* 'at', respectively), while in (b) and (c) it is etymologically a body-part noun (*bolo* 'hand, arm' and *kùn* 'head', respectively). The semantics and pragmatics of these constructions, however, are different; we will return to this issue in section 2.6.1 (see also Claudi 1986).

2.1.3 The Companion (or Accompaniment) Schema

The extension of this schema, according to which the possessee is conceptualized as a kind of companion, can be described with the following formula:

(17) X is with Y > X has, owns Y

As is obvious from this formula, languages that use this pattern as a conceptual template are likely to encode the possessor as the subject and the possessee as a comitative complement. The example *She is with child*, illustrates the structure of this schema (Ultan 1978:35). The following are examples of Accompaniment:

(18)   //Ani (Central Khoisan, Khoisan; Claudi 1986:16)
!xû   thíyà-n   /gábì-n-   ka   nũĩ
chief many   pipe-C.PL-with   sit
'The chief has many pipes.'

Luo (Western Nilotic, Nilo-Saharan; Stafford 1967:18)
Joluo   nɪ   gɪ   tɪm   mabɛyɔ.
Luo:people   COP   with   habit   good.PL
'The Luo have good customs.'

Khalkha (Mongolian-Tungusic, Altaic; Ultan 1978:35)
xür   daxa-tai
man.NOM   fur- COM
'The man has a fur.'

Guugu Yimidhirr (Pama-Nyungan; Haviland 1979:58)
ngayu   galga-dhirr   ngayu   buurray-irr
1.SG.NOM   spear-COM.ABS   1.SG.NOM   water- COM.ABS
'I have a spear. I have water.'

Portuguese (Freeze 1992:587)
O   menino   esta   com fome.
the child   is   with hunger
'The child is hungry.' (Lit.: 'The child is with hunger.')

Somali has an item *leh-yahay* 'have' which is verbal to some extent but is not treated as a 'full verb' by most Somali grammarians. This item is composed of the particle *leh* which, diachronically, consists of the comitative marker *la* followed by a copula verb, plus the copula verb *-ahay*. Synchronically, this item is an unanalyzable marker of verbal possession, but Serzisko (1984:176) interprets it synchronically as well as a combination of a comitative marker and a copula. That this item can be traced back to the Companion Schema is suggested, *inter alia*, by word order: as in canonical instances of this schema, the possessor is encoded as the subject and the possessee as the complement, as can be seen in (19a). Note that *leh* also occurs without the copula, e.g. in 'belong'-constructions like (19b)(see 1.2 above).

(19)   Somali (Cushitic, Afro-Asiatic; Serzisko 1984:179ff.)
       (a) Naag- ta   baabuur   ay-   ay   leh-dahay.
           woman-ART   car   FOC-3:F   have.3:F
           'The woman has a car.'
       (b) Guri- gaan   yaa   leh?   Hooya- day   baa   leh.
           house-DEM   FOC   have   mother-F.my   FOC   have
           'Whose house is this? It is my mother's.'

In the Venda construction in (20) below, the (a) sentence expresses the original concept of a comitative relation, while the (b) sentence is primarily associated with permanent possession.

(20)   Venda (Bantu, Niger-Congo; Poulos 1990:386–7)
       (a) Ro vha ri na   vhana   mulovha nga   masiari.
           we be we with children yesterday INSTR afternoon
           'We were with children yesterday afternoon.'
       (b) Ndi na   modhoro.
           I.be with motor-car
           'I have a car.'

The difference between accompaniment and possession in (20) can be shown e.g. by paraphrasing (20a) with 'The children were with us yesterday' and (20b) with 'The car is mine'. The following example from Ngalakan, which Hengeveld (1992:165–6) gives as an instance of his 'proprietive predication type', is also suggestive of Accompaniment, where the possessee is introduced by the discontinuous marker *bata . . . yi?* 'with':

(21)   Ngalakan (Gunwinyguan; Hengeveld 1992:166)
       Buru- bata-   gaka- yi?.
       3.NSG-PROPRIETOR-brother-PROPRIETOR
       'They have brothers.'

A perhaps unusual form of the Companion Schema involving a marker of emphasis (EMPH) has been reported from Mandinka, which, like all other Mande languages, has a verb-final syntax:

(22)   Mandinka (Mande, Niger-Congo; Creissels 1979:138)
       n niŋ kòleyaa le   mu
       I with difficulty EMPH it:is
       'I have problems'

Locker (1954:503–4) characterizes the Companion Schema with the formula *I am with something* (*Je suis avec une chose*) and he observes that it is highly restricted in its occurrence, being largely confined to Bantu and other African languages. While this schema is in fact most widely found in Bantu languages in particular and Niger-Congo languages in general, it is none the less of worldwide distribution (cf. Dixon 1980:324–5; Heine, Claudi and Hünnemeyer 1991:116ff.; Kilian-Hatz and Stolz 1992). Stolz (1994:54) considers it possible that underlying the use of this schema there is a metaphor A POSSESSEE IS A COMPANION.

While the schema *Possessor is with Possessee* is the one usually encountered, there are claimed to be exceptions. Creissels (1979:132) observes that in some African languages it is possible to reverse the order of possessor and possessee, that is, to use the propositional formulas *Possessor is with Possessee* and *Possessee is with Possessor* as functionally equivalent expressions. He presents examples (23a) and (23b) to illustrate this claim. Furthermore, Yimas has two comitative-based 'have'-constructions, where one, exemplified by (23c), corresponds to the canonical Companion pattern, while the other, exemplified by (23d), appears to be suggestive of a *Possessee is with Possessor*-schema (Michele Emanatian, p.c.). Note, however, that the latter appears to be only a minor construction that is never preferred to the former and is confined to alienable possession (Foley 1991:306). Finally, Gulf Arabic also has a comitative-based construction where the possessor is encoded as a comitative argument and the possessee (cf. (23e)) agrees with the verb (*Saar* 'become') in gender.

(23)   (a) Nuer (Western Nilotic, Nilo-Saharan; Creissels 1979:132)
j'n à   kè yaŋ OR yaŋ à   kè j'
he exists with cow   cow exists with him
'He has a cow.'

(b) Mangbetu (Central Sudanic, Nilo-Saharan; Creissels 1979:132)
nia   nekinga-ro   OR nekinga a mi- ro
you.are bike-   with   bike   is you-with
'You have a bike.'

(c) Yimas (Papuan; Foley 1991:305)
arm kantk-n   amyak?
water with- 1SG COP. 2.SG
'Do you have kerosene?'

(d) Yimas (Papuan; Foley 1991:306)
arm ma-na-taŋ-taw-n?
water 2.SG. S-DEF-COM-sit-PRES
'Do you have kerosene?'

(e) Gulf Arabic (Semitic, Afro-Asiatic; Holes 1990:95–6)
Saar-   at 9indah   Diifaan
became-3.F with.him guests
'He had guests.'

It would seem that some of these examples need a more detailed analysis before they can be taken as evidence in favour of Creissels' claim. The Nuer example may illustrate this point. Creissels adopted example (23a) from Crazzolara (1933:92), who in fact presents the two sentences as functionally equivalent alternatives. What Creissels fails to observe, however, is, first, the case marking and, second, the function of the preposition *kè* in (23a). Crazzolara (1933:63–6) observes that the item *j'n* represents the 'full sized form' of the personal pronoun ('he, she, it'), while *j'* represents the 'middle sized form' of the same pronoun, and he adds that the 'full sized form' is essentially the subject pronoun while the 'middle sized form' is used to mark direct and indirect objects. The item *kè* is a multi-purpose preposition whose functions include, *inter alia*, that of a comitative and of a locative marker. Comparing the structures exemplified in (23a) with comparable Nuer examples in Crazzolara's grammar, one is led to conclude that the two sentences of (23a) differ considerably in both their structure and their literal meaning: the literal meaning of *j'n à kè yaŋ* can be rendered as 'He is with a cow', while that of *yaŋ à kè j'* is 'A cow is (at the place) where he is.' This means that only the former sentence is an instance of the Companion Schema, while the latter is a straightforward instance of Location, where the possessee is encoded as the subject and the possessor as a locative complement.

Thus, rather than being at variance with the canonical pattern of the Companion Schema, (23a) supports the claim made here that each source schema is strongly associated with a fixed morphosyntactic pattern. Note also that according to Leon Stassen (p.c.) all examples of *Possessee is with possessor* that he is familiar with are 'belong'-constructions of the type *Possessee belongs to Possessor* rather than 'have'-constructions.

The Companion Schema and its effects on the development of 'have'-constructions has been described more recently in a number of studies (see especially Boeder 1980:207–12; Kilian-Hatz 1992; Stolz 1993, 1994). While, prior to its grammaticalization as a possessive schema, it is a flexible and variable structure in many languages, once grammaticalized it tends to become fixed and invariable in the form sketched in (17) above.

2.1.4 The Existence Schema

The term 'Existence Schema' may be misleading since it subsumes two kinds of propositions: one that has a one-argument structure of the form *Y exists*, let us call it 'nuclear existence', and another one that has a two-argument structure of the form *Y exists with reference to X*, which could be called 'extended existence' since it appears to be historically derived from the former by adding a second argument. As we will see below (especially

58 *The process*

section 2.3), nuclear existence does not provide a source for predicative possession; rather it may itself be derived from 'have'-constructions. Extended existence, however, is a common source for predicative possession. In the following chapters the term 'Existence' will refer exclusively to extended existence.

The formula *Y exists with reference to X* is an abstract one that has no direct correspondence to actually occurring linguistic structures; rather the formula stands for three types, which we will call the Genitive, the Goal, and the Topic Schemas.

2.1.4.1 The Genitive Schema

Clark (1978:115) found the genitive case to be used for the possessor in the following languages: Classical Armenian, Bengali, Chuvash, English, German, Hindi, Panjabi, and Yoruba. As these examples suggest, however, presence of the genitival morphology is not sufficient to distinguish schemas: there are two contrasting schematic structures that tend to involve such morphology for their expression (see 2.4 for more details). One of these is discussed below under the label Equation Schema. The second is the one looked at here.

The Genitive Schema is characterized by the fact that the possessor is encoded as a genitival modifier of the possessee. This schema exploits existing means of encoding possessive relations between thing-like entities, that is, attributive possession, for the expression of propositional forms of encoding possession. The schema involves a one-place propositional structure, as sketched in (24); examples can be found in (25).

(24)   X's Y exists > X has Y

(25)   K'ekchi' (Mayan, Penutian; Freeze 1992:589)
       wan   iš-   soʔsol-   č'ič'   li   išq.
       COP.LOC   3.GEN-dragonfly-metal   the   woman
       'The woman has a helicopter.' (Lit.: 'The woman's helicopter is.')

       Yanomama (Chibchan, Chibchan-Paezan; Migliazza 1972:125)
       kama e   şama ki-a   ki reh
       he   GEN   tapir there:is Q
       'Does he have a tapir?' (Lit.: 'Does his tapir exist?')

       Turkish (Lyons 1967:395)
       Kitab-im var
       book- my existent
       'I have a book.'

Locker (1954:502) describes the Genitive Schema under the formula *My X exists* (*Mon ... existe*). The examples he provides include Quechua *llamay canmi* ('my lama is') 'I have a lama', and Huailou (New Caledonia) *û na wi na nō xivu* ('yes, there is a word of us two') 'we have something to say'.

2.1.4.2 The Goal Schema
The structure of the Goal Schema can be described by means of the following formula:

(26)   Y exists to/for X > X has, owns Y

This schema typically consists of a verb of existence or of location, where the possessor is encoded as a dative/benefactive or goal case expression and the possessee typically as a subject constituent. Since dative/benefactive markers are frequently derived from allative/directional markers, the latter functions may also be part of the case marker figuring in the Goal Schema. This applies, for example, to the suffix *-ni* occurring in the Japanese example below (see Makino 1968:4). The following are examples of this schema:

(27)   Bolivian Quechua (Quechuan, Andean; Bills, Vallejo and Troike 1969:186)
waska tiya- puwan.
rope   exist-for.me
'I have a rope.'

Palestinian Arabic (Freeze 1992:585)
kan   ʿind il   walad ktaab.
COP.TNS   to the boy book
'The boy had a book.'

Tamil (Dravidian; Ultan 1978:33)
ena-kku oru nalla naay (irukkiratu).
me- DAT   a   good dog   is
'I have a good dog.'

Japanese (Korean-Japanese, Altaic; Makino 1968:4)
John-(ni)-wa kuruma-ga ar-ru.
John to   car   is
'John has a car.'

Kashmiri (Indic, Indo-European; Kachru 1968:35–36)
šɪːlas   čhu   dɔd
Sheela:DAT COP   milk
'Sheela has milk.'

Malayalam (Dravidian, Elamo-Dravidian; Asher 1968:99)
avan   oru vit   unt
him.DAT one house is
'He has a house.'

Breton (Celtic, Indo-European; Orr 1992:252–3)
ur velo c'hlas am   eus
a bike blue to:me is
'I have a blue bike.'

Languages having a case morphology are likely to use the Dative marker or its nearest equivalent for encoding the possessor. In Ik, for example, the verb employed is the locative copula i-, the possessor is encoded by means of the Dative (Goal) suffix -k^e and the possessee noun phrase appears in the Absolute case, which usually marks the clausal object:

(28)   Ik (Kuliak, Nilo-Saharan; Heine 1983:157)
    (a) iá   ho- k^e
        exist house-DAT
        'S/he is in the house.'

    (b) iá   hoa   ńci- k^e
        be.at:3.SG house I   -DAT
        'I have a house.' (Lit.: 'There is a house to/for me.')

A characteristic shown by the Goal Schema in Hungarian is that there is agreement in person (optionally also in number) between the possessor and the possessee, whereby the possessee noun phrase has a pronominal suffix on it agreeing with the possessor noun phrase:

(29)   Hungarian (Biermann 1985:85)
    nek- em   van macská-m
    DAT-1.SG is   cat-   1.SG
    'I have a cat'

    nek-ed   van macská-d
    DAT-2.SG is   cat-   2.SG
    'You have a cat.'

    a   fiú-nak   van macská-ja
    the boy-DAT is   cat-   3.SG
    'The boy has a cat'

In a number of works, the Location and Goal Schemas are not distinguished, rather both are treated as reflecting one and the same general structure. While in fact in some languages it turns out to be hard to distinguish between the two (see below), it is hoped that the present discussion has made it clear that they represent different cognitive patterns. This is suggested most clearly by languages which distinguish the two schemas both diachronically and synchronically, as is the case, for example, in Ewe (see 2.6.2 below).

Instances of the Goal Schema are also found in some Romance languages, cf. (30). As we noted in chapter 1, the Goal Schema was grammaticalized in different directions: while it has given rise to a 'have'-construction in Latin, a 'belong'-construction emerged in French.

(30) Latin (Lyons 1967:392)
      Est Johanni   liber.
      is John.DAT book.NOM
      'John has a book.'

      French
      Le livre est à moi.
      the book is to me
      'The book is mine.'

Instead of a dative or benefactive case marker, some languages have an object case marker in 'have'-constructions, and we tentatively group the relevant constructions together with the Goal Schema. Ultan (1978:34) notes, for example, that Classical Tajik uses the direct object postposition *ro* to indicate the possessor, for example *uu-ro yak pisar bul* 'he had one son'. It would seem that there are reasons for such a grouping. Turkana, for example, has a construction that is suggestive of the Goal Schema, but there is no equivalent of a dative case marker in this language, and conceivably for this reason, the Absolute case is used instead. Note that the Absolute case marks both direct and indirect objects and what in other languages is encoded by means of dative case inflections is likely to be marked in Turkana by means of the Absolute case. In accordance with canonical constructions of the Goal Schema, the possessee appears as the sentence subject (in the Nominative case) in Turkana:

(31) Turkana (Eastern Nilotic, Nilo-Saharan; Dimmendaal 1983:82)
      e-yaká-sı   ayɔ́ŋ`   ŋá-atuk.
      3–be- PL I.ABS PL-COW.NOM
      'I have cows.'

2.1.4.3 The Topic Schema

A third instance of Existence involves constructions where the possessor is presented as a kind of clausal topic or theme: it appears as a topic or theme constituent in clause-initial position, but it also figures as a possessive modifier of the possessee in addition. The resulting schematic structure can be sketched in (32); some examples are found in (33).

(32)   As for X, Y (of X) exists > X has, owns Y

(33)   Lango (Western Nilotic, Nilo-Saharan; Noonan 1992:148)
òkélò gwók'kɛ́rɛ̂ pé
Okelo dog.his 3.NEG.exist
'Okelo doesn't have a dog.'

Luiseño (Uto-Aztecan; Steele 1977:115ff.)
noo=n no-paaʔaʃ ʔawq
I= CLIT my-brother is
'I have a brother.'

Since the topicalized constituent tends to acquire properties of a subject and to be increasingly grammaticalized as a subject, the result is a construction having two subjects; Seiler (1983:60) therefore proposes the term 'double subject strategy' for such cases (see 2.5.3). Note, however, that not all instances of what has been called 'double subject' or 'multiple subject constructions' (see e.g. Kuno 1973:62–78) belong here. We will return to this issue in the next chapter (3.2).

In the Uto-Aztecan language Cahuilla there are three different instances of the Topic Schema. The first, exemplified by (34a), has *mí-yax-wen* '(it) is somehow, (it) exists' as a predicate. The second, exemplified by (34b), uses the predicate form *híw-qal* '(it) is living, (it) exists' and serves to establish possession involving kinship terms, while the third has the verb *qál* 'to be placed (somewhere), to exist' as its predicate and takes humans as possessors and cultural implements as possessees, as in (34c).

(34)   Cahuilla (Uto-Aztecan; Seiler 1983:58)
(a) wíkikmaĺ-em hem- wákʔa míyaxwen
    bird-   PL their wing exists
    '(The) birds have wings'

(b) néʔ né-pas   híw.qal
    I   my-older:brother he.live.DUR
    'I have a brother'

(c) néʔ ne-cípatmal qál
    I   my-basket   placed
    'I have a basket'

While *qál* has the semantics of a locative verb, it functions as a one-place predicate in (34c), behaving like a verb of existence. Thus, we are dealing with what Seiler calls double subjects. Locker (1954:501–2) was perhaps the first to clearly propose Topic as a distinct pattern of forming 'have'-constructions. He describes it by means of the formula *As far as I am concerned, it exists* (*En ce qui me concerne, il existe*). He observes that the Topic Schema is found mainly in the Far East, and he gives Japanese, Mongolian, and Khmer as examples.

The three schemas that we have subsumed under the label Existence may form one of the minor schemas and, as such, they appear to be fairly common. Gabu, for example, has grammaticalized the Companion Schema (*X is with Y*; Santandrea 1965:118) as its major schema, but uses the Genitive Schema in addition, as is suggested by (35a). Similarly, in Gisiga the Location Schema appears to provide the main pattern for verbal possession, as in (35b), but in the examples provided by Lukas there are also instances of the Genitive Schema, as in (35c).

(35) (a) Gabu (Ubangi, Niger-Congo; Santandrea 1965:119)
aduturu dii lɔ mbi
dog   my is there
'I have a dog.'

(b) Gisiga (Chadic, Afro-Asiatic; Lukas 1970:37, 145)
du   'a və-   ɗo
millet at body-my
'I have millet'

(c) hagam- ɗo da
hoe-   my exist
'I have a hoe'

Stassen (1995) discovered a construction type having the form *X exists, Y exists* which has been grammaticalized to a 'have'-construction (*X has Y*). On the basis of the evidence provided it does not become entirely clear what the source schema is, yet the most plausible hypothesis would be that we are dealing with a special instance of the Topic Schema, first, because the word order involved is possessor–possessee and, second, because the possessee is presented in the form of an existential predication. Note further that in the following example from Zapotec there is cross-referencing between possessor and possessee which, while not an obligatory property of the Topic Schema, nevertheless is commonly associated with it. What distinguishes this kind of structure essentially from other instances of the Topic Schema is the fact that the theme or topic is presented as a clause rather than a noun phrase.

(36)   Ixtlan Zapotec (Zapotecan, Oto-Manguean; Stassen 1995)
        doa tu jrudi,   doa tu beku to   kye
        exist one gentleman, exist one dog small his
        'A certain gentleman had a little dog' (Lit.: 'There was a gentleman, there was his little dog')

2.1.5   The Source Schema

The structure of this schema can be described by means of formula (37a) and an example is found in (37b). What is perhaps the main linguistic property of this schema is that the possessor is expressed as an ablative participant, typically encoded as a marker denoting notions such as 'from', 'off', 'out of', etc.

(37)   (a) Y exists (away) from X > X has, owns Y

        (b) Slave (Athabaskan, Na-Dene; Rice 1989)
            ts'ét'ú   nets'e.
            cigarette   you.from
            'Do you (sg.) have cigarettes?'

As we will see in chapter 3, the Source Schema provides an important conceptual template for expressions for attributive possession in European languages. As a source for predicative possession, however, this schema appears to be virtually irrelevant. The examples we were able to find are of the kind to be observed in Ik: in this Ugandan language, Goal provides the major source for 'have'-constructions, as exemplified in (38a). In negative forms, the possessor is encoded in the Ablative case and the construction is seemingly an instance of the Source Schema, cf. (38b). Note, however, that the verb employed in negative possession (*bɪra-*) requires its locative complement to be in the Ablative case, as can be seen in (38c). Very likely therefore, the use of the Ablative in the negative possessive construction is due to a lexical property of the verb *bɪra-* rather than being suggestive of the Source Schema.

(38)   Ik (Kuliak, Nilo-Saharan; Heine 1983:157)
        (a) iá   hoa   ńci-kᵉ
            exist house.NOM I- DAT
            'I have a house' (Lit.: 'There exists a house to/for me')

        (b) bɪra   hoa   ńcu-u
            absent.be house.NOM I- ABL
            'I have no house' (Lit.: 'There exists no house from me')

(c) bɪra   ho-   o
    absent.be house-ABL
    'S/he is not in the house'

2.1.6   The Equation Schema

The second main pattern of predicative possession that involves some genitival-possessive morphosyntax is called the Equation Schema. Its structure is outlined in (39).

(39)   Y is X's (property) > Y belongs to X

'Equation Schema' does not mean that we are dealing with an identity between Y and X, and Watkins (1967:2193) therefore describes this schema as predicating an 'identity of inequality'. Nevertheless, we will retain that term since the notion of equation or identity appears to have provided the structural template on which the schema is built.

While the Genitive Schema has a one-place propositional structure, the Equation Schema has two places (Y and $X's$). This schema differs from all other schemas, first, in that it does not involve conceptual shift, that is, its source meaning is essentially the same as its target meaning. Second, whereas other schemas, with few exceptions, give rise to 'have'-constructions, the Equation Schema is invariably associated with 'belong'-constructions. Nevertheless, it can be found in many languages worldwide, cf. English *The book is John's* (Lyons 1967:391, 1977:722). Further examples of this schema are:

(40)   Russian (Lyons 1967:394)
         Kniga moja
         book my
         'The book is mine.'

         Mandarin Chinese (Lyons 1967:393)
         Shū shì, wǒ-de.
         book be   me-of
         'The book is mine.'

Conceivably, an equation may also be derived from the Source Schema, that is, a structure where the possessor is presented by means of an ablative or related morphology (see 3.1 below). A Spanish example might be *ese lapiz es del profesor* 'This pencil belongs to the teacher' (Thomas Stolz, p.c.), even though it may well be that this Spanish 'belong'-construction derives directly from the genitival construction rather than from the Source

Schema. On the whole, however, the Source Schema is irrelevant for predicative possession, though not for attributive possession, as we will see in chapter 3.

The possessor may be encoded as a possessive modifier of a dummy noun whose lexical meaning is likely to be 'property' or 'thing', as illustrated in the following example:

(41) Ewe (Kwa, Niger-Congo)
 Ʊ̃ lá nyé tɔ nye.
 car the be property my
 'The car belongs to me.'

Instances of the Equation Schema usually exist side by side with instances of other schemas, where Equation is a means of presenting definite possessees. The following example of the Equation Schema is taken from Swahili (42b), whose main source of 'have'-constructions is derived from the Companion Schema (42a):

(42) Swahili (Bantu, Niger-Congo)
 (a) Ni-na   saa.
   1- be.with watch
   'I have a watch.'

 (b) Saa   ni y-   angu.
   Cl.9:watch be CL.9–my
   'The watch is mine.'

Watkins (1967; cf. Clark 1978:115–16) argues that in Indo-European, the Goal and the Equation Schemas were used to indicate different types of possession, the former being associated with temporary possession, without necessarily implying ownership, while the latter was used for 'true ownership'. The former is illustrated by (43a), where the possessor is encoded in the Dative case (*Johanni*) and the latter by (43b), where the possessor appears in the Genitive case (*Johannis*). We will return to this issue below.

(43) Latin (cf. Watkins 1967; Clark 1978:115–16)
 (a) Liber est Johanni.
   'John has a book.'
 (b) Liber est Johannis.
   'The book is John's.'

Clark (1978:115) observes that the two cases generally used for the possessor are the dative and the genitive. This statement in itself is not sufficient to provide any clues as to which schemas are involved, since both the Genitive and the Equation Schemas are likely to involve a genitival morphology and, as we will see below (2.3, 2.4), the two schemas tend to be associated with different possessive notions. The Latin example (43b) provided above is an instance of Equation since it is suggestive of the schematic structure *Y is X's (property)*, while the Genitive Schema is based on the schematic structure *X's Y exists*, that is, we are dealing with a two-argument structure in the former case and a one-argument structure in the latter.

2.1.7 Discussion

In a number of languages, the Genitive Schema provides the primary means of expressing inalienable possession, while alienable possession is expressed by means of other schemas. Ik has grammaticalized the Goal Schema for both inalienable and alienable verbal possession (see above). In the case of permanent and inalienable possession, Ik has developed an alternative expression type in addition based on the Genitive Schema, i.e. the possessor is encoded as a Genitive modifier of the possessed noun phrase; cf. the following examples:

(44)   Ik (Kuliak, Nilo-Saharan; Heine 1983:157)
    (a) iá   hoa   nci-k^e.
        be.at:3.SG house 1.SG-DAT
        'I have a house (not necessarily my own).'
    (b) iá   hoa   nci- i.
        be.at:3.SG house 1.SG-GEN
        'I have a house (inalienable).' (Lit.: 'My house exists.')

Similarly, Anywa uses the Goal Schema for alienable possession, as in (45a). Inalienable possession again is expressed by the Genitive Schema if the possessor is known to the hearer (45b) and Topic if the possessor is either unknown or has not been mentioned in the preceding discourse (45c):

(45)   Anywa (Western Nilotic, Nilo-Saharan; Reh 1994a)
    (a) yàa, jìr-ā   dá   gwèl.
        yes, to-me exist money
        'Yes, I have money.'
    (b) dá   cí-   ɛ́.
        exist wife:of-3:SG
        'He has a wife.'

(c) ojʌk dá cí-   '.
    Ojak exist wife:of-3:SG
    'Ojak has a wife.'

Furthermore, in Hindi, the Location Schema appears to be used for alienable possession, as in (46a), and the Genitive Schema for inalienable possession, as in (46b) and (46c) (see Freeze 1992:591).

(46)   Hindi (Indo-European; Freeze 1992:591)
    (a) larkee-   kee   paas   kuttaa hai.
        boy.OBL-GEN proximity dog   COP.3.PRES
        'The boy has a dog.' (Lit.: 'By the boy is a dog.')
    (b) meree   doo   bhaii   hãĩ.
        my.PL   two   brother COP.3.PL
        'I have two brothers.' (Lit.: 'My two brothers are.')
    (c) baccee-   kee   dãāt   safeed hãĩ.
        child.OBL-GEN.PL   teeth   white   COP.3.PL
        'The child has white teeth.' (Lit.: 'The child's white teeth are.')

A slightly more complicated situation is found in Kpelle. In this West Atlantic language, expressions of alienable possession are derived from the Location Schema of the form *Y is in X's hand*, as illustrated in (47a) below. Inalienable possession is derived from a pattern that, on the surface, is exactly the same except that the phrase *X's hand* (*yée-ì*) is replaced by the phrase *its surface* (*m̀à*), as can be seen in (47b).

(47)   Kpelle (West Atlantic, Niger-Congo; Welmers 1973:316)
    (a) sɛŋ-kâu   káa   ń- yée-   ì
        money   be.at   my-hand-LOC
        'I have money.'
    (b) ń- yée   feerɛ káa   m̀à
        my-hand   two   be.at its.surface
        'I have two hands'

According to Welmers' description, however, there is a decisive difference between the two constructions: The phrase *káa m̀à* in (47b) has been grammaticalized to a marker expressing the notion '(there) exist(s)', and (47b) could therefore also be translated as 'my two hands exist'. This has led to a different way of possessor–possessee encoding, according to which the possessor appears as a nominal modifier of the subject noun phrase. The Kpelle sentence (47b) is thus structurally similar to the Ik sentence (44b), considering the fact that Kpelle is a verb-medial (SVO) and Ik a verb-initial (VSO) language. Note that, like the Ik example, the Kpelle instance of the Genitive Schema is confined to expressions of inalienable possession involving kinship terms, body-parts, or the item 'God' (Welmers 1973:316).

Instances of the Location and the Goal Schemas may have strikingly similar structures, in that (a) the possessee is encoded as the sentence subject, (b) the possessor noun phrase has a form that resembles the locative morphology, and (c) the predicate consists of a copula-like verb. That, nevertheless, the two must be distinguished is suggested by observations such as the following: first, if both schemas are associated with a locative morphology to mark the possessor, then the locative concept expressed is static (to be translated by 'at, by', etc.) in the case of the Location Schema, while it expresses some goal-orientation ('to, for,', etc.) in the case of the Goal Schema. Second, the possessor is presented as a complement in the former but as an adjunct in the latter case. Third, while in many languages verbs expressing location ('be at') and existence ('exist, be there') are homophonous, some languages do distinguish the two. In Ewe, the former is *le* and the latter *lee* or *lii* and, accordingly, the former occurs in instances of the Location Schema, as in (48a) and the latter in instances of the Goal Schema, as in (48b).

(48)   Ewe (Kwa, Niger-Congo; Felix Ameka, p.c.)
    (a) ga   le   así   nye.   (Location Schema)
        money be.at hand my
        'I have money.'

    (b) ga   sia   é   lii   ná m.   (Goal Schema)
        money this FOC exist to me
        'I have the money (I want to spend).'

It goes without saying that the above source schemas do not account for all expressions of verbal possession in the languages of the world. First, there are constructions whose conceptual source is no longer accessible on the basis of synchronic evidence (see below). We will refer to these expressions as etymologically opaque or, in short, as *opaque expressions*. Second, grammatical or typological descriptions are not always detailed enough to allow for a reconstruction of source schemas. Descriptive statements commonly found in the relevant literature, like 'possession is expressed by means of the element "to be"', are too general and, hence, not very helpful for our purposes, considering the fact that such elements are likely to figure in all source schemas except Action.

Third, while the schemas outlined above can be said to present the major

70   *The process*

and statistically predominant sources for 'have'-constructions, there are also a number of less common patterns that are employed for encoding predicative possession. One schema that provides a rich source for the development of various types of grammatical categories, but appears to be virtually irrelevant as a source for 'have'-constructions, is the Source Schema, as we saw above (2.1.5).

Another pattern is characterized by the use of a more or less grammaticalized item denoting 'owner' or 'possessor.' Typically that item can be described with reference to a grammaticalization chain extending from a relational noun at one end to a derivational affix at the other. Example (49) illustrates the use of such an item. The derivative suffix -tɔ 'owner' in (49) appears to be derived from the relational noun tɔ́ 'father', and in some languages, nouns meaning 'father' and/or 'mother' have been grammaticalized to possessive markers. In Gulf Arabic, for example, certain kinds of inalienable possession are expressed by a noun + noun construction where the first noun is *abu* 'father of' or *ʔumm* 'mother of'. While this construction is used essentially for attributive possession, it also appears to figure in predicative statements, as is suggested by (50).

(49)   Ewe (Kwa, Niger-Congo)
       xɔ-   tɔ   wo- nyé.
       house-OWNER 3.SG-is
       'He is a house owner; he has a house.'

(50)   Gulf Arabic (Semitic, Afro-Asiatic; Holes 1990:96–7)
       il-musajjila   ʔumm   mikrufuun   thaabit.
       the-tape-recorder mother (of) microphone fixed
       'The tape-recorder has a built-in microphone.'

In Malay, the item *punya* 'to have' is a reduced form of *empu-punya* 'its owner'. Hopper (1986:132) observes that 'the original syntax was (and often still is) of the form *rumah ini saya punya* "this house I [am] its owner", requiring the possessed object to be a definite topic'.

Another kind of source pattern that is encountered occasionally is described by Hengeveld (1992:168–9) as the 'predicative quantifier predication type', where the predicate nucleus consists of or includes some quantifying item, as can be seen in the following examples:

(51)   Navajo (Na-Dene; Hengeveld 1992:168)
       Shi- béeso 'ádin.
       1.SG-money none/zero
       'I have no money.' (Lit.: 'My money is zero'.)

(52)   Fijian (Oceanic, Austronesian; Hengeveld 1992:168)
       Sā   rua na   nodra lawa.
       EMPH two ART their net
       'They have two nets.' (Lit.: 'Their nets are two.')

Furthermore, one might wish to mention the particles and affixes to be found in many languages that may be translated by means of 'having' and that tend to be described as proprietive markers, for example in Djaru, Warrungu, and Anindilyakwa (Tsunoda 1996). Note also that Stolz (1994:54–5) considers it possible that side by side with the Companion Schema there is a closely related schema according to which the possessee is introduced as an instrument rather than as a companion.

Finally, Locker (1954:501) observes that there are languages, such as Tamil, Laotian, and Quileute, that employ the same construction for 'be'-relations and for 'have'-relations. There are in fact a few languages for which a similar situation has been reported; see, for example, Munro (1990:23–4) on the Kawaiisu language of south-central California. It would seem, however, that the situation to be found in these languages deserves a more detailed analyis. The only example that we are personally familiar with where exactly the same construction is used for equation and/or existence possession is Kenya Pidgin Swahili. When ambiguity may arise, however, the Companion Schema is employed, which is also the major source for 'have'-constructions in Standard-Swahili. Thus, example (53) may be an instance of either equation/identity or possession. But in contexts where it remains unclear which of the two meanings is intended, (53) is replaced by (54) to express possession.

(53)   Kenya Pidgin Swahili (Bantu, Niger-Congo)
       Ochieng' iko mpishi.
       Ochieng' be cook
       (i) 'Ochieng' is a cook.' (ii) 'Ochieng' has a cook.'

(54)   Ochieng' iko na   mpishi.
       Ochieng' be with cook
       'Ochieng' has a cook.'

These are but a few examples of the kinds of constructions that may be found in addition to the source schemas discussed above; for further examples see Locker (1954). As we will see in more detail in chapter 4 (4.4), the verbal items figuring as a predicate nucleus in the various schemas do not all exhibit the same degree of grammaticalization; rather, they can be arranged along the following scale, where the leftmost pole represents the least and the rightmost pole the most grammaticalized situation (see Devitt 1990:103, 113).

(55)   Postural>Locative>Existential>Copula with a   >General
       verb   verb   verb   temporary sense copula

If the discussion in the preceding paragraphs may have led to the conclusion that each language is associated essentially only with one of the source schemas distinguished then such a conclusion would be partly right and partly wrong. It is right in so far as, within a given language, one schema is likely to be favoured as a means of expressing predicative possession; we will refer to such a schema as the *major schema* (see 2.5.1). A cursory look at a larger number of languages suggests that the areal distribution of major schemas is not accidental, rather it correlates to some extent with geographical parameters. Languages in Europe, for example, have, at least over the last two millennia, drawn primarily on the Action Schema for developing 'have'-constructions, while people in central and southern Africa have preferred the Companion Schema instead.

Nevertheless, the conclusion alluded to above is also misleading in that, as we argue here, the various schemas belong to the universal pool of human conceptualization, where the term 'universal' has two different aspects. On the one hand, it refers to our claim that all schemas are potentially available to all speech communities worldwide. On the other hand, it means that, rather than selecting only one out of the entire pool of schemas, a given community may simultaneously draw on several or even all schemas for the expression of possessive notions. As we will see in more detail in 2.6, it is quite common for a given language to derive expressions for predicative possession from three or more different schemas.

Furthermore, even if one particular schema is strongly favoured in a given language, as is the case in English, there tend to be constructions derived from alternative schemas that serve as paraphrases for possessive constructions. We may illustrate this observation with reference to the approach used by Bendix (1966) to deal with what he calls 'A has B' constructions in English. Bendix distinguishes two kinds of such constructions, which he calls, respectively, the inherent and the general 'A has B', a classification that largely corresponds to our inalienable/alienable distinction (see 1.2 above). The former is characterized by using kinship and body-part terms, as well as a number of other relational nominals, for 'B', that is, for the possessee. His general construction includes all those possessive relations that are not inherent. The general construction is defined by means of the following formula (the symbols are those used by Bendix (1966:39)):

(56) B is X A B→A has B
where X=*with*,
         for,
         to+Verb (+/−Z), or
         Locative Preposition (+/−Z), and
Y may be null.

This formula can be interpreted roughly in the following way: there is a regular relationship between 'A has B' and 'B is X A B', whereby the former is derived by paraphrasis from the latter. Now, as the examples provided by Bendix (1966:39-45) show, the kinds of paraphrase from which 'A has B' is said to be derived are mostly constructions that are suggestive of the schemas that in other languages provide the main source for conventionalized 'have'-constructions. Thus, the following examples presented by Bendix appear to be instances of the Location (57a) and the Goal Schemas (57b), respectively.

(57) (a) The name you want is on this list. → This list has the name you want.
      (b) The hardest task will be for John. → John will have the hardest task.

In a similar way, Bendix (1966:45ff.) defines inherent 'A has B' by means of formula (58), exemplified by (59).

(58) There is a C   + C is A's B   → A has a B.

(59) There is a son + the son is John's son. → John has a son.

Like general 'A has B', inherent 'A has B' is claimed to exhibit a regular relationship of paraphrase and, consequently, is claimed to be derived from a sequence of an existential ('There is a C') and an equative construction ('C is A's B'). Once again we notice that there is a 'have'-construction that is said to be systematically related to two of the source schemas described in the previous sections, viz. the Existence (*Y exists*) and the Equation Schemas (*Y is X's*), respectively.

It is immaterial for our purposes whether we believe, as Bendix (1966) does, that the paraphrase relationships sketched above are part of the conventionalized morphosyntax of English and, furthermore, that these relationships can be accounted for by deriving 'have'-sentences from other kinds of schematic structures. What is of interest here is the fact that even in a language like English, which has grammaticalized only a small number out of the total range of source schemas, virtually all of these schemas surface in certain constructions and can be interpreted as providing paraphrases for 'have'-sentences. To summarize, there are at least three different ways in which a source schema may be linked with the domain of possession: either it develops into the major 'have'-construction in that language, or it provides any of the minor constructions that express only a limited range of possessive notions and/or occur in specific contexts only, or else it concerns constructions whose primary function is to express such notions as location, goal, etc., but which in certain uses may be understood to express some possessive notion or, alternatively, to provide a convenient paraphrase for such a notion.

The various schemas looked at above differ from one another in a number of ways. First, they exhibit contrasting conceptual properties: notions such as action and location do not seem to have any salient properties in common. Second, they clearly differ in their relative degree of abstractness. This is suggested, for example, by the conceptual derivation patterns obtaining between schemas. Thus, instances of the Action and the Location Schemas can give rise to Existence while the opposite does not seem to happen. This is suggested by the lexical development from action verbs (e.g. 'give') to existential verbs (cf. German *Es gibt kein Bier* ('it gives no beer') 'There is no beer'), or from locative verbs ('be somewhere', 'live, remain, stay somewhere') to existential verbs. Similarly, action verbs may give rise to expressions for accompaniment, that is, to comitative markers (see Heine, Claudi, and Hünnemeyer 1991).

There is a widespread assumption to the effect that the Action Schema as a source model for 'have'-constructions constitutes a relatively late acquisition in the languages of the world. As we will see below (section 2.7), such an assumption is without foundation. While prevalent in Europe, the Action Schema is not the most frequently employed source for possession. Nevertheless, this schema does occur in virtually all parts of the world, in a similar way as the other source schemas do. Such a conclusion can be reached, for example, when looking at the quantitative data of a survey carried out by Dirk Otten (1992) on 'have'-constructions in African languages. According to this survey, the Action Schema is made use of in 14 out of 93 languages, that is, in roughly 15 per cent of the languages considered.

Similar observations were made in the course of our own survey. This survey is based on a world-wide sample of 100 languages; the nature of the sample can be derived from the details presented in the Appendix of this

Table 2.2. *Source schemas for 'have'-constructions in 100 languages according to continents. (Only major schemas are considered; note that there are some languages that have more than one major schema.)*

Source schema	No. of major schemas					Total	Percentage
	Europe	Asia	Africa	America	Indian/ Pacific Ocean		
Action	3	1	9	1	1	15	13.6%
Location	5	8	9	1	–	23	20.9%
Companion	–	–	7	3	4	14	12.7%
Genitive	–	2	4	5	5	16	14.6%
Goal	3	11	4	1	3	22	20.0%
Topic	–	4	1	3	3	11	10.0%
Opaque and other schemas	1	–	3	5	–	9	8.2%
Total	12	26	37	19	16	110	100%

work. The sample includes languages from most of the major language families and from all major regions of the world. While an attempt was made to have as much linguistic and geographical diversity as possible represented in the survey, no claim is made that the sample is in fact 'representative' of the world's languages at large. The distribution of source schemas according to continents is shown in Table 2.2. As can be seen in this table, the Action Schema accounts for only 13.6% of the have-constructions in the 100 languages of the sample.

The figures presented in Table 2.2 are suggestive of a relatively weakly contrasting geo-linguistic profile: contrary to what has been observed in other domains of grammaticalization (cf. Heine 1994a), the choice of source schemas for possession does not seem to be influenced strongly by areal forces. Nevertheless, there are a few correlations that one might wish to look at in more detail in future research, such as the following:

(a)　The primary source schemas in European languages are Action and Location, all other models being largely irrelevant, perhaps with the exception of the Goal Schema.

(b)　The primary source for 'have'-constructions in Asiatic languages is Existence: 17 out of 26 languages in our sample, that is, roughly two out of three, have one of the three variants of Existence, i.e. Genitive, Goal, or Topic, as their conceptual source. Existence constitutes altogether the most frequent source domain: every third 'have'-construction in our sample (34 %) can be traced back to any of its three variants.

(c) In Africa on the other hand, Existence is not very common as a source model for 'have'-constructions; rather, Location, Companion, and Action appear to provide the primary choices.

The preceding paragraphs have shown that possessive expressions are not original, rather that they are invariably derived from expressions having non-possessive meanings. The development concerned is called grammaticalization, which we will now look at in more detail.

2.2 Grammaticalization

By grammaticalization we mean a process whereby a linguistic expression E, in addition to its conventional meaning M_1, receives a more abstract and more grammatical meaning M_2. With M_1 we refer here to the meaning of the source schemas discussed in the previous section (2.1) and with M_2 to the possessive meanings these source schemas acquire.

The process from M_1 to M_2 has been described by students of grammaticalization in a number of ways: it has been analyzed in terms of metaphorical and/or metonymic transfer, or of pragmatic mechanisms involving inferencing or implicatures or, in more general terms, as context-induced reinterpretation. We will not go into details here; the reader is referred to the relevant literature for more information (Heine, Claudi and Hünnemeyer 1991; Traugott and Heine 1991a; 1991b; Hopper and Traugott 1993; Bybee, Perkins, and Pagliuca 1994). We will argue, however, that the process has both a cognitive and a pragmatic component, and that the former can be described with reference to metaphorical extension while the latter has to do with context manipulation. Possession is an abstract concept in that it is hard to define in non-linguistic terms. It is therefore not surprising that people use certain conceptual templates to refer to it. We have described the templates that are at issue here in the preceding section and have called them event schemas.

A car that belongs to me may be described as one that is regularly found to be located close to me (Location), that I drive (Action), that I am accompanied by (Companion), or that is there for me (Goal). And it is therefore

2.2 Grammaticalization

not surprising that source schemas such as Location, Action, Companion, or Goal serve as templates or metaphorical vehicles for referring to possession.

While it seems justified therefore to account for the transition from source schema to possession in terms of metaphor, we are not dealing with metaphor in the conventional sense, but rather with a phenomenon that has been referred to as 'emerging metaphor' (Heine, Claudi, and Hünnemeyer 1991:60–2), that is, with a kind of metaphorical extension that does not arise as a spontaneous act of transfer from one domain of conceptualization to another but emerges gradually in the course of years or even centuries. The driving force behind this kind of metaphorical extension is context extension. At the initial stage, the expression concerned exclusively denotes the literal meaning of the source schema. Subsequently, the expression is increasingly used in contexts which allow for a possessive interpretation until this interpretation becomes the primary and, eventually, the conventional one. Since, in the course of this process, both interpretations are possible, a situation of overlapping meanings arises, and it is only at the final stage, when the possessive meaning is conventionalized, that the expression can be interpreted exclusively with reference to possession. The effects this process has on the linguistic material employed for encoding the various source schemas are considerable. Some of them are now looked at in turn.

One of these effects concerns *decategorialization*. With the new function that the source schema assumes, the items making up the source schema tend to lose their erstwhile properties. For example, a locative preposition is meaningful as long as it is part of a locative expression. Once, however, that expression comes to be consistently associated with another function, like possession, the preposition is likely to lose the properties of its category in that context, such as the ability to be exchangeable with other items belonging to the same category, for example, alternative locative prepositions. In the end, the preposition will no longer bear any relationship to locative morphology and will have no significance other than being part of a possessive expression. And the same applies to the other items figuring in that locative expression.

The way different exponents of source schemas give rise to new symbols whose only function is to express verbal possession can be illustrated with the following example from Ancient Egyptian, taken from Claudi (1986:18–20). Late Egyptian (approx. 1574 to 715 BC) developed a pattern of possessive expression based on the auxiliary *wn* 'there is, there are' and the preposition *m.dj* 'near, with', as can be seen in (60). The further development of these two items and, ultimately, their fusion is sketched in (61), the result being a possessive verb *wɛntɛ, wɛnta-* 'have' in Coptic, a later form of Egyptian. This development is remarkable in that an original Location Schema gave rise to what might be called a 'pseudo-Action Schema' (Ulrike Claudi, p.c.), that is, to a structure resembling 'have'-constructions derived from the Action Schema. We are dealing with a process corresponding closely to what Hagège (1993) describes as a development from a 'be'- to a 'have'-construction. A comparative process can be observed in Cornish, as we shall see in 2.4. The process concerned is briefly discussed in 2.5.3 under the label 'transitivization.'

(60) Late Egyptian (Afro-Asiatic; Erman 1933:247; Claudi 1986:19)
 n   wn   m.dj-f   is - t
 NEG be   with-3.SG.M crew-F
 'He doesn't have a crew.'

(61) Late Egyptian
 m.dj > mtw > ɛntɛ, ɛnta-
       wn >   wɛn
              wɛn+ɛnta- > Coptic wɛnta-,
              wɛn+ɛntɛ >   wɛntɛ
                                'have'

(62) Coptic (Egyptian, Afro-Asiatic; Claudi 1986:19)
 wɛnta-f
 have- 3.SG.M
 'he has'

A number of authors have drawn attention to the hybrid status of 'have'-verbs in European languages. French *avoir*, Benveniste (1960:120–1) observes, has a number of properties of a transitive verb: it takes an object and is inflected for person, number, tense, etc. On the other hand, it lacks other verbal properties, such as the ability to passivize or to denote a process. Such a situation is in fact to be predicted when the Action Schema is grammaticalized to a possessive construction. Once the predicate nucleus of the schema, say, a verb like 'take,' 'seize,' or 'keep' comes to consistently serve the expression of possession, it no longer refers to actions but rather to states. Accordingly, it is likely to be decategorialized to an item that denotes states rather than processes, that is no longer associated with agents, and that may no longer passivize. The result then is a structure that Benveniste calls a *'pseudo-transitif'*.

In connection with decategorialization there is another development that may be referred to as *specialization* (Hopper 1991:22ff.). The Location Schema, for example, may have a number of different instantiations, like being usable with different kinds of locative concepts, for example *X is at/on/in/near to Y*. With the development of a pattern of verbal possession, the construction becomes increasingly petrified, that is, fixed and invariable: it may no longer be used with different locative markers. Thus, while the source schema may be associated with several kinds of locative concepts, the morphology used to mark possession tends to become restricted to one specific concept. The following example illustrates this evolution. According to Freeze, verbal possession in Hindi is associated exclusively with the marker *paas*, as in (63b), while some other postpositions can be used in the case of non-grammaticalized uses of the Location Schema, as in (63a).

(63) Hindi (Indic, Indo-European; Freeze 1992:584)
(a) kamree- mẽẽ aadmii hai.
 room.OBL-in man is
 'There is a man in the room.'

(b) larkee- kee paas kuttaa hai.
 boy.OBL-GEN proximity dog is
 'The boy has a dog.' (Lit.: 'By the boy is a dog.')

Specialization may also be achieved by possessor topicalization: a common process that is likely to affect those schemas that have the possessor encoded in a position other than the clause-initial one, has the effect that the possessor noun phrase is moved to the clause-initial position. The source structures affected are primarily the Location and the Goal Schemas. Since this process has to do with the pragmatics of information processing rather than with grammaticalization, it is not further analyzed here; we will, however, return to it briefly in 2.5.

While the processes sketched above can be universally observed in the transition from source schema to possession, other developments may, but need not, occur. One of them has been described in the literature as *erosion* (Heine and Reh 1984). The effect of this phenomenon can be described as follows. The morphological material employed to encode a source schema may be appropriate when it comes to expressing concepts such as location or accompaniment, where every morpheme has its well-defined function. Once the relevant expression comes to denote possession, however, part of that material may be felt to be redundant and, hence, may be eliminated (see Heine 1993 for a more detailed account). Thus, not infrequently, elements like locative markers or copulas are shortened or disappear entirely once a source schema turns into a possessive expression.

A few examples may illustrate this process. In Ewe, the main expression of verbal possession is based on the Location Schema having the form *Y is in X's hand*, as can be seen in (64). Note that location is marked by means of two different markers, viz. the locative copula *le* 'be at' and the postposition *me* 'in'. With the grammaticalization of this schema to a 'have'-construction, the postposition was obligatorily eliminated, as can be seen in (65).

(64) Ewe (Kwa, Niger-Congo)
 ga le así- nye me.
 money be.at hand-my in
 'Money is in my hand.' (*'I have money')

(65) ga le así- nye.
 money be.at hand-my
 'I have money.' (*'Money is in my hand')

An alternative explanation for this process is volunteered by Westermann (1907). He argues that nouns that are conceived of as expressing locative concepts may not take (locative) postpositions. Now, with the grammaticalization of the concrete noun *así* 'hand' to a locative concept, as in (65), *así* may no longer receive any postposition. Note that Westermann's interpretation does not contradict our account in terms of erosion as a grammaticalization process; rather we view it as an indication that grammaticalization may be triggered simultaneously by other kinds of processes. Thus, the linguistic criterion proposed by Westermann may explain, for example, why it was the locative postposition, rather than any other item, that disappeared.

In other languages again it is not the locative marker but rather the erstwhile main verb that is eliminated in the process of grammaticalization. Wukari might be an example of such a language. The Takum dialect of Jukun presents a canonical instance of the Companion Schema for verbal possession, where the main verb is *syì* 'sit, live' and the comitative notion is expressed by the marker *bá* 'be with', as shown in (66). In the closely related Wukari dialect, however, it would seem that the main verb *syì* has been eliminated, as is suggested by examples like (67).

(66) Takum (Benue-Congo; Niger-Congo; Welmers 1968; Dirk Otten 1992)
 kú syì bá zà.
 3.SG live be.with guinea-corn
 'He has guinea-corn.'

(67) Wukari (Benue-Congo; Niger-Congo; Welmers 1968; Dirk Otten 1992)
   kú bá zá.
   3.SG be.with guinea-corn
   'He has guinea-corn.'

According to Claudi (1986), Zande has gone even one step further than Ewe and Wukari in that it has not only grammaticalized the noun *be* 'hand, arm' to a preposition, but it also allows for an optional deletion of the copula verb (*du*). Thus, neither the verbal element nor the locative marker is required any longer for the expression of verbal possession, as can be seen in (68).

(68) Zande (Ubangi, Niger-Congo; Claudi 1986)
   kpakpari (du) be ko
   hat   (exist) hand his
   'He has a hat' (Lit.: 'A hat is in his hand')

Loss of coding material belonging to the source schema is likely to start in frequently used, 'unmarked' tense forms before it spreads to other items. The structure *ku-wa na* 'to be with' of the Companion Schema, for example, is retained in Swahili except in the most unmarked present tense form, where the locative copula *ku-wa* 'be' is omitted, as the comparison between the past tense form in (69a) and the present tense form in (69b) shows.

(69) Swahili (Bantu, Niger-Congo)
   (a) a- li- ku- wa na wa- ke wa- wili.
       3.SG-PAST-INF-be with CL.2-wife CL.2-two
       'He had two wives.'

   (b) a- na wa- ke wa- wili.
       3.SG with CL.2 wife CL.2-two
       'He has two wives.'

In Luo, the locative copula *nɪ* 'be (at)' is used obligatorily before the comitative preposition *gɪ* (or *kɔd*) 'with' if the possessor is a noun, but the copula is omitted when the possessor is a personal pronoun:

(70) Luo (Western Nilotic, Nilo-Saharan; Stafford 1967:18)
   (a) Mɛsa nɪ gɪ tiende aŋwɛn.
       table COP with legs four
       'A table has four legs.'

   (b) Wan gɪ chiemo maŋeny.
       we with food many
       'We have much food.'

```
Structure   Development Stage
              I    II   III

Source        A    A
Target             B    B
```
Figure 2.1 The Overlap Model.

Second, rather than using some specialized locative morphology for marking the possessor, that morphology tends to be eliminated altogether. The effect is that, while in non-grammaticalized uses of the Location Schema there is some locative marker like an adposition or an inflection, the corresponding possessive construction lacks such a marker. The following (a)-sentences are instances of the former and the (b)-sentences instances of the latter.

(71)   Tagalog (Meso-Philippine, Austronesian; Freeze 1992:585)
       (a) may   gera sa   ewropa.
           COP.LOC   war   in   Europe
           'There is war in Europe.'

       (b) may   relos aŋ   naanai.
           COP.LOC   watch ART mom
           'Mom has a watch.'

(72)   Shanghainese (Sino-Tibetan; Freeze 1992:585)
       (a) (lʌlʌ) vɔŋts   lidʌw   yu   i-   tsʌ   mɔ.
           (in)   building   inside COP   one-CLFR   cat
           'There's a cat in the building.'

       (b) ŋow   yu   i-   tsʌ   mɔ.
           I   COP   one-CLFR   cat
           'I have a cat.'

Another implication has already been alluded to above. As in other cases of grammaticalization, the transition from a concrete source schema (A) to a more abstract target schema (B) involves a stage of overlapping structures (AB), where the two schemas co-occur and create a situation of ambiguity. This situation, described in Heine (1993:48ff.) as the Overlap Model, is sketched in Figure 2.1; a similar model, referred to as the 'polysemous view of semantic change', has been developed independently by Wilkins (1996).

It need not be the case, however, that all three stages are actualized in a given situation; it may happen, for example, that the development does not proceed beyond Stage II, that is, that Stage III is never reached (Elizabeth Traugott, Nigel Vincent, p.c.). We may illustrate the nature of the process with the following example from Russian. The data is taken from Isačenko (1974b), although the interpretation differs slightly from his.

(73)   Russian (Isačenko 1974b:45–7)
    (a) Lámpa stoít u okná.
        'The lamp stands by the window.'

    (b) Mašina u Péti.
        'The car is with/at Peter.'

    (c) Sejčás u Márkovyx gripp.
        (i) 'There is flu at the Markovs.'
        (ii) 'The Markovs have the flu now.'

    (d) U Péti est' mašina.
        'Peter has a car.'

Utterances (73a) and (73b) may be interpreted as instances of the Location Schema; they are suggestive of Stage I in our Overlap Model, where u is intepreted by Isačenko as an adessive preposition and the structure [u+Genitive+'be'] expresses the schematic content Y is at X. Essentially the same content is also expressed by (73c), at least as long as meaning (i) is implied. (73c) has, however, a second meaning (ii) in addition which is suggestive of the Possession Schema X has Y. Thus, (73c) is suggestive of the overlap Stage II (AB), which can be predicted whenever a source schema (which is the Location Schema in this Russian example) gives rise to a target schema (Possession). (73d) is interpreted exclusively with reference to this target schema, which, as far as the description by Isačenko (1974b:45ff.) suggests, is an instance of Stage III. (Note that Isačenko [1974b:46] uses a different perspective in describing the meaning of utterances like (73d), which he characterizes as a 'relation of concern or implication'.)

Lyons (1967:394; 1968a:395) says that, whether we are dealing with a locative construction, as in (73b), or a possessive one, as in (73d), depends very largely upon whether the referent in the [u+Genitive] prepositional phrase 'is a personal noun or not.' But this is not the only contextual factor that is relevant for the distinction between the two constructions. As is suggested by the contextual frame structure involved, the transition from Location Schema to Possession Schema in Russian appears to have been triggered by three properties that also played a role in other languages for which similar processes have been recorded. First, it required that *u* be associated with human referents. Second, it was confined to utterances having a 'be'-predicate (or zero), that is, the transition did not take place if other verbs were involved, as in (74).

(74)   Russian (Isačenko 1974b:46)
         U Péti vstrečájutsja artísty.
         'Actors meet at Peter's place.'

And third, it involved a reversal of the topic–comment structure or, to use Isačenko's terminology, it required the [*u*+Genitive] prepositional phrase to stand in the initial topic position. Whenever the prepositional phrase does not occupy the initial position, as in (73b), we are dealing with instances of location rather than of possession.

We have ignored the fact that there is a second, less common, 'have'-construction in Russian involving the verb *imet'*. This construction, which is an instance of the Action Schema (*imet'* can be traced back to the root **em-* 'take'; Creissels 1996:154), is claimed to be a recent one (Isačenko 1974b:50ff.), but this view is not shared by all authors (cf. Guiraud-Weber 1996:147–8). To summarize, the transition from Location to Possession Schema can be understood as an instance of frame extension where specific contexts give rise to new semantic interpretations and eventually to a new contextual frame.

But there are three other factors that appear to have been underestimated in many previous works, in addition to the semantics of the noun within the prepositional phrase and the nature of the topic–comment structure involved. First, time is essential, that is, the time that is required for the conventionalization of a new grammatical pattern. Second, what may have been a contributing factor is language contact, that is, areal influence exerted by some neighbouring language or languages. Third, what can also have been involved is something that one may simply call a creative act: some languages have exactly the same structural conditions as Russian, still, the process that occurred in Russian did not take place in these languages, that is, a creative act did not take place whereby a possessive concept was expressed in terms of a locative concept.

At least two contrasting positions have been maintained regarding the relationship between the locative and the possessive constructions in (73b) and (73d), respectively. Lyons (1967:394) observes that the possessive construction is 'patently related to locatives', but it does not become entirely clear what the phrase 'patently related' exactly stands for. For Isačenko, the

2.2 Grammaticalization 85

two are essentially unrelated: 'But synchronically, the "implicational" *u* in Russian is homonymous with the adessive *u*' (Isačenko 1974b:46). In accordance with similar findings made in other languages worldwide, we claim that the two constructions are related in a specific way: the possessive construction can be assumed to be historically derived from the locative construction. Isačenko (1974b:46) observes that diachronically 'the relation of the "implicational" preposition *u* with the adessive preposition *u* is very likely, but cannot be established by historical evidence'. Looking at other languages that have grammaticalized locative constructions to possessive constructions, we may say that it would be very surprising indeed if it should turn out that the two were not diachronically related, more precisely, if the possessive meaning were not historically derived from the locative meaning.

In addition we may argue that the two are also synchronically related, mainly for two reasons. First, there is no clear-cut boundary separating the two; rather, they are linked by an intermediate stage of overlap, exemplified by (73c), which can be interpreted alternatively with reference to both constructions. Second, the two can also be linked by invoking the traditional notion of complementary distribution: while canonical instances of the possessive construction have human possessors, use 'be' as their predicate, and have the [*u*+Genitive] prepositional phrase in topic position, canonical instances of corresponding locative constructions are characterized by the absence of any or all of these three properties.

Possessive expressions typically involve human possessors. We noticed in chapter 1 that, of all possessive notions distinguished, it is permanent possession which has the highest degree of prototypicality, and permanent possession is characterized by the presence of human possessors. A common line of grammaticalization concerns in fact the development from permanent possession to inanimate possession, whereby a construction serving the expression of utterances like (75a) comes to be extended to also be used for utterances like (75b).

(75)   (a) Nathaniel has short legs.
       (b) A coffee-table has short legs.

In accordance with the Overlap Model sketched in Figure 2.1 above, at Stage I of the process leading from source schema to possession, the construction concerned is almost invariably associated with human possessors. A significant new stage is reached when instead of a human/animate possessor, an inanimate possessor can occur. Such a situation can be observed in Estonian, which has grammaticalized the Location Schema using the verb 'be' and the possessor in the adessive case. The two utterances in (76) are structurally identical, but (76a) is an instance of the source schema and (76b) of the target schema, as the English translations indicate. That the possessive utterance in (76b) is an instance of Stage III is suggested by the following facts. First, Lehiste (1969:325ff.), using a Fillmorian case grammar approach, observes that the sentence-initial constituents in the adessive case correspond to different underlying argument roles, namely to a LOCATIVE role in (76a) and a DATIVE role in (76b). Second, whereas (76a) would answer the question 'What is on the table?', (76b) would be the appropriate answer to the question 'What does the father have?' Third, it seems that the possessive schema is firmly associated with the possessor constituent in initial position. Thus, while the order of the two arguments figuring in (76) can be reversed if the locative source schema is involved, as in (77a), this does no longer seem possible if possession is implied, as in (77b). Fourth, the possessive schema is no longer confined to human possessors, as can be seen in (78), which, according to Lehiste (1969:328), is also an instance of possession, in that it is an answer to the question 'What does the table have?', rather than 'Where are the four legs?' And finally, the case marking used for the possessor may appear a second time in the same clause for a constituent marking the function characteristic of the source schema. Thus, in Estonian the adessive has been grammaticalized as a possessor marker; at the same time it is still used as a locative marker, as can be seen in (79), where both functions co-occur in the same sentence.

(76) Estonian (Finnic, Uralic-Yukaghir; Lehiste 1969:325–9)
    (a) laual   on   raamat
        table.ADESSIVE 3.SG.be book.NOM
        'On the table is (a) book.'
    (b) isal   on   raamat
        father.ADESSIVE 3.SG.be book.NOM
        'Father has (a) book.'

(77) (a) raamat   on   laual
        book.NOM 3.SG.be table.ADESSIVE
        'The book is on the table.'
    (b) *raamat   on   isal
        ?'The book is on the father.'

(78) laual   on   neli   jalga
     table.ADESSIVE 3.SG.be four.NOM leg.PART
     'The table has four legs.'

(79) emal   on   toit   laual
      mother.ADESSIVE   3.SG.be food.NOM   table.ADESSIVE
      'Mother has food on the table.'

As I have outlined elsewhere (Heine 1992), the stages are not discrete entities; rather the transition from one to another is gradual. One factor concerns the semantics of context selection, for example whether the meaning of a given utterance is more compatible with context A rather than with B. The following example from Estonian may illustrate the kinds of factor involved. As we observed above, Estonian has grammaticalized the Location Schema as its major construction of verbal possession. The two utterances in (80) are morphosyntactically identical, yet (80a) triggers the Location Schema and (80b) the Possession Schema, because the combination 'table' and 'book' is likely to invoke the former while the combination 'table' plus 'four legs' within the same clause is more likely to be interpreted with reference to the latter or, to use the wording of Lehiste (1969:329): 'we know that a table may "possess" four legs, but may not "possess" a book except in some metaphoric, poetic sense'.

(80) Estonian (Lehiste 1969:328–9)
      (a) laual   on   raamat
          table.ADESSIVE   3.SG.be book.NOM
          'On the table is a book.'
      (b) laual   on   neli   jalga
          table.ADESSIVE   3.SG.be four.NOM   leg.PART
          'The table has four legs.'

All the processes sketched above lead from concrete to more abstract meanings and from a relatively free and flexible morphosyntax to fixed patterns of expressing predicative possession. Thus, the structures described observe a basic principle of grammaticalization, according to which this process is unidirectional (see Heine, Claudi, and Hünnemeyer 1991). There is, however, one issue that seemingly poses a problem to this principle, and this problem concerns the conceptual nature of the possessor. We observed above, for example with reference to the Estonian example, that once a possessive schema has evolved, the development tends to be from permanent to inanimate (inalienable) possession, which again entails a shift from human to non-human possessors. An important shift to be encountered in many instances of grammaticalization is in fact one according to which expressions for human concepts come to be used also for concepts that are inanimate. This shift is described by Heine, Claudi, and Hünnemeyer

(1991) with reference to what they call the PERSON-to-OBJECT metaphor. It can be observed, for example, in the process of auxiliation (see Heine 1993): when main verbs, for example *go* or *use*, give rise to auxiliaries (*be going to, used to*) they are likely to lose their association with human subjects and accept inanimate subjects. Similarly, one major way of developing grammatical concepts of spatial orientation is by extending expressions for parts of the human body (e.g. *my back*) to inanimate items (*in back of the house*).

The problem we have in mind relates to cases such as the Russian example cited above: it concerns the shift from the Location Schema to possession. This shift typically leads from a source structure like (81a) via an intermediate structure (81b) to the target structure (81c).

(81)   (a) Y is located at X
        (b) Possessee Y is located at Possessor X's place
        (c) X has/owns Y

In (81a), X is a concept that bears no special association with human concepts; it would seem in fact that it normally refers to inanimate locations. In (81b) and (81c), however, X refers essentially only to human concepts. What this suggests is that the shift from location to possession entails a process whereby typically inanimate locations come to be reinterpreted as human possessors. The question of how this problem is to be handled in grammaticalization theory requires a separate treatment.

For the evolution of the Action Schema there is some historical evidence from European languages, especially from Spanish. The Spanish verb *tener* 'hold, keep' became the predicate of the Action Schema and, by the fifteenth century, had replaced *haber* as the predicate of 'have'-constructions. The evidence available on the evolution of *haber* and *tener* in Spanish (cf. Pountain 1985) suggests the following scenario of possessive concepts, which is in line with parameters of grammaticalization such as degree of increasing abstractness:

(82)   Action Schema > Physical > Permanent > Inalienable
        ('hold, keep')   possession   possesssion   possession

That the distinction between a temporary and a permanent situation is a cross-linguistically significant one, and that expressions for the former may be extended to also encode the latter, can be illustrated with another example involving the development of copular constructions. On the basis of comparative reconstructions in a number of genetically unrelated languages, Devitt (1990) concludes that one common path to be observed in the evolution of copulas can be described in the form of a scale, that we presented above (2.1, (55)). Part of this scale is a development from copulas having a temporary sense to general copulas, i.e. copulas having no temporal limit.

2.3 Targets

In section 2.1, a small range of event schemas was described that can be held responsible for the development of possessive constructions. The process leading to these constructions was the topic of section 2.2. In the present section our concern is with the targets of this process, that is, with the meaning of the resulting constructions. Part of the problem to be looked at concerns the question of whether or in which way this meaning is related to that of the respective source schema from which it is derived, in other words: are there any significant correlations between sources and targets?

In the introductory chapter, a characterization of prototypical instances of possession was attempted, and these instances, called possessive notions, form the basis of our analysis of the semantics of possessive constructions (1.3). For the convenience of the reader, these notions and the abbreviations used to refer to them are listed in (83).

(83) Salient possessive notions
　　　Physical　　　　　　　(PHYS)
　　　Temporary　　　　　　(TEMP)
　　　Permanent　　　　　　(PERM)
　　　Inalienable　　　　　　(INAL)
　　　Abstract　　　　　　　(ABST)
　　　Inanimate inalienable　(IN/I)
　　　Inanimate alienable　　(IN/A)

Possessive constructions differ considerably with regard to the notions they express. As we saw in chapter 1.2, the English 'have'-construction is commonly used with all notions except inanimate alienable possession. Other English expressions for predicative possession again are confined essentially to one notion only, viz. to permanent possession. Thus, *own*-predications, or the Equation Schema (*Y is X's (property)*) can be used in utterances like (84a) but not necessarily in (84b), (84c), or (84d), which are suggestive, respectively, of inalienable, abstract, and inanimate inalienable possession.

(84)　　English
　　　　(a) I own a car.　　　　　　　The car is mine.
　　　　(b) ?I own two sisters.　　　　?Two sisters are mine.

(c) ?I own a cold.	?The cold is mine.
(d) ?My house owns two bedrooms.	?Two bedrooms are my house's.

While in English there are no constructions that are compatible with all seven possessive notions, other languages do have such constructions. In Swahili, for example, the standard 'have'-construction is (-*li*-) *na* ('(be) with'), which is used for all seven notions, at least by most speakers.

The various schemas differ in a number of ways from one another, both in their source and their target structure. The Action Schema, for example, contrasts with all other schemas in that its predicate nucleus clearly has a lexical content, involving such items as 'take', 'seize', etc. All other source schemas have a predicate nucleus that is schematically simplified, in that it expresses such concepts as location, existence, equation or identification, or accompaniment. Even if such predicates are derived from fully lexical items, for example, postural or motion verbs, at the time when they serve as sources for possessive notions they can be assumed to have lost most of their lexical content.

A distinction can also be made between source schemas that are basic and those that are extended, i.e. that have an additional participant grafted onto them. Basic schemas are Action and Location. All others are extended: they contain a comitative adjunct in the case of the Companion, a dative, allative or benefactive adjunct in the case of the Goal, or a genitival modifier in the case of the Genitive or the Equation Schemas.

With regard to the target schemas of possession, perhaps the most salient distinction is that between schemas that encode the possessor as the clausal subject and those that do not. The former are Action and Companion. All others have the possessor as an oblique case expression, be it a locative, a dative, or a genitival modifier. These contrasts are summarized in Table 2.3.

The preceding discussion raises questions such as the following:

(a) Is it possible to predict whether a given schema will give rise to a 'have'- or a 'belong'-construction?
(b) Are there any correlations between the source schemas and the possessive notions derived from them?

Question (a) allows at least for a partial answer. In some cases a straightforward correlation appears to exist: the Location Schema (*Y is located at X*) invariably leads to 'have'-constructions. Equation (*Y is X's*) again is invariably the source of 'belong'-constructions. This fact has already been noticed by Benveniste (1960:123), who observed that in Indo-European languages like Latin, Homeric Greek, Vedic, or Hittite, the Goal Schema is

2.3 Targets

Table 2.3. *Contrastive properties of source schemas for predicative possession.*

	Semantics of predicate nucleus	Structure of source schema	Participant encoded as subject
Action	Lexical	Basic	Possessor
Location	Non-lexical	Basic	Possessee
Companion	Non-lexical	Extended	Possessor
Genitive	Non-lexical	Extended	Possessee
Goal	Non-lexical	Extended	Possessee
Topic	Non-lexical	Extended	Possessee
Equation	Non-lexical	Extended	Possessee

used for 'have'-constructions while the Equation Schema is used for 'belong'-constructions (*prédicat d'appartenance*).

The situation is more complicated in the case of Action (*X takes Y*) and Goal (*Y exists to/for X*): they may give rise to either construction. Whether the Action Schema develops into a 'have'- or a 'belong'-construction depends crucially on the argument structure of the verb: if the verb requires a complement that is human then a 'belong'-construction results. If, on the other hand, the verb is associated with a human subject and an object that is typically inanimate then a 'have'-construction is likely to emerge.

The relevance of this generalization can be illustrated by means of languages distinguishing the two kinds of Action constructions by means of active–passive diathesis. In Nama (Khoekhoe) of the South African Khoisan family, for example, exactly the same form of the Action Schema is used for both 'have'- and 'belong'-constructions. What distinguishes the two is the fact that the verb *'uu* 'take' appears in the active voice when 'have'-expressions are involved, but in the passive voice (*'uu-he*) when 'belong'-expressions are involved; the subject (more precisely: the sentence topic) is typically human in the former case but inanimate in the latter (Heinz Roberg, p.c.; see 1.2 above).

No such predictions seem possible for example in the case of the Goal Schema: it has given rise to both 'belong'- and 'have'-constructions (see above; cf. Benveniste 1960:123). What is obvious is that the development from Goal Schema to 'have'-construction requires the subject to become regularly associated with indefinite referents (see below); it remains unclear, however, as to what conditions must be met for that to happen.

Table 2.4. *Typical correlations between source schemas and 'have'- and 'belong'-constructions.*

Source Schema	'Have'-c.	'Belong'-c.
Action	+	+
Location	+	−
Companion	+	−
Genitive	+	−
Goal	+	+
Topic	+	−
Equation	−	+

The remaining Existence schemas, that is, Genitive and Topic, appear to lead invariably to 'have'-constructions. The overall correlations obtaining between source schemas and the two kinds of construction are summarized in Table 2.4.

The distinction between 'have'- and 'belong'-constructions raises another problem that we have touched upon already in section 1.2. Irrespective of the particular source schema involved, the two tend to give rise to drastically different semantic structures: the meaning of 'belong'-constructions is confined to the notion of permanent possession. 'Have'-constructions, on the other hand, tend to express an array of different possessive notions. Cross-linguistically, we appear to be dealing with two fundamentally different types of linguistic items, one that is essentially 'monosemous' and another that is 'polysemous'; we will return to this issue in section 5.3.

Question (b) is more difficult to answer. One might say that, in principle, any schema may give rise to any possessive notion and there is in fact ample evidence to support such a statement. On the other hand, a few probabilistic generalizations seem possible, such as the following:

(i) The Location Schema is most likely to be associated with physical and temporary possession.

(ii) The Existence schemas again, that is, Genitive, Goal, and Topic, are more likely to be associated with permanent and inalienable possession.

(iii) The Companion Schema is claimed to be more likely to express physical and temporary or, more generally, alienable possession rather than inalienable possession (Kilian-Hatz and Stolz 1992:4; Stolz 1994:53).

(iv) Finally, there is a strong negative correlation: the Existence schemas are very seldom recruited for the expression of physical possession.

These generalizations, while probabilistic in nature, account for a number of situations in genetically and areally unrelated languages. Telugu, for example, has grammaticalized the Location Schema to an expression for physical and temporary possession, as illustrated in (85a), while other notions, such as permanent possession (85b), inalienable possession (85c) and (85d), or inanimate inalienable possession (85e) are derived from the Goal sub-schema of Existence.

(85) Telugu (Dravidian; Bhaskararao 1972:164–5)
 (a) pennu va:ḍi-daggara undi
  pen him at is
  'He has a pen.' (=He has a pen with him, which may not necessarily belong to him.)

 (b) pennu va:ḍi-ki undi
  pen him- to is
  'He has a pen (which belongs to him).'

 (c) reṇḍu kaḷḷu na:-ku unna:y
  two eyes me-to are
  'I have two eyes.'

 (d) iddau pillalu na:-ku unna:ru
  two children me-to are
  'I have two children.'

 (e) kommalu ceṭṭu-ki unna:y
  branches tree- to are
  'The tree has branches.'

A similar situation appears to exist in Hungarian (Biermann 1985), where Location (using the case suffix *-on*) is associated with physical and inanimate possession, while Goal (using the case suffix *-nak*) is employed for such notions as permanent, inalienable, and abstract possession.

It remains to be investigated whether there is some general limit to the number of distinct possessive constructions any one language will mark. Which possessive notion is present in a given example depends on a number of factors. One common factor concerns the referentiality of the possessee. 'Have'-constructions typically involve indefinite possessees and whenever the possessee is definite, a temporarily limited type of possession, be it physical or temporary possession, is likely to emerge. The following Ewe sentence denotes physical possession when the possessee is definite, i.e. when it refers to either a person (=proper name) or else is qualified by the definite marker *lá* 'the' (4b). When the possessee is indefinite, however, the meaning is one of permanent possession (4a):

(86) Ewe (Kwa, Niger-Congo; Ameka 1991:207)
 (a) dɔ   lii   ná Kofí.
     work exist to Kofi
     'Kofi has work.'

 (b) dɔ   lá   lii   ná Kofí.
     work the exist to Kofi
     'Kofi has work to do (=the work is there for Kofi).'

The same situation obtains when Location is involved. With an indefinite possessee, the resulting meaning is one of permanent possession, as in (87a), while with a definite possessee, physical possession is implied:

(87) Ewe (Kwa, Niger-Congo; Ameka 1991:215)
 (a) ga   le   Kofí sí.
     money be.at Kofi hand
     'Kofi has money.'

 (b) ga   lá   le   Kofí sí.
     money the be.at Kofi hand
     'The money is with Kofi.'

According to one of the main principles of grammaticalization, the evolution of grammatical forms leads from relatively concrete meanings to increasingly abstract meanings (concerning the notion 'abstractness', see Heine, Claudi, and Hünnemeyer 1991). This would mean that the structures serving as sources for 'have'-constructions are less abstract than the resulting structures. If possession is a more abstract concept than any of the concepts from which it is historically derived, then this has to do with the fact that possession 'goes beyond what is perceptible', a stolen apple does not look different from any other apple (Miller and Johnson-Laird 1976:558).

As we argued above, the development from source to target schema is unidirectional, that is, we do not expect a 'have'-construction to give rise to location, action, or any of the other source concepts. There is, however, one seeming counter-example to the unidirectionality principle. Now, occasionally it happens that expressions for predicative possession may also give rise to existential expressions, as in the following examples from French and Spanish:

(88)　French
　　　(a) Possession
　　　　　Il a   deux enfant-s.
　　　　　he has two child- PL
　　　　　'He has two children.'

　　　(b) Existence
　　　　　Il y a   deux enfant-s.
　　　　　it there has two child- PL
　　　　　'There are two children.'

(89)　Spanish
　　　Hay   un médico en este pueblo?
　　　exist.3.SG a doctor   in that town
　　　'Is there a doctor in this town?' (Hist.: 'Has it a doctor in that town?')

The structures exemplified in (88b) and (89) are probably not independent of one another; Nigel Vincent (p.c.) suspects that both can be traced back to Late Latin. But similar situations, where a 'have'-verb used in a third-person singular form gives rise to an existential expression, can be found in a number of languages, cf. Bulgarian *ima* ('it has') 'there is' (Tania Kouteva, p.c.), or sub-standard German *Da hat es zwei Kinder* ('there has it two children') 'There are two children.' Not infrequently, the third-person singular pronoun functioning somehow as a subject dummy has a locative reference. In Bantu languages, for example, which almost invariably use the Companion Schema for predicative possession, it is the locative classes 16 (*pa), 17 (*ku), and 18 (*mu) that provide the subject marker, as illustrated below.

(90)　Bantu languages
　　　(a) Swahili (Bantu, Niger-Congo)
　　　　　ni-na   chakula.   Ku-   na   chakula.
　　　　　I- be:with food   LOC:CL.17-be:with food
　　　　　'I have food.'   'There is food.'

　　　(b) Shona (Bantu, Niger-Congo; Brauner 1993:53)
　　　　　ndìné   bhúkú.   kú-   nè   zúvá.
　　　　　I:be:with book   LOC:CL.17 be:with sun
　　　　　'I have a book.'   'It is sunny.' (Lit.: 'There is sun.')

That we are not dealing with a reversal of directionality of the kind [existence>possession>existence] is suggested by the following observations. We do not know of any language where existence as a 'nuclear' schema (*X exists*) provides the source for predicative possession (see 2.1 above). Rather, it is an existential expression *plus* some additional participant, encoded as an oblique case expression, that provides the source for possession. This additional participant may be a dative case adjunct (*Y exists to/for X*), a genitive expression (*X's Y exists*), or a topic or theme constituent (*As for X, Y (of X) exists*). Thus, rather than dealing with a violation of the unidirectionality principle, the overall development is in fact unidirectional and can be sketched as follows:

(91) Existence   > Possession > 'Nuclear' existence
      (Y exists with   (X has Y)   ('it has Y'>Y exists)
      reference to X)

As we mentioned in 2.1, the term 'Existence' is used in this work always in its extended sense (i.e. *Y exists with reference to X*).

2.4   How to reconstruct schemas

On the basis of the observations made in the previous sections we will now highlight a few criteria that may be helpful for reconstructing the evolution of the various patterns of predicative possession. The approach used here resembles to some extent established methods of historical reconstruction. As we observed in chapter 1, grammaticalization is a diachronic process, even if it can be interpreted as well as a synchronic process, and its reconstruction therefore must be verifiable or falsifiable by means of diachronic evidence. It is related, for example, to both the comparative method and internal reconstruction in that it is also concerned with etymological continuity. This means, for example, that the Swahili 'have'-expression -*wa na*, which has been reconstructed as being an instance of the Companion Schema (*X is with Y*), must be etymologically a combination of the copula verb -*wa* 'be' and the comitative preposition *na* 'with'. At the same time, this Swahili construction must also be in accordance with the syntactic properties that instances of the Companion Schema exhibit across languages, such as encoding the possessor as the clausal subject and the possessee as the object or complement. Thus, in addition to historical continuity in the morphophonological substance employed, there must also be typological consistency in that the syntactic pattern characterizing the Companion Schema is the same across languages. Finally, schema reconstruction must also be in accordance with the principles of grammaticalization. For example, in the development from lexical to grammatical markers, the forms employed may undergo erosion (Heine 1993), that is, the phonetic substance used for encoding the possessive construction may be shorter than the comitative construction from which it is derived, while the opposite is unlikely to happen. To summarize, the approach sketched in the present section cannot be reduced to any of the traditional methodologies commonly employed for linguistic reconstruction (cf. Bynon 1994:4471–2).

For most of the languages of the world there exist no early written documents and historical reconstruction therefore has to rely exclusively on synchronic evidence. Still, when reconstructing the source from which a given 'have'-construction is derived we rarely encounter any problems: in most cases there are clear linguistic clues that enable us to determine the schema that had served as a conceptual template for the 'have'-construction concerned. These clues can be immediately derived from the linguistic properties associated with each schema and relate to the morphology and/or the syntax employed for encoding possessive constructions.

We may illustrate the procedure adopted by using a particularly difficult example, viz. the English *have*-construction. Suppose there was no historical evidence on it: how to reconstruct the schema from which it is derived? There is morphological and syntactic evidence that enables us to reconstruct the source structure concerned: the fact that in expressions like *I have no money* the possessor is the subject and the possessee the object suggests that this construction cannot be derived from Location or Goal, or from Equation. The only remaining schemas are Action and Companion. In the latter case one would expect that the possessee noun has some comitative or related morphology on it. Since neither applies, the only logical conclusion is that this construction is derived from the Action Schema. There is in fact evidence to support such a hypothesis. First, among all the schemas distinguished, the Action Schema is virtually the only one that gives rise to transitive structures where the possessor is encoded as the subject and the possessee as the object. Second, the etymology of the verb *have* is such that it can be reconciled exclusively with the Action Schema: as we noted above, this verb is historically derived from an action verb meaning 'take, seize'. To summarize, even in a case like the 'have'-construction, where the native speaker is no longer aware of any relationship between this construction and its conceptual source, it is possible to determine that source and to explain why the English 'have'-construction has the kind of morphosyntax it does. One of the implications of this observation will be discussed in section 5.4.

98 The process

But there are other problems that may arise in the reconstruction of schemas. One of these problems is discussed in 2.5.3 under the label 'transitivization'. Like English, the Celtic language Cornish has a 'have'-verb, also exhibiting a kind of transitive structure. Still, as Stassen (1995) shows, this construction, exemplified in (92c), does not go back to the Action but rather to the Goal Schema (*Y exists for/to X*); its earliest diachronic stage is exemplified in (92a). For reasons to be discussed in more detail below (2.5.3; see also Hagège 1993:66ff.), the erstwhile structure has been reinterpreted as a transitive construction. An earlier form of the reinterpreted construction is found in (92b), while (92c) illustrates the final stage where there now is a kind of 'have'-verb.

(92)   Cornish (Celtic, Indo-European; Stassen 1995)
    (a) Ancow a -s   byth
        death to-you be.3.SG.FUT

    (b) Why   a -s   beteugh   ancow
        2.SG.NOM to-you be.2.SG.FUT death

    (c) Why   asbeteugh   ancow
        2.SG.NOM have.2.SG.FUT death
        'You will have death: you will die.'

As is to be expected in such cases, there remain some relics that allow us to identify the historical source of the construction: the prefixal element *as-* ('to-you') in (92c) still bears witness to the fact that we are dealing with an instance of the Goal rather than the Action Schema. A comparable example is found in Coptic, as we saw in 2.2. To conclude, while the presence of a transitive (or better: 'pseudo-transitive') 'have'-verb is strongly suggestive of the Action Schema, there are also alternative ways in which such verbs may arise. We shall return to this issue in 2.5.3.

Usually, however, schema reconstruction is less difficult. In many cases, reconstruction is made easy by the fact that both the source and the target schemas coexist in the relevant language, and that the process leading from source to target is still accessible in the form of contextually differentiated synchronic variation. We may illustrate the nature of this process and its synchronic correlates with the following examples from Bisa.

(93)   Bisa (Voltaic, Niger-Congo; Naden 1982:212)
    (a) A   ta   m   par- o.
        he exist my house-at
        'He is at my house.'

    (b) Wusu ta-   w.
        God   exist-at
        'God exists.'

(c) Mʋʋ lu   ta- w.
    my wife exist-at
    'I have a wife.'

These utterances, taken from modern Bisa, each represent a different stage in the evolution of the major 'have'-construction in this language. (93a) is suggestive of the initial stage: it contains a locative verb *ta* and a locative postposition *-o* (*-w* after vowels), and is suggestive of the Location Schema (*Y is at X*). Once the locative complement is omitted, as in (93b), a one-argument clause structure results and we arrive at the second stage, which is an instance of what we called above (2.3) an expression of 'nuclear' existence (*Y exists*). The postposition *-o*, now attached to the verb, survives as a relic of the first stage. The final stage is reached when the subject receives a possessive modifier. We are now dealing with an instance of extended existence, that is, of the Genitive Schema (*X's Y exists*), which is reinterpreted as a Possession Schema (*X has Y*) in accordance with a canonical process described in 2.1. This means that the possessee is encoded as the subject, the possessor as a genitival modifier, and the locative/existence verb *ta* plus postposition (*-o*) acts as a kind of 'have'-verb, as in (93c). To conclude, we are dealing with a pattern of conceptual shift that involves two steps, summarized below as (94a) and (94b), respectively.

(94)   (a) Location > 'Nuclear'
                      existence
        (b) 'Nuclear' + genitival > Possession
            existence   modifier

As elsewhere in this work, we have to emphasize that the three stages do not represent discrete steps, rather they are linked to each other in a chain-like manner (cf. Heine 1992). For example, parts of the earlier structures are carried over to later stages, like the postposition *-o*. Note also that, while (93c) expresses predicative possession, it has not entirely lost its earlier meanings. Thus, Naden (1982:212) observes that (93c) can also be understood as meaning 'My wife is here/is alive', that is, with reference to the two earlier stages.

In this example from Bisa we have made use of two independent parameters to arrive at the reconstruction proposed. One of them makes use of observations on diachronic regularities, such as the observation that locative expressions frequently give rise to existential meanings while the opposite is unlikely to happen. The second parameter is based on the assumption that contextually defined synchronic variation may, and frequently does, reflect patterns of diachronic evolution.

Case encoding may also be of help in reconstructing the schema that must have been involved in the case of opaque constructions. Late Egyptian (approx. 1574 to 715 BC), for example, had a construction involving the auxiliary *wn* 'there is, there are' plus the preposition *m.dj* 'near, with', where the possessor was introduced by this preposition and the possessee was encoded as the sentence subject (Claudi 1986):

(95) Late Egyptian (Afro-Asiatic; Erman 1933:247; Claudi 1986:19)
wn   pr   m.dj jt   n   mwt- j
be   house with father of mother-my
'My grandfather has a house.'

The fact that the preposition *m.dj* has 'with' as one of its senses might suggest that we are dealing with a comitative constituent and, hence, with an instance of the Companion Schema. However, the structure of possessor–possessee encoding is that of canonical instances of the Location Schema; note also that the second sense of *m.dj*, 'near', appears to have a locative base. It would therefore seem more plausible that this Late Egyptian construction is derived from the Location Schema.

Similarly, in modern Welsh, the preposition *gan* or *gyda* 'with' is used in a 'have'-construction exemplified by (96). That we are dealing with an instance of the Location Schema, rather than with Companion, is again sugggested by the structure of case encoding: one would expect the possessor to be the subject and the possessee the complement in the case of Companion (='I am with dog') but the other way round in the case of Location (='A dog is at my place'). Second, while Companion appears to be insignificant as a source for predicative possession in Welsh and other Celtic languages, Location provides perhaps the main source in these languages. Thus, in spite of the meaning of the preposition, Companion can virtually be ruled out as a source.

(96) Modern Welsh (Orr 1992:252)
Mae ci   gennyfi.
is   dog with:me
'I have a dog.'

Kanuri presents a more complicated case. In this Nigerian language there are a number of 'have'-constructions. One of them uses the suffix -(*C*)*à* as a kind of adjectivizer (Norbert Cyffer, p.c.). This suffix, which is described by Hutchison (1980) as an associative postposition (ASSOC), can be assumed to have a comitative meaning 'with' as its source, as exemplified in (97a), and possessive constructions like (97b) are seemingly straightforward instances of the grammaticalization of the Companion Schema, whereby a structure like *X is with Y* serve as a structural template to express the possessive schema *X has Y*.

(97) Kanuri (Saharan, Nilo-Saharan; Hutchison 1980:328ff.; Norbert Cyffer, p.c.)
    (a) tádà+nzə́+à   kádìo
        child-his-ASSOC came
        'She/he came with her/his child.'

    (b) Módù kèké+ nzə́+à
        Modu bicycle-his-ASSOC
        'Modu has/owns a bicycle.'

There are, however, reasons to assume that such an interpretation is inaccurate. Among the various grammaticalizations that the associative postposition has undergone (cf. Hutchison 1980), one is that of an existential marker ('there is/are'), exemplified in (98a), and it appears that it is this marker that was responsible for the emergence of a pattern of predicative possession. The source schema concerned, therefore, was the Genitive Schema (*X's Y exists*), as can be seen in (98b). Diachronically, (98b) can therefore be assumed to mean 'his bicycle exists'. The transition from structures like (98b) to structures like (97b) is one not infrequently observed when a nominal possessor is added as a clause-initial topic, thus giving rise to an instance of the Topic Schema (*As for X, (X's) Y exists*).

(98) Kanuri (Saharan, Nilo-Saharan; Hutchison 1980:326, 328)
    (a) kâusù+à
        heat- ASSOC
        'There is heat, it is hot out.'

    (b) kèké+ nzə́+à
        bicycle-his-ASSOC
        'He has/owns a bicycle'

To conclude, morphological evidence is not always a reliable indicator for conceptual source schemas. What is required in addition is information on the extent to which the morphological items concerned are grammaticalized at the stage when they are recruited as a source for possessive expressions. The whole issue needs, however, further analysis since there are a few cases, like some of the Celtic ones, where an alternative reconstruction in terms of the Companion Schema appears to be equally plausible (Thomas Stolz, p.c.).

Many typological observations that have been made by some previous authors on the relationship between 'have'-constructions and other kinds of construction in the same language are inadequate because they take care of part of the propositional content involved. Thus, a statement to the effect that a copula verb figures in a given construction for predicative possession is not of much help, since copula verbs may be involved in most schemas distinguished here. Such a statement is, however, not entirely useless since it allows us with a high degree of probability to rule out at least one schema, namely Action, which is unlikely to be associated with the use of copula verbs. More useful, however, are observations such as the following:

(a) The presence of a comitative marker on the possessee, be it an adposition, a clitic, or a case inflection, is strongly suggestive of the Companion Schema.
(b) The presence of a locative marker on the possessor constituent is suggestive of the Location Schema, and the presence of a benefactive/dative marker of the Goal Schema.
(c) The presence of a verb meaning 'take', 'seize', 'keep', 'hold', 'obtain', 'get', 'acquire', etc. is strongly suggestive of the Action Schema.

That such morphological evidence is in fact crucial for reconstructing source schemas can be illustrated with the following example taken from Claudi (1986:16–18). Lotuxo, an Eastern Nilotic language spoken in the southern Sudan, has two functionally equivalent 'have'-constructions both having the verb *-won* 'exist' as a predicate. The two differ from one another in that one uses the comitative preposition *ikɔ* 'with' while the other uses the (locative) preposition *jo* 'near'. On the basis of what has been observed above we are led to reconstruct the former as being derived from the Companion (*X is with Y*) and the latter from the Location Schema (*Y is located at X's place*). If such a reconstruction is to be historically adequate it should be supported by other evidence in addition. One piece of evidence should come from word order behaviour: since the possessor (X) is encoded as the subject in the Companion but as a locative complement in the Location Schema, we would expect the two Lotuxo constructions to have contrasting patterns of participant marking. And this is exactly what we find: The *ikɔ*-construction has the possessor as the subject and the possessee as a comitative complement, while the *jo*-construction has the possessee as the subject and the possessor as a locative complement, as can be seen in (99).

(99)   Lotuxo (Eastern Nilotic, Nilo-Saharan; Tucker and Bryan 1966:484; Claudi 1986:17)
    (a) Companion Schema
        o- won Lɔyɛ́ ikɔ lonyi.
        3.SG-exist Loye with son
        'Loye has a son.'

    (b) Location Schema
        o- won lonyi jo Lɔyɛ́.
        3.SG-exist son near Loye
        'Loye has a son.'

That the two constructions are in fact derived from the respective concrete source schemas can be shown with the following examples which illustrate the non-possessive source structures involved:

(100)   Lotuxo (Eastern Nilotic, Nilo-Saharan; Claudi 1986:18)
    (a) Companion Schema
        e -t- oŋo ni ikɔ iye.
        1.SG-PFV-stay I with you
        'I stay (together) with you.'

    (b) Location Schema
        e -t- oŋo ni jo iye.
        1.SG-PFV-stay I near you
        'I stay with you (at your place).'

Sometimes we get additional clues from the kinds of possessive notion expressed. Thus, if any of the above constructions expresses physical or temporary possession then this is more likely to be the one derived from Location (see above). Now, as the above examples show, both Lotuxo constructions can express permanent possession. But, whereas the *ikɔ*-construction appears to be confined to the expression of permanent possession, the *jo*-construction is used for temporary possession in addition, as in (101) below: (101b) expresses the meaning that the cattle that Loye has may also include those that are lent to him by a relative or a neighbour.

(101)   Lotuxo (Eastern Nilotic, Nilo-Saharan; Claudi 1986:17)
    (a) o -won Lɔyɛ́ ikɔ nesuŋ aryai.
        3.SG-exist Loye with cattle many
        'Loye has/owns much cattle (i.e. he is rich).'

    (b) o -won nesuŋ aryai jo Lɔyɛ́.
        3.SG-exist cattle many near Loye
        'Loye has much cattle.'

104 *The process*

Most problems are encountered when it comes to establishing whether a given construction is an instance of the Location or the Goal Schema: both schemas encode the possessee as the sentence subject and the possessor as some oblique case expression, both tend to use a kind of copula verb, and both may involve some locative case marking. The following example from Ik illustrates the nature of this problem, where (102a) has a locative and (102b) a (temporary) possessive meaning.

(102) Ik (Kuliak, Nilo-Saharan; Heine 1983:155–7)
    (a) ia imá ho- k^e
        is.at child house-DAT
        'The child is in the house.'

    (b) ia ima ntsí-k^e.
        is.at child him-DAT
        'He has a child (not his own).'

What accounts for the different semantics of the two utterances is the fact that the Goal complement is inanimate in (102a) but human in (102b). The presence of the locative copula *ia* is suggestive of the Location Schema, while the use of the Dative (Goal) inflection suggests an interpretation in terms of the Goal Schema.

2.5 Language-internal variation

2.5.1 *Major vs minor schemas*

On the basis of a world-wide language survey, Clark (1978:99) concludes that while there are a few languages that have two word orders for possessive constructions, the vast majority have only one. The question is what exactly this means, considering the fact that in most languages we are familiar with there are both verbs that present the possessor as a subject or topic (e.g. English *have*) and verbs that present the possessor as a complement (e.g. *belong*).

A distinction that may be more useful for typological and other cross-linguistic studies is one that divides possessive constructions and their respective sources into major and minor schemas. Major schemas can be described with reference to the following interrelated characteristics:

(a)   They exhibit a minimum of contextual restrictions.
(b)   Typically they involve both human and inanimate possessors, or both alienable and inalienable relations.

(c) They cover a number of the possessive notions distinguished in Section 1.3.

Minor schemas lack these characteristics, that is, they are restricted in their occurrence, they exhibit certain constraints on the semantic properties of the possessor or the possessee or both, and they are associated with only a limited number of possessive notions, frequently only with one notion.

In many languages we did not meet any problems in tracing a boundary between the two kinds of schema. English, for example, has only one major schema, viz. the Action Schema involving the verb *have*. All other possessive constructions, such as the '*own*'- and the '*belong*'-constructions, have the characteristics of minor schemas. In addition there are contextually restricted and/or semantically specialized constructions. As we will see below, however, there are languages where it turns out to be hard if not impossible to determine what the major schema is. This observation deserves attention, considering the fact that most cross-linguistic surveys we are familiar with are based exclusively on what we call here major schemas, while minor ones are generally ignored, that is, the assumption made in such surveys is that each language necessarily has one major schema.

We will come back to the distinction between major and minor schemas in section 2.6; at this stage, a few further examples may suffice to illustrate the nature of the distinction. It would seem that its significance differs from one language to another. Krongo, spoken in the western part of the Republic of Sudan, for example, has an opaque construction involving the possessive verb -*àná* 'have' which is confined essentially to the expression of alienable possession (more correctly, to instances where the relation between possessor and possessee is not 'presupposed'; see Reh 1985:324 for details). Still, this appears to be the construction that best exhibits the characteristics (a), (b), and (c) proposed above; hence we consider it to be the major schema of this language. There is a second construction, involving the Action Schema based on the action verb *t-àllà* 'carry', which does not conform to (a): it appears to be overwhelmingly restricted to utterances which are compatible with the lexical semantics of this verb, as in (103a), even though Reh (1985:326) also recorded a sentence like (103b), where this is no longer the case.

(103) Krongo (Kordofanian, Nilo-Saharan; Reh 1985:326)
    (a) nk-   állà   áalì   k- í- k- ötù.
        CONN:PL-carry wounds LOC-PL-PL-head
        'And they have wounds on their heads.'

(b) m-állà Kàkká músò kí- còorì.
    3–carry Kaka   flour LOC-house
    'Kaka has flour in his house.'

Once a construction is associated with a wider range of possessive notions it is likely to have fewer contextual constraints than do constructions expressing a limited range of possessive notions. Bisa has two 'have'-constructions. One, illustrated by (104b), is derived from the Genitive Schema (*X's Y exists*), a source form of which is presented in (104a). This construction expresses a number of possessive notions including abstract possession, as can be seen in (104c), and it may be negated by replacing the locative/existential verb *ta* 'to exist, be in' with the discontinuous marker *ba . . . -y/-i*, as in (104d).

(104)   Bisa (Voltaic, Niger-Congo; Naden 1982:212–13)
        (a) Wusu ta- w.
            God   exist-at
            'God exists.'

        (b) Mʊʊ lu   ta- w.
            my wife exist-at
            'I have a wife.' (Or: 'My wife is here/is alive.')

        (c) A   gweli   ta- w.
            her beauty   exist-at
            'She is pretty.'

        (d) A   fʊ- si   ba-   w-i.
            his thing-any NEG:exist-at-NEG
            'He has nothing.'

A second Bisa construction is derived from the Companion Schema, where again the locative/existential verb *ta* is employed, with the possessee being introduced by the postposition *n* 'with', as in (105).

(105)   Bisa (Voltaic, Niger-Congo; Naden 1982:213)
        A ta   busoo n   guta.
        he exist money with big
        'He has lots of money.'

This construction appears to be much more restricted in the range of possessive notions it is associated with. At the same time, it is largely restricted to cases 'where something additional follows the basic core of the clause,' like *guta* in (105) above. Furthermore, this construction may not be negated (Naden 1982:213). Hence, we will say that Genitive is the major and Companion a minor schema in Bisa.

2.5 Language-internal variation

It goes without saying that the presence of a given construction does not exclude the possibility that the same language makes use of more than one pattern of predicative possession for the expression of one and the same possessive notion. Synonymy, or at least 'near-synonymy', based on contrastive source schemas is in fact quite widespread. A number of Slavic languages are characterized by the co-existence of an earlier Location-derived and a later Action-derived construction, as illustrated by the following examples (cf. Isačenko 1974b; Orr 1992).

(106) Slavic languages (Orr 1992:250–1)
Ukrainian
u mene je hroši   OR   ja maju hroši
at me   is cash   I   have cash
'I have cash.'

Belorussian
u mjane jość brat   OR   ja maju brata
at me   is   brother   I   have brother
'I have a brother.'

While the presence of one major schema only within a given language might be the expected case, some languages have grammaticalized more than one major schema. In such languages, there are two, or even more, schemas that are conceptually and contextually largely equivalent for the expression of predicative possession. In Lezgian, for example, the Location and the Goal Schemas provide functionally equivalent models for predicative possession. The predicate nucleus is *awa* 'be, exist', and the case function is expressed, respectively, by the Postessive (POESS) suffix -q^h ('behind', Location Schema) and the Dative suffix -z (Goal Schema):

(107) Lezgian (Caucasian; Haspelmath 1993:89, 93)
   (a) Ada-z   xtul-   ar awa.   Goal
       she-DAT   grandchild-PL   be.in   Schema

OR (b) Ada-aq^h xtul-   ar awa.   Location
       she-POESS   grandchild-PL   be.in   Schema
   'She has grandchildren.'

Similarly, Claudi (1986:17) observes that Lotuko uses, at least in some contexts, the Location and the Companion Schemas as functionally equivalent constructions for verbal possession (see 2.4 above).

In Hungarian, the Goal Schema (108a) can be used as what Kiefer (1968:63) calls a 'paraphrase' of the Location Schema (108b) for verbal possession. Note that the Goal Schema, though not the Location Schema, shows possessor agreement on the possessee.

108 *The process*

(108) Hungarian (Kiefer 1968:63)
    (a) A   házon   van tetö   Location Schema
        the house.on is   roof
        'The house has a roof.'

    or (b) A   háznak   van teteje   Goal Schema
           the house.to is   roof.its
           'The house has a roof.'

In Somali, the Companion Schema based on the verbal *leh-yahay* 'have' (<*'be with') provided the main source for verbal possession. There is also, however, a minor schema based on the Action Schema, involving the verb *qab-* (*qab-ayya*) 'hold, take'. The use of the latter schema is functionally equivalent with the former one in some contexts. Thus, (109a) and (109b) appear to be largely synonymous.

(109) Somali (East Cushitic, Afro-Asiatic; Serzisko 1984:195)
    (a) Naag   ma   leh-dahay?   Companion Schema
        woman   Q   have:2.SG
        'Do you have a woman?' (='Are you married?')

    or (b) Naag   ma   qabtaa?   Action Schema
           woman   Q   hold:2.SG
           'Are you married?'

According to Freeze (1992:587), the Action Schema (based on the verb *ter* 'take, hold') and the Companion Schema are 'normal alternatives' in Portuguese, as in (110):

(110) Portuguese (Freeze 1992:587)
    (a) O   menino tem fome.   Action Schema
        the child   has hunger
        'The child is hungry.'

    or (b) O   menino esta com   fome.   Companion Schema
           the child   is   with hunger
           'The child is hungry.'

The relationship between source schemas and the kinds of possession associated with each of them is a complex one (see 2.3 above). Some schemas are more likely to give rise to alienable, as opposed to inalienable, possession and, statistically, some schemas are more likely to be associated with major than with minor schemas. The Companion Schema, for example, is said to be more likely to express physical and temporary or, more generally, alienable possession than inalienable possession (Kilian-Hatz and Stolz 1992:4; Stolz 1994:53). In many languages having several different 'have'-constructions each of these constructions may be derived from a different schema. This, however, is not always the case, rather one and the same schema may be recruited repeatedly for the same purpose; we will return to this point in 2.6 below.

2.5.2 Competing schemas

From the foregoing discussion we learn that it is quite common for languages to have two or even more different 'have'-constructions. It is equally common that these constructions overlap in their use, that is, that different constructions express one and the same possessive notion, even if in some contexts there may be semantic contrasts between these constructions. In fact, a situation where each construction was associated with a different range of possessive notions, that is, where these constructions were used in mutually exclusive environments, would be the exception rather than the rule. Our data do suggest indeed that functional differentiation as a principle of structuring the grammar of possession in a given language is of minor significance compared to the two main parameters considered here, viz. schema choice and grammaticalization.

What appears to happen quite commonly, however, is that, with the rise of a new 'have'-construction, the existing one gradually comes to be restricted to specific uses, most of all to the expression of abstract possession. Throughout the recorded history of Latin prose, the Goal Schema of the type *mihi est liber* 'I have a book' was strongly associated with abstract possession (Löfstedt 1963:75). The Action Schema, based on the use of the verb *habere* 'have', whose lexical meaning was 'to hold', emerges in Old Latin, where *habere* still competes with other verbs such as *possidere*. In its earliest uses, the *habere*-construction was largely confined to expressions having concrete possessees, but relatively early the construction also began to cover inalienable possession both of the body-part- and the kinship-type, and instances of abstract possession emerge in the texts of Cato (e.g. *spem habere* 'to have hope') and Cicero (*timorem habere* 'to have fear'; Löfstedt 1963:76–7). Since the Christian era, constructions of the type *opus mihi est* are increasingly replaced by *opus habeo* (Löfstedt 1963:76–8).

The replacement of *habere* (>*aver*) by *tenere* (>*tener*) in Spanish dates back to the twelfth century, but this evolution appears to be rooted in developments that took place much earlier: in Latin, *tenere* figured in some possessive expressions (Löfstedt 1963:79).

110 *The process*

Conversely, while the use of the Goal Schema as the major 'have'-construction declined during the Latin period, Löfstedt (1963:80) maintains that it did not disappear entirely, rather that it is retained, for example, in the Rumanian construction of the form *îmi este frica* ('to me is fear') 'I am afraid', where it is associated with abstract possession. Note, however, that in Rumanian and French there are also modern versions of the Goal Schema that are not immediately derived from the Latin construction, examples being Rumanian *cartea este a tatalui* 'the book belongs to my father', and French *la maison est à moi* 'the house belongs to me'. These more recent innovations are 'belong'-constructions and, hence, they denote permanent, rather than abstract or any other kind of possession. It would be worth investigating whether the French 'belong'-construction might not be due to Celtic substrate influence (Nigel Vincent, p.c.).

2.5.3   *Peculiar structures*

With the grammaticalization of concrete source schemas to more abstract expressions of possession, a development is triggered that leads to the rise of a number of morphosyntactic peculiarities in the languages concerned. These peculiarities are of two kinds. First, they concern the emergence of new morphosyntactic structures that may have no parallel elsewhere in the language, that is, that cannot be accounted for with reference to rules commonly applicable in that language. Second, these peculiarities may also be typologically significant in that the new morphosyntactic structures cannot be reconciled with typological regularities across languages. We will illustrate some of these peculiarities in this section.

Most of them appear to be due to a process that we will loosely refer to as 'transitivization'. As we shall see below (2.7), the development from concrete source schema to possession is likely to activate forces that have the effect that definite participants are placed before indefinite ones, and animate participants before inanimate ones. The hypothetical endpoint of this process is a predication structure having the following characteristics:

(a)   The possessor precedes the possessee.
(b)   The possessor has properties of a subject and the possessee of a clausal object.
(c)   The possessor is definite and the possessee indefinite.

Nevertheless, what we usually find are situations where 'have'-constructions retain some properties of their conceptual source, but in addition acquire some properties characteristic of the 'transitivization' process. The result is a structure that has been described by Heine, Claudi, and Hünnemeyer (1991:231–3) as a 'hybrid form': the possessive construction concerned combines the properties of its non-possessive conceptual source with the target properties listed in (a) through (c) above. We will now illustrate the nature of such hybrid forms with examples from a few genetically and areally unrelated languages.

Until the nineteenth century, Hungarian had a 'have'-construction derived from the Action Schema, involving the transitive verb *bír-* 'rule' as a predicate nucleus. This verb was grammaticalized to a marker of predicative possession, roughly corresponding to 'have'-verbs in other European languages. Thus, Biermann provides the following passage, taken from the writings of the poet Sándor Petöfi (1823–49):

> Hungarian (Biermann 1985:12)
> bír- om végre Juliská-m- at
> have-I finally Julia- my-ACC
> 'Finally [after the longed-for wedding], I have my Julia.'

This instance of the Action Schema is no longer in use; the major pattern of predicative possession in modern Hungarian is provided by the Goal Schema (*Y exists for/to X*). The structure that this pattern normally shows is sketched in (111a); an example is found in (111b).

(111) Hungarian (Biermann 1985:13)
    (a) Possessor -nak van Possessee-PRON
            DAT is

    (b) a férfi-nek van ház- a.
        the man-DAT is house-3.SG
        'The man has a house.'

The possessee noun phrase is encoded in the Nominative case (marked by zero) and has an obligatory pronominal suffix (PRON) agreeing with the possessor in person, optionally also in number.

While the case morphology of (111a) exhibits a clause structure Dative – Verb – Nominative, the actual use patterns are at variance with such a structure. Rather, these patterns are suggestive of a process whereby the Dative-marked possessor noun phrase (henceforth: the possessor) has gained a number of subject properties and, in a parallel fashion, the Nominative-marked possessee noun phrase (the possessee) has lost some properties that one would expect from canonical subjects in Hungarian. This claim is based on the following observations made by Biermann (1985:96ff.):

112   *The process*

(a) Like canonical subjects in the Nominative case, the possessor can be deleted if its reference has been established by the preceding discourse.
(b) Like subjects, the possessor is normally referred to in the following discourse by means of zero anaphora, while the formal subject, that is, the possessee, is likely to use a demonstrative (*az*) for anaphoric reference, as do non-subject participants.
(c) The possessor triggers agreement on the possessee.
(d) The possessor is definite and is likely to act as the clausal topic, while the possessee is indefinite and rarely has a topic function.
(e) The possessor is what Biermann (1985:135) calls a fully specified noun phrase while the possessee is not.

To summarize, the Hungarian 'have'-construction has developed a form that has no immediate parallel elsewhere in the clausal syntax of the language. Even if some of its characteristics can also be observed in other parts of the language, the construction as a whole is '*sui generis*', as Biermann (1985:83) calls it.

Processes of shift, as in this Hungarian example, appear to be most dramatic in the case of 'have'-constructions derived from the Goal Schema. Hebrew offers another example of such a case: Its major 'have'-construction is a canonical instance of the Goal Schema, as illustrated in (112). There are, however, two varieties of modern Hebrew: colloquial Israeli Hebrew (henceforth: colloquial Hebrew) and Normative Literary Hebrew (henceforth: literary Hebrew), and the process has affected only colloquial Hebrew.

(112)   Literary Hebrew (Ziv 1976:130)
        haya   lemoshe   shaon   shveycari.
        was.3.M   to.Moshe   watch:M   Swiss:M
        'Moshe had a Swiss watch.'

The possessee (*shaon shveycari* 'Swiss watch') is the formal subject, while the possessor (*lemoshe* 'to Moshe') is an oblique participant. In colloquial Hebrew, the possessee has lost most subject properties while the possessor appears to be gaining in subject properties. This process is reflected in the following developments observed by Ziv (1976:144):

(a) As (112) shows, the possessor normally precedes the possessee. Note that this applies to both literary and colloquial Hebrew.
(b) Whereas in literary Hebrew the definite nominal possessee occurs in the subject case, i.e. the Nominative, it is assigned the Accusative case marker *et* in colloquial Hebrew.

(c) In literary Hebrew, the possessee controls verb agreement; in colloquial Hebrew, however, the definite nominal possessee loses control of verb agreement.

(d) In literary Hebrew, the nominal possessee can undergo subject raising to subject position; the definite possessee of colloquial Hebrew, however, does not normally undergo subject raising.

(e) In some cases, the nominal possessor is now emerging in normal subject position, i.e., before the verb *haya*.

To summarize, the definite possessee of colloquial Hebrew has been reanalysed as a non-subject, if not as a direct object, while the possessor has acquired subject properties. Note, however, that this process is largely confined to definite possessees; it has not (yet) affected indefinite possessees. The result is a hybrid 'have'-construction in colloquial Hebrew, a construction that has neither a clear subject nor a clear object.

Similar observations have been made by Hagège (1993). His concern is on the one hand with the transition from possession to tense, aspect, and modality – a process that we will return to in chapter 4. On the other hand, he is concerned with what he calls the reanalysis of 'be structures' as 'have structures'. With regard to the latter process, Hagège (1993:66ff.) presents in particular the following examples:

(a) Nineteenth-century Manchu, an Altaic language, developed its Goal Schema (*Y exists for/to X*) into a 'have'-construction whereby the possessor loses the Dative case marking and is reanalysed as the subject of the clause.

(b) A comparable evolution can be observed in Maltese, a vernacular form of Arabic. As the description by Comrie (1981:212–18) suggests, this language has grammaticalized the Location Schema to a 'have'-construction, more specifically a sub-schema of Location that we have briefly sketched in section 2.1 (see especially example (11a)). The structure of this sub-schema is reprinted for convenience in (113), while (114a) provides an example that can be assumed to illustrate the locative source and (114b) the possessive target structure of the 'have'-construction of Maltese.

(113) Y is at X's home > X has, owns Y

(114) Maltese (Semitic, Afro-Asiatic; Comrie 1981:213)
    (a) Il-ktieb għandu.
        the.book at.his.house
        'The book is at his house.'

114 *The process*

(b) Għandu   ktieb.
    at.his.house book
    'He has a book.'

The evolution is summarized by Comrie in the following way:

> We can now characterize the historical development from Proto-Arabic (presumably the same, in these respects, as Classical Arabic) to Maltese as follows: in the possessive construction, subject properties have been transferred diachronically from the possessed noun phrase to the possessor, until finally the possessed noun phrase has no subject properties, while the possessor has all subject properties except the form of the verb agreement that it triggers (Comrie 1981:217).

The final stage of this general evolution is reached when a transitive 'have'-verb emerges, as appears to have happened in Cornish, as Stassen (1995) says; we have summarized his discussion in 2.4 above.

The grammaticalization of concrete source schemas to possessive expressions is not only responsible for peculiar constructions that contrast with regular patterns of building discourses, it may also give rise to 'exotic' typological situations. Such a situation is presented by what has been described as double subject marking: it tends to arise when the Topic Schema (*As for X, (X's) Y exists*) is involved.

In Luiseño, the Topic Schema has given rise to a sentence structure having two subject-like constituents. Thus, in (115), the constituents *noo=p* and *nopaa?aš* exhibit a number of morphosyntactic properties that justify calling them both subjects.

(115)   Luiseño (Takic, Uto-Aztecan; Steele 1977:114)
        noo=p   nopaa?aš   ?awq
        I=clitic my:brother is
        'I have a brother.'

The way the evolution of this 'have'-construction in Luiseño is to be conceived can be sketched by means of the following scenario, reconstructed on the basis of generalizations on grammaticalization processes (see especially Heine, Claudi, and Hünnemeyer 1991). At Stage Zero, there is only a single subject. This stage is still widely attested in the language, as in the following example.

(116)   Luiseño (Takic, Uto-Aztecan; Steele 1977:124)
        nopuuš konokniš
        my:eye green
        'My eyes are green.'

2.5 Language-internal variation

At Stage I, topicalized subjects are introduced, giving rise to a structure *As for X, X does Y*. This structure has had a number of influences on language use patterns, described in more detail by Steele (1977); it can be held responsible in particular for a pattern of predicative possession, where the verb is 'be (here)' and the topic constituent comes to refer to the possessor and the subject to the possessee, the resulting structure being something like *As for X, X's Y is (here)*. Initially, however, this structure expresses location (or existence) rather than possession, as in (117), where *noo* 'I' is an independent pronoun (Steele describes (117) as a good 'if quite uncommon expression.').

(117) Luiseño (Takic, Uto-Aztecan; Steele 1977:125)
noo nopaaʔaš ʔawq
I my:brother is
'My brother is here.'

At Stage II, a possessive meaning is introduced when the topic is a noun rather than a pronoun. In such a case, ambiguity arises in that the construction could be interpreted alternatively with reference to the locative source and the possessive target meaning, as can be seen in (118).

(118) Luiseño (Takic, Uto-Aztecan; Steele 1977:125)
xwaan popaaʔaš ʔawq
John his:brother is
(a) 'John's brother is here.'
(b) 'John has a brother.'

At Stage III, ambiguity is resolved by the use of a clitic pronoun placed after the topic agreeing in number and person with the subject of the clause: whenever this clitic is placed, the possessive reading is the only one possible, as in (119).

(119) Luiseño (Takic, Uto-Aztecan; Steele 1977:114, 125)
xwaan=up popaaʔaš ʔawq
John=clitic his:brother is
'John has a brother.'

Possession is then extended to inalienable possessees such as body-part terms, as in (120). Note that in constructions like (120), a formal predicate is no longer required.

(120) Luiseño (Takic, Uto-Aztecan; Steele 1977:124)
noo=p nopuuš konokniš
I=clitic my:eye green
'I have green eyes.'

This evolution entails a number of concomitant grammaticalization processes that have been discussed in the relevant literature (see Givón 1979; Heine and Reh 1984). One of these processes involves the fossilization of the pronominal clitic: when following independent pronouns, the clitic loses the ability to agree with the subject in number and person and turns into an invariable marker in its third-person singular form *up* (reduced to *-p* after vowels). With the phrase 'loses the ability' we wish to indicate that the process is not yet completed: it is still possible to use the agreement clitic, as can be seen in (121a), while (121b) represents the fossilized stage. Thus, the alternatives in (121) are suggestive of the Overlap Stage (see section 2.2 above), which is a predictable component of grammaticalization. Steele (1977:122) says, however, that (121a) is 'much less common' than (121b), which might be taken as an indication that the proccess of fossilization is close to reaching completion.

(121)   Luiseño (Takic, Uto-Aztecan; Steele 1977:114,122)
    (a) noo=n   nopaa?aš   ?awq
        I=1SG:clitic:pronoun my:brother is
        'I have a brother.'
    (b) noo=p nopaa?aš   ?awq
        I=clitic my:brother is
        'I have a brother.'

Another process involves syntacticization, whereby constituents serving discourse pragmatic functions, like topics or themes, come to develop into syntactic constituents, like subjects. The erstwhile topic in the Luiseño 'have'-construction is no longer primarily associated with topic features, to the extent that Steele describes it as a subject and the invariable *up* as being increasingly reinterpreted as a subject marker.

The result is that in such constructions, Luiseño now has two subjects. Note, however, that instances of double-subject constructions are not confined to predicative possession. They may also arise, for example, in attributive possession when, in predications involving body-parts as subjects, the possessor is presented as the clausal theme rather than as a possessive modifier; for an example involving Mandarin Chinese, see Chappell (1996).

These are but a few examples that illustrate the kind of peculiarities that may arise when possessive constructions evolve. Many other examples could be added; suffice it to mention that possessive constructions themselves may give rise to other grammatical forms such as aspect categories and, in the course of this evolution, may be grammaticalized as ergative structures (Trask 1979:398ff.; but see also Hagège 1993). We will return to this issue in chapter 4.

2.6 Schemas and possessive notions

The main theme of the preceding sections was the relationship between event schemas and the possessive constructions derived from them. In section 2.5 we were also dealing with the way two or more schemas may interact within the same language. In the present section we will be concerned with the question of what all this means with reference to the overall situation of predicative possession in a given language. To this end, a couple of languages for which sufficient information is available are looked at in greater detail.

2.6.1 Manding

Manding belongs to those languages that have made maximal use of one schema only for creating possessive expressions: It has exploited the Location Schema for four different 'have'-constructions. Manding belongs to the Mande group which, according to Greenberg (1963a), constitutes one of the branches of the Niger-Congo sub-family of Congo-Kordofanian but which, according to more recent lines of research, may be a distinct sub-family of Congo-Kordofanian, on the same genetic level as Niger-Congo. Manding has a number of closely related dialects, the main ones being Bambara, Dyula, Mandinka, and Maninka. Unless otherwise stated, the data discussed below are from Bambara, the *de facto* national language of Mali.

Like many other languages, Manding has developed a conventionalized 'belong'-construction based on the Equation Schema (*Y is X's (property)*), which is essentially confined to the expression of permanent possession, as illustrated in (122).

(122) Manding (Mande, Niger-Congo; Bird 1972:5)
       mobili ` bɛ   Bàba bolo, ngà à   ta   tɛ.
       car   the be.at Baba hand but his possession NEG
       'Baba has the car, but it's not his.'

Our main concern, however, is with the various 'have'-constructions (as opposed to 'belong'-constructions or forms of attributive possession; see chapter 1.2 above), that is, with constructions expressing notions like 'I have a watch/a cold'. Among the many forms the Location Schema takes, the four structures exemplified in (123) are agreed by most authors to provide the standard patterns for 'have'-constructions.

(123) Manding (Mande, Niger-Congo; Bird 1972:1; Kastenholz 1988:199; Mohamed Touré, p.c.).
    (a) wari ` bɛ Baba kùn.
        money the AUX Baba head
        'Baba has the money (on him).'

    (b) wari ` bɛ Baba bolo.
        money the AUX Baba hand
        'Baba has the money.'

    (c) wari ` bɛ Baba fɛ̀.
        money the AUX Baba at
        'Baba has the money.'

    (d) mura bɛ Baba la.
        catarrh be.at Baba at
        'Baba has a cold.'

All four constructions may have definite or indefinite possessees, and they have identical conceptual and syntactic structures, as sketched in (124).

(124) Conceptual structure: Possessee is at possessor's place
       Syntactic structure: NP_1 bɛ NP_2 Postposition

In negative utterances, *bɛ* is replaced by *tɛ*. The constructions differ from one another in the use of postpositions: *fɛ̀* is a straightforward locative postposition, while *bolo* 'arm, hand' and *kùn* 'head' are body-part nouns that have been grammaticalized to locative postpositions. The constructions also differ with regard to the possessive notions they are associated with. We will now look at each of them in turn.

Following Bird (1972), Kastenholz describes the meaning of the *kùn*-construction as involving 'control' (of the possessor over the possessee) and 'existence'. Neither of these properties would seem to characterize this construction appropriately because the same can be claimed for virtually all constructions discussed here, at least in some of their uses. Furthermore, Bird (1972:4) says that *kùn*, but not *bolo* or *fɛ̀*, has properties of a locative. This statement appears to be of little value either since, first, all 'postpositions' figuring in 'have'-constructions are locative in their source uses (see above) and, second, since, when having human 'objects', *kùn* invariably expresses physical possession rather than location, as in example (125a); Bird (1972:5) notes that 'the money must be on Baba's person at the moment of speaking' when *kùn* is used. That *kùn* may not be used with permanent possession is shown by the fact that (125b) is not a well-formed sentence.

(125) Manding (Mande, Niger-Congo; Bird 1972:5)
    (a) wari   te   Bàba kùn, ngà à be   so.
        money the be.at.NEG Baba head but it be.at house
        'Baba doesn't have the money, but it's at home.'

    (b) *wari   bɛ   Bàba kùn, ngà à be   so.
        money the be.at   Baba head but it be.at house

Of all constructions, however, *kùn* has retained the largest portion of its source meaning and, accordingly, exhibits more contextual constraints than the other constructions. *bɛ – kùn* literally means 'be on (one's) head' and, while the construction has been extended to uses where no actual carrying on one's head is involved, its use has not been generalized to all instances of physical possession; rather it requires that the possessed item be small enough that it could still be carried on one's head. Sentence (126) is therefore not a well-formed utterance. Bird (1972:4) notes, however, that, if we conceive of the car as a toy, or of Baba as a giant, then (126) might be acceptable.

(126) Manding (Mande, Niger-Congo; Bird 1972:4)
    ? mobili `   bɛ   Baba kùn.
      car   the be.at Baba head
      'Baba has the car.'

The meaning of the *bolo*-construction is described by Bird (1972) and Kastenholz (1988) with reference to the feature 'control'. They find this feature also to be present in the *kùn*- and *fɛ̀*-constructions, but, while the latter two have other distinguishing features in addition, the *bolo*-construction is said to lack such features (see below). Kastenholz (1988:200) refers to the latter as the 'minimally marked (kind of) possession'. The *bolo*-construction encompasses a wide range of possessive notions. It expresses physical possession in (127a), temporary possession in (127b), permanent possession in (127c) and, like *fɛ̀*, also inalienable kin possession in (127d), though not inalienable body-part possession.

(127) Manding (Mande, Niger-Congo; Bird 1972:5; Kastenholz 1988:200; Mohamed Touré, p.c.)
    (a) mobili bɛ   n   bolo, nkà ne ta tɛ.
        car   be.at my hand but mine NEG
        'I have a car (at my disposal), but it isn't mine.'

(b) i   ka kiriyon bɛ   n   bolo nkà à bɛ   so.
    you of pencil be.at my hand but it be.at house
    'I have your pencil, but it is at home.'

(c) wari   bɛ Bàba bolo, ngà à bɛ   so.
    money the be.at Baba hand but it be.at house
    'Baba has the money, but it's at home.'

(d) mùso bɛ   n   bolo.
    woman be.at my hand
    'I have a wife.'

Physical possession is expressed by the *bolo-* but not by the *fὲ*-construction. (128a), which is an instance of permanent possession, is therefore acceptable while (128b), volunteered by Bird, is not, since it would be suggestive of physical possession.

(128)   Manding (Mande, Niger-Congo; Bird 1972:5)
    (a) wari   bɛ Bàba fɛ, ngà à bɛ   so.
        money the be.at Baba at but it be.at house
        'Baba has the money, but it's home.'

    (b) *wari   tɛ Bàba fɛ̀, ngà à bɛ   so.
        money the be.at.NEG Baba at but it be.at house
        ('Baba doesn't have the money, but it's home.')

In (129a), for example, the possessed item is one to be 'consumed', (129b) may therefore not be used according to Kastenholz (1988). Note, however, that our consultant Mohamed Touré considered *fὲ* to be compatible with physical possession and, hence, did accept (129b) as an appropriate utterance. (130) can occur with both postpositions, but when *fὲ* is used, as in (130b), the sense expressed is one of permanent possession: the sentence would be uttered, for example, by someone having legal title to the field (cf. Kastenholz 1988:197).

(129)   Manding (Mande, Niger-Congo; Kastenholz 1988:197)
    (a) dɔ̀lɔ bɛ   à bolo.
        beer be.at his hand
        'He has beer.'

    (b) *dɔ̀lɔ bɛ   à fɛ̀.
        beer be.at his at

(130)   (a) dugukolo bɛ   n   bolo.
            field   be.at my hand
            'I have a field (e.g. for use).'

        (b) dugukolo bɛ   n   fɛ̀.
            field   be.at my at
            'I (legally) own a field.'

2.6 Schemas and possessive notions

In addition, *fὲ* also expresses inalienable kin possession, in a way similar to *bolo*, as in (131a), plus body-part possession, as in (131b); Kastenholz (1988:199) observes that '*bólo* et *fὲ* sont employés pour établir une relation possessive entre époux et épouse, amants, parents et enfants, frères et soeurs, etc'.

(131) Manding (Mande, Niger-Congo; Kastenholz 1988:200; Mohamed Touré, p.c.)
    (a) dénw   bɛ   à   fὲ.
        children be.at his at
        'He has children.'

    (b) bolo belebele-w bɛ   à   fὲ. (*bolo, *kun, *la)
        hand big-   PL be.at his at
        'He has big hands.'

The use of *la* in possessive expressions is referred to by Kastenholz (1988:194) as being essentially locative. We do not see, however, why *la* should be more strongly associated with locativity than any of the other 'postpositions'. Consider the following examples:

(132) Manding (Mande, Niger-Congo; Kastenholz 1988:194)
    (a) sèn naani bɛ   tabali ` la.
        leg four be.at table the at
        'The table has four legs.'

    (b) fànga bɛ   òmàsakɛ la.
        power be.at king   at
        'The king has the power.'

    (c) minnɔgɔ bɛ   ù   la.
        thirst   be.at their at
        'They have thirst (=are thirsty).'

    (d) fàrigan tɛ   à   la tugun.
        fever   be.at.NEG her at
        'She has no longer any fever.'

None of these examples is clearly suggestive of location as a noticeable sense of the *la*-construction. Kastenholz's characterization of these examples as involving a part–whole relationship would seem to be more appropriate. One may wonder, however, whether in examples like (132c) and (132d) we are not dealing with abstract possession, considering the fact that thirst and fever would not seem to qualify as typical items figuring in part–whole relations. We will assume that the *la*-construction serves the expression of inanimate inalienable possession on the one hand, and of abstract possession on the other. We will return to the contrasting meanings of these constructions below.

None of these four constructions serves the expression of inanimate alienable possession – a concept that does not appear to be associated with possession in Manding. Rather this concept is encoded by means of other constructions having a locative basis. Thus, while (133a) uses the *la*-construction, since it is an instance of inanimate inalienable possession, all other examples in (133) require the locative postposition *kɔnɔ* 'in, belly'.

(133)   Manding (Mohamed Touré, p.c.)
    (a) fenɛtiri bɛ   so   la.   (*bolo, *kùn, *fɛ̀)
        window be.at house at
        'The house has a window.'

    (b) tàbali naani bɛ   so   kɔnɔ. (*bolo, *kùn, *fɛ̀, *la)
        table four be.at house in
        'The house has four tables in it; there are four tables in the house.'

    (c) mɔ̀gɔ caman bɛ   dùguba kɔnɔ. (*bolo, *kùn, *fɛ̀, *la)
        people many be.at town in
        'The town has many inhabitants; there are many people in the town.'

It goes without saying that the boundary between alienability and inalienability is culturally determined to a large extent and, hence, differs from one society to another. For example, while 'cold' in (134a) is treated as alienable and receives the postposition *kɔnɔ*, 'nest' in (134b) is treated as an inalienable part of a tree.

(134)   Manding (Mohamed Touré, p.c.)
    (a) nɛnɛ bɛ   so   kɔnɔ.   (*la)
        cold be.at house in
        'The house is cold.'

    (b) nyaga bɛ   jiri la.
        nest be.at tree at
        'The tree has a nest in it.'

The range of possessive notions each of the four 'have'-constructions of Manding is associated with is summarized in Table 2.5.

Note that the generalizations contained in Table 2.5 are not shared by all speakers of the language. Some variation is apparent in the case of the *fɛ̀*-construction, which is compatible with physical and temporary possession for some speakers but not others. Furthermore, although these generalizations hold true for what we argue are 'prototypical instances' of the possessive notions concerned, they may not be applicable in a specific case. For

2.6 Schemas and possessive notions

Table 2.5. *The main possessive constructions in Manding and the notions expressed by them. (Abbreviations: KI=kinship, BO=body-part. For other abbreviations, see section 1.3.)*

Construction	Source Schema	PHYS	TEMP	PERM	INAL KI	INAL BO	ABST	IN/I	IN/A
bɛ – kùn	Location	+	–	–	–	–	–	–	–
bɛ – bolo	Location	+	+	+	+	–	–	–	–
bɛ – fɛ̀	Location	+/–	+/–	+	+	+	–	–	–
bɛ – la	Location	–	–	–	–	–	+	+	–

example, according to Table 2.5, the *kùn*-construction is confined to physical possession, yet we find examples like (135), where it expresses inalienable (body-part) possession. There are usually reasons for such a treatment. In this particular instance, the reason is that the postposition *kùn* is derived from the body-part noun *kùn* 'head' and that the semantics of its lexical source has not entirely disappeared. Thus, in the case of possessees that are part of the head, the postposition *kùn* may be used side by side with *fɛ̀*.

(135) Manding (Mande, Niger-Congo; Mohamed Touré, p.c.)
      kùn- sigi jàmanjan bɛ   à   kùn/fɛ̀.
      head-hair long   be.at his head/at
      'He has long hair.'

What Table 2.5 suggests is that the various constructions are associated to some extent with mutually exclusive environments, and that there appears to be some principle of functional differentiation at work. One remarkable exception can be seen in the case of *bolo* and *fɛ̀*, which are both used for the expression of permanent and inalienable kinship possession. This fact has led a number of Manding grammarians to claim that *bolo* and *fɛ̀* can be used interchangeably (cf. Kastenholz 1988:193); as we saw above, such a claim is unfounded.

2.6.2 Ewe

The Ewe language of south-eastern Ghana and southern Togo has developed a bewildering variety of possessive constructions. With the exception of Companion, all source schemas are grammaticalized for this purpose. That the Companion Schema has been spared may be surprising, considering the fact that it is one of the most commonly exploited schemas in African languages, especially in the Niger-Congo family, to which Ewe belongs (see Table 2.2; see also Otten 1992).

Like Manding, Ewe has grammaticalized the Equation Schema as its main 'belong'-construction, which is based on the structure Y nyé X tɔ ('Y is X's') 'Y belongs to X'. The morphological items figuring in this construction are the equational copula nyé 'be' and the nominal tɔ 'property'. In accordance with the conceptual structure of this schema, the possessee is encoded as the subject and the possessor as a complement, and the possessee is typically definite, as can be seen in (136). This construction is confined to the expression of permanent possession.

(136) Ewe (Kwa, Niger-Congo)
       ga-   a   nyé tɔ   nye.
       money-the is   property my
       'The money belongs to me.'

What might be called the major 'have'-construction in Ewe is an instance of the Location Schema; it has the form Y le X ası́ ('Y is at X's hand'). The noun ası́ 'hand' figuring in this construction is reduced to sı́ following e.g. a possessive pronoun. An example of this construction is presented in (137).

(137) Ewe (Kwa, Niger-Congo)
       ga   le   Kofi sı́.
       money   be.at Kofi hand
       'Kofi has money.'

Six different stages can be reconstructed diachronically in the grammaticalization of the le . . . ası́-construction. All these stages are still found in modern Ewe. At Stage I, which represents the source structure, the construction expresses location rather than possession, and it is used in its full form, that is, the noun ası́ 'hand' and the possessor are linked by the possessive particle pé, and ası́ is headed by the locative postposition me 'in', as in (138a). The second stage is preserved in two different forms, both of which have undergone what we called erosion in section 2.2: either the postposition me is deleted, as in (138b), or else the possessive particle pé is deleted, as in (138c). None of these three examples expresses permanent possession; (138a) and (138b) have locative semantics while (138c) is an instance of physical possession. Example (138d) exhibits the fully grammaticalized morphosyntax in that both the postposition and the possessive particle have been eliminated, but, since the possessee is definite, the

2.6 Schemas and possessive notions   125

possessive notion expressed is that of physical possession. Only when the possessee is indefinite, as in (138e), does the construction express permanent possession. The latter construction has also been extended to express inalienable possession involving both kinship and body-part terms, as in (138f), but the extension has not gone so far as to allow for inanimate possessors. Thus, (138g) is not a well-formed utterance; to turn it into an acceptable sentence, the locative source schema involving postpositions such as ŋú 'outside' or me 'in' would be required, as in (138h).

(138)   Ewe (Kwa, Niger-Congo)
     (a) akɔdú eve le   Kofí pé sí   me.
          banana two be.at Kofi of hand in
          'Two bananas are in Kofi's hand.'

     (b) (Ameka 1991:205)
          ba   le   Kofí pé así.
          mud be.at Kofi of hand
          'There is mud on Kofi's hand.'

     (c) Ʋu lá nyé tɔ   nye gaké fífíá lá   é-le.at Kofí sí   me.
          car the is   property my but   now DEF it.is   Kofi hand in
          'The car is mine but right now Kofi has it.'

     (d) (Ameka 1991:207)
          ga   lá le   Kofí sí.
          money the be.at Kofi hand
          'The money is with Kofi.'

     (e) ga   le   Kofí sí.
          money be.at Kofi hand
          'Kofi has money.'

     (f) (Ameka 1991:204)
          tɔ́   le   ɖeví má sí.
          father be.at child that hand
          'That child has a father.'

     (g) *Ʋɔtrú eve ko   le   xɔ   siá sí.
          door two only be.at house this hand
          (*'This house has only two doors.')

     (h) Ʋɔtrú eve ko   le   xɔ   siá ŋú.
          door two only be.at house this outside
          'This house has only two doors.'

The evolution underlying this process can be sketched as in Table 2.6. Stage I is characteristic of free and unconstrained language use. Stage II and all subsequent stages represent fossilized morphosyntactic structures that in some way or other violate productive collocation rules of Ewe. The

Table 2.6. *The main stages in the development from location to possession in Ewe. (For the abbreviations, see chapter 1.3).*

Stage	Example	Construction	Meaning	Notion
I	a	le ... ame pé así me be.at person of hand in	'be in one's hand'	LOC
II	b	le ... ame pé así	'be in one's hand'	LOC
III	c	le ... ame así me	'have on oneself'	PHYS
IV	d	le ... ame así +definite possessee	'have on oneself'	PHYS
V	e	le ... ame así +indefinite possessee	'have, own'	PERM
VI	f	le ... ame así +indefinite possessee	'have, own'	INAL

constructions of Stages III and IV still have some locative component, and in their capacity as expressions of physical possession they compete with other locative constructions that also have assumed the function of denoting physical possession. Thus, Ameka (1991:207) notes that the following two utterances are 'pragmatically equivalent':

(139)   (a) ga lá le Kofi sí.
           money the be.at Kofi hand
           'The money is with Kofi.'

      (b) ga lá le Kofi gbɔ́.
           money the be.at Kofi side
           'The money is with Kofi.'

In constructions like (139a), the erstwhile noun (*a*) *sí* 'hand' appears to have joined the paradigm of locative postpositions such as *gbɔ́* 'side, at', and Ameka (1991:205) observes that this noun 'has become grammaticalized as a postposition expressing a spatial relational meaning'.

At Stage V, the construction has lost its association with location and physical possession and corresponds closely to prototypical possession, that is, to permanent possession; at Stage VI it has been extended to an additional notion, namely that of inalienable possession.

To summarize, the evolution just sketched is characterized by two main processes, namely the erosion of certain markers and conceptual extension. We are now in a position to account for the following properties of *le ... así* as a 'have'-construction expressing permanent possession:

(a) The morphosyntax of this construction is that of a locative construction, but it differs from the latter in that it lacks the possessive linking particle *pé* 'of' and the postposition *me* 'in'.
(b) The possessee must be indefinite.
(c) The possessor must be a human participant.

A second 'have'-construction in Ewe has the form *Y lii ná X* ('*Y exists for X*'). It is a canonical instance of the Goal Schema; the following is an example:

(140) Ewe (Kwa, Niger-Congo; Ameka 1991:214)
sítsopé aɖéké mé lii ná m o.
refuge none NEG exist for me NEG
'I don't have any (place of) refuge.'

The copula verb *lii* or *lee* 'exist' is probably etymologically related to the locative copula *le* 'be at' (Ameka 1991:211), but the details need not concern us here; note that in non-present tenses, *lii* is replaced by *nɔ anyí*, a verb meaning 'sit down', which has been grammaticalized to an existence copula. At Stage I, this construction expresses existence rather than possession, as in (141):

(141) Ewe (Kwa, Niger-Congo; Ameka 1991:211)
tʊgbé- wó lee.
ancestor-PL exist
'Ancestors exist/are there.'

At Stage II, the existential copula *lii* is followed by an adjunct introduced by the benefactive preposition *ná* 'for, to', which is derived from the verb *ná* 'give, donate'. The resulting meaning is close to that of physical possession in that it refers to a temporary association between possessee and possessor, as in (142):

(142) Ewe (Kwa, Niger-Congo; Ameka 1991:215)
dɔ lá lee ná Kofí.
work the exist for Kofi
'The work is there for Kofi (he will have to do it).'

Stage III represents the grammaticalized situation of inalienable possession, exemplified below:

(143) Ewe (Kwa, Niger-Congo; Ameka 1991:214)
fofó kplé dadá lii ná ɖeví má.
father and mother exist for child that
'That child has a father and a mother.'

128   *The process*

Table 2.7. *The main stages in the development from existence to possession in Ewe.*

Stage	Construction	Meaning	Notion
I	lii exist	'exist'	Existence
II	lii ná ame exist for somebody +definite possessee	'be there for somebody'	Temporary association
III	lii ná ame +indefinite possessee	'have, own'	INAL
IV	lii ná ame +indefinite possessee	'have, own'	ABST
V	lii ná ame +indefinite possessee	'have, own'	IN/I

As in the case of the *le . . . así*-construction, full grammaticalization was confined to contexts involving indefinite possessees. Thus, with definite possessees (including proper names), the Stage II meaning of temporary association is retained, as can be seen in (142) above. The *lii ná*-construction has, however, gone one step further in that it has been extended to inanimate possessors, as in (144):

(144)   Ewe (Kwa, Niger-Congo; Ameka 1991:215)
        nuwúwú lii   ná núsianú.
        end   exist for everything
        'Everything has an end.'

The evolution of the Goal Schema is summarized in Table 2.7.

There is another 'have'-construction in Ewe which is also an instance of the Goal Schema but combines the properties of the Goal and the Location Schemas. It has the structure *Y le Z ná X* ('Y be at Z for X'). An example of its source structure, where Z is formally marked as a definite participant, is provided in (145a), and an example of its possessive use in (145b).

(145)   Ewe (Kwa, Niger-Congo; Ameka 1991:217)
        (a) aha le   ze- á- me ná mi.
            wine be.at pot-the-in for you (PL)
            'There is wine in the pot for you (PL).'
        (b) srɔ̃   eve le   apé- me ná ŋútsu má.
            spouse two be.at home-in for man   that
            'That man has two wives at home.'

2.6 Schemas and possessive notions

This mixed construction has also been grammaticalized beyond the stage of temporary possession: as the following example provided by Ameka suggests, it can express permanent possession:

(146) Ewe (Kwa, Niger-Congo; Ameka 1991:219)
xɔ eve le gẽ ná áma srɔ̃.
house two be.at Accra for Ama spouse
'Ama's husband has two houses in Accra.'

The Action Schema is of far less importance than the preceding schemas. Still, a number of verbs, like xɔ 'get, receive', lé 'catch, hold', can be used with this schema, usually to express temporary possession. As we would predict, instances of this schema encode the possessor as the sentence subject and the possessee as the object, as in the following example:

(147) Ewe (Kwa, Niger-Congo; Ameka 1991:225)
áma xɔ pe blá-eve.
Ama get year tie-two
'Ama became/is twenty years old.' (i.e. 'Ama has twenty years')

Ameka (1991:225) treats the relevant constructions as instances of 'temporary possession' and most, though not all, examples given by him are in fact suggestive of physical or temporary possession. These constructions are in the initial stages of grammaticalization, and in many of their uses it is debatable whether indeed we are dealing with instances of possession rather than with lexical uses of the verbs concerned.

There is, however, one form of the Action Schema that has been grammaticalized to a larger extent. This form has the verb kpɔ́ 'see' as a predicate. As in the case of possessive utterances derived from the Location and the Goal Schemas, grammaticalization has taken place in one specific context only, namely when the possessee is indefinite. Thus, (148a) is an instance of a possessive expression while (148b) is not since it contains a possessee which is definite. But the presence of an indefinite possessee is not a sufficient condition for the presence of a 'have'-construction; in more general terms it seems that a possessive interpretation is only possible when the situation involved is non-specific. (148c) is therefore not a 'have'-construction since the adverbial phrase le afimá 'there' is suggestive of a specific situation.

(148) (a) é- kpɔ́ ga ŋútɔ́.
s/he see money very
'He has/got a lot of money.'

(b) é- kpɔ́ ga   lá.
    s/he see money the
    'He saw/found the money.'

(c) é- kpɔ́ ga   ŋútɔ́ le afīmá.
    s/he see money very at there
    'He saw/found the money there.'

The Action Schema has not, however, led to the rise of a genuinely productive pattern of a 'have'-construction. Even the kpɔ́-construction, which has been grammaticalized to an expression of permanent possession, is only of limited productivity. Ameka (1991:227) observes that this construction serves 'to express possession of material things like ga 'money' and dɔ́ 'work', as well as abstract attributes and states such as ŋúsẽ 'strength' or vovo 'free'. In this respect, the kpɔ́-construction differs from the le . . . ası́-construction, which is fully productive within the limits sketched above.

The canonical patterns looked at above have also served as a template for additional forms of possessive expressions. Following Hopper (1991) we will refer to this phenomenon as layering, which he defines thus: 'Within a broad functional domain, new layers are continually emerging; in the process the older layers are not necessarily discarded, but may remain to coexist with and interact with new layers' (Hopper 1991:22). Layering is the synchronic result of successive grammaticalization of forms which contribute to the same domain (Hopper and Traugott 1993:124). We will now look at some common patterns of layering in Ewe.

The Goal Schema has given rise to a pattern of expression called inchoative possession by Ameka (1991:222), but which might equally well be described as resultative possession: inchoative possession means 'that something has come into the possession of the possessor.' According to this pattern, instead of the existential verb lii 'exist', the verbs bɔ́ 'abound', sɔgbɔ 'be plentiful', and susɔ 'be left, remain' are used as a predicate, and instead of the Goal preposition ná 'for, to', the adjunct is introduced by means of the allative preposition ɖé 'to' and the postposition (a)sí 'at', as in the following examples:

(149)   Ewe (Kwa, Niger-Congo; Ameka 1991:224)
   (a) núɖuɖu bɔ́   ɖé yiyi   sí   ŋútɔ́.
       food   abound to spider hand much
       'Yiyi (the spider) had a lot of food.'

   (b) lɔri- wó sɔgbɔ   ɖé é- sí.
       lorry-PL be.plentiful to his-hand
       'He has several lorries.'

(c) kokló atɔ̃ ko- é susɔ ɖé así- nye.
hen five only-FOC remain to hand-my
'I have only five hens left.'

Layering has been particularly creative in the case of the Location Schema, leading to two different lines of grammaticalization. In accordance with this schema, the possessor is encoded as a locative constituent headed by the postposition (*a*)*sí* (which, as we saw above, is derived from the noun *así* 'hand'). Now, however, instead of the copula verb *le* 'be at', dynamic verbs such as *ɖó* 'reach', *sū* 'grasp', and *ká* 'get to, touch' are used. The resulting possessive meanings are described by Ameka (1991:222) as inchoative possession (see above). Since the Location Schema provided the template for this line of grammaticalization, the participant coding is that predictably associated with this schema: the possessee is encoded as the subject and the possessor as the complement of the clause, as can be seen in the following examples:

(150)   Ewe (Kwa, Niger-Congo; Ameka 1991:222–4)
  (a) agble-a   sū   Kofí sí.
      farm-the grasp Kofi's hand
      'The farm has become Kofi's.'

  (b) ... mɔ́-zɔ-ga   kplé nú-ɖu-ga   ká   wó   sí.
      travel.money and food.money touch their hand
      '... they got money for travel and food expenses.'

  (c) ga   ɖó   áma   sí.
      money reach Ama's hand
      'Ama has become rich.'

A second kind of layering involving the Location Schema concerns the locative notion rather than the predicate: Instead of the postposition *así* 'hand', a number of other postpositions, such as *gbɔ́* 'side, at', *dzí* 'top, on', or *ŋú* 'outside', are used depending on relevant contextual constraints. The meaning expressed is physical possession; in no case does this structure lead to expressions for permanent possession. Consider the following examples:

(151)   Ewe (Kwa, Niger-Congo)
  (a) ga   le   ŋú   nye.
      money be.at outside my
      (i) 'I have money on me.'
      (ii) 'I owe (somebody) money.'

  (b) wo   ágbalẽ le   gbɔ́ nye.
      your book   be.at side my
      (i) 'I have your book.'
      (ii) 'Your book is with me.'

(c) dɔ   le   dzí nye.
    work be.at   top my
    'I have a lot of work (to do).'

The various constructions looked at above differ with regard to the possessive notions they express, as can be seen in Table 2.8.

Table 2.8. *The main constructions of predicative possession in Ewe and the notions expressed by them.*

Construction	Source schema	Kind of possession						
		PHYS	TEMP	PERM	INAL	ABST	IN/I	IN/A
le – así	Location	−	−	+	+		−	−
le – así me	Location	+	+	−	−			
le – me, ŋú	Location	+	+	−	−		+	+
lii ná	Goal	+	+				+	+
nyé – tɔ	Equation	−	−	+				
kpɔ́	Action			+		+		

2.6.3 Conclusions

The data on Manding and Ewe presented above provide a number of insights into the structure of possession. They suggest, for example, that the distinction between major and minor schemas proposed in section 2.5 is one that may be useful for typological surveys and prescriptive treatments of language, but its significance for understanding the way possession is expressed in a given language is limited: neither Manding nor Ewe has a construction that would unambiguously qualify as a major schema. We referred to the *le . . . ásí*-construction of Ewe as representing the major pattern of expressing predicative possession. We did so on the basis that, first, this construction appears to be used most frequently in texts for conveying possessive concepts and, second, because in grammatical descriptions it is characterized as representing the standard expression for predicative possession. Yet, with regard to the number of possessive notions associated with it, the *le . . . ásí*-construction would not qualify as a 'major' schema, as can be seen in Table 2.8.

Manding and Ewe are suggestive of a type of language characterized by a specific way of encoding possession. On the one hand, there are languages where there is only one construction (e.g. the 'have'-construction in

2.6 Schemas and possessive notions 133

English), taking care of most or all of the spectrum of possessive notions, even if there are other constructions in addition to cover parts of the spectrum. In Manding and Ewe, however, the spectrum is divided up among different constructions. Whether this typological contrast is suggestive of basic differences in the way possession is conceptualized, remains to be investigated.

Throughout this work we have assumed that the seven possessive notions distinguished can be associated with the domain of possession, on the grounds that, at least in some languages, they receive the same forms of expression that 'canonical' instances of possession do. At the same time, we have avoided delimiting this domain, assuming that it has the structure of a prototype with genuinely fuzzy boundaries. As the Ewe data presented above suggest, there are in fact examples where it remains unclear whether we are actually dealing with instances of possession. Such examples concern most of all expressions in the initial stage of grammaticalization, where these expressions can simultaneously be interpreted with reference to either their non-possessive source or to possession. In accordance with the Overlap Model sketched in chapter 2.2, such ambiguous situations are in fact to be expected in the genesis of possessive constructions: whether utterances such as (151b) should be interpreted as instances of location or of physical possession is a question that can be answered conclusively only with reference to the speaker's intentions and/or the context in which that utterance was made.

The Manding case is suggestive of a recursive renewal process involving one and the same source schema, viz. Location. Each of the four 'have'-constructions is suggestive of a different development stage. If we classify these constructions according to their relative age of grammaticalization, then the following scenario of development may be established: the *la*-construction is the oldest one, being associated with abstract and inanimate possession, that is, with notions that usually are the last ones to be grammaticalized. It must have been followed by the *fὲ*-construction, which denotes permanent and inalienable possession, thus occupying a middle range of possessive notions. The *bolo*-construction must be of roughly the same age, but, in addition to the notions covered by the *fὲ*-construction, it also denotes temporary and physical possession, which are the first to be affected by grammaticalization. Finally, the *kùn*-construction represents the most recent stage: it is confined to expressing physical possession, which is the first to be affected when the Location Schema is pressed into service for the expression of possession. Note that the two youngest constructions, i.e. the *kùn-* and the *bolo-*constructions, are exactly the ones that still have transparent lexical semantics: their literal meaning is, respectively, 'be on one's head' and 'be in one's hand'.

A Manding-type situation, where one and the same source schema was used time and again for various possessive constructions, can in fact be observed in a number of languages. The following examples may further illustrate this type. In Kabiye, the Companion Schema, involving the comitative preposition *ná* (or *nɛ*), has given rise to three different 'have'-constructions, whose predicate nuclei are, respectively, *wɛ-ná* ('be with'), *tɪná* (diachronically: **tɪ* 'owner'+*ná* 'with'), and *nɛ* 'with', as exemplified by (152a), (152b), and (152c), respectively.

(152) Kabiye (Voltaic, Niger-Congo; Lébikaza 1991)
    (a) Kao wɛ-ná   líidiyé
        Kao be-with money
        'Kao has money.'

    (b) Kao tɪná kalímiyé
        Kao own chicken
        'Kao is the owner of the chicken.'

    (c) ... mɛ́-nɛ   me-líidiyé
        I- with my-money
        '... I have money.'

The preceding discussion was meant to reveal some of the dynamics and diversity characterizing the growth and uses of possessive constructions. This dynamics is reflected in the recursive development of new modes of expressing possession which are grafted onto older modes. In languages like Ewe, virtually all source schemas are recruited for this purpose, while in other languages one and the same schema is used repeatedly to create new forms for possessive meanings, a paradigm case being Manding. This dynamics is responsible for the fact that in many languages a host of different constructions exist, expressing the same kind of possession.

2.7   Further issues

While the syntax of a given possessive construction can largely be predicted once we know the event schema from which it is derived, there are some additional factors that also influence the shape of possessive constructions.

Perhaps the most important factor concerns two discourse-pragmatic principles that may determine the linear arrangement of linguistic expressions for predicative possession. These are (see 2.5.3 above; cf. Clark 1978):

(i) Definite participants tend to precede indefinite ones.
(ii) Animate participants tend to precede inanimate ones.

Some of the effects these principles have on the structure of predicative possession are discussed in section 2.5.3. That the principles are not only relevant to predicative possession can be illustrated with the following example involving attributive possession in English. Hawkins (1981:257) observes that, whereas the utterances in (153) and (154a) are acceptable, that of (154b) is less so. He attributes this to the fact that if the possessor and the possessee are human, both structures of attributive possession in English, [NP's N] and [the N of NP], are possible. If, however, one of them is human and the other is not, the structure in which the human participant comes first (i.e. (154a)) will be more acceptable than the corresponding structure in which the human participant comes second ((154b)). This would be in accordance with the pragmatic principle (ii) proposed above.

(153) English (Hawkins 1981:257)
(a) Mary's brother
(b) the brother of Mary

(154) (a) Mary's car
(b) ?The car of Mary

In the case of the Action and the Companion Schemas, no problems exist with these principles since the syntax of these schemas is in accordance with the two principles. In the case of the other schemas, however, the principles are at variance with basic word order constraints, since, in such schemas, typically inanimate and indefinite possessee arguments precede human and definite possessors, and the possessor is not the subject, as is suggested by the structure of source schemas summarized in Table 2.9.

Table 2.9. *Typical participant encoding in 'have'-constructions according to source schema.*

Source Schema	Possessor	Possessee
Action	Subject	Object
Location	Locative complement	Subject
Accompaniment	Subject	Comitative adjunct
Genitive	Genitive modifier	Subject
Goal	Dative adjunct	Subject
Topic	Theme, subject	Subject

Languages differ with regard to the way they resolve this conflict between word order constraints and the discourse-pragmatic principles. One widespread strategy is to topicalize the possessor, with the effect that arguments having a locative or dative morphology appear in clause-initial position when expressing possessors though not when expressing other kinds of participants; some languages where such a situation obtains were looked at above (cf. 2.5.3).

In her survey of word order characteristics of possessive constructions, Clark (1978:94–102) comes up with generalizations such as the following:

(a) Unlike existential and locative constructions, possessive constructions do not usually show regular word order alternations according to the definiteness of the constituent expressing the possessee.

(b) She found a clear predominance of the order possessor–possessee in her language sample: in 32 of the 33 languages this was the dominant word order pattern, the only exception being Klamath.

(c) In spite of the predominance of languages with possessor–possessee word order, the verb in possessive constructions shows agreement with the possessee, rather than the possessor, in the majority of languages of Clark's sample (1978:102).

These patternings can be accounted for with reference to the two principles outlined above. Note, however, that the principles take care of but a limited part of the word order behaviour of possessive constructions. The kind of source schema involved is more important. Observation (b), for example, is in accordance with principle (ii), according to which animate participants tend to precede inanimate ones. (b) is also in accordance with the Action and the Companion Schemas, but at variance with the remaining schemas. Thus, we can make the following probabilistic prediction: in a language that has chosen the Location or the Goal Schema, the order will be possessee–possessor; but, since possessed items are typically inanimate while possessors are typically human/animate, we nevertheless may not be surprised if the order is reversed in accordance with principle (ii). However, since this principle is optional, it can be ignored in a given language. This means that we may also find indefinite (possessee) nominals preceding definite (possessor) nominals, as in the following example from Ewe involving the Location Schema (see 2.6.2 above). Note that in this example, the formal subject *ga* 'money' is obligatorily indefinite. This means that the use of the definite article *lá* would not result in an expression for permanent possession.

(155) Ewe (Kwa, Niger-Congo)
       ga   le   Kofi sí.
       money be.at Kofi hand
       'Kofi has money.'

To conclude, a knowledge of the source schema concerned allows us to understand not only why there are exceptions to principles like the ones outlined above, but also that there are good reasons for such exceptions to be there.

The cognitive forces that can be held responsible for schema choice are still largely unclear. One factor may be language contact in general and creolization in particular. Bickerton (1981:66–7) observes that over a wide range of creole languages, the same lexical item is used for constructions of nuclear existence ('there is') and 'have'-constructions. His examples include Guyanese Creole, Haitian Creole, Hawaiian Creole English, Papiamentu, and São Tomense. Two examples may suffice to illustrate this striking convergence:

(156) Creole languages (Bickerton 1981:66–7)
       Guyanese Creole
       dem get wan uman we get gyal-pikni
       'There is a woman who has a daughter'

       Papiamentu
       tin   un muhe cu   tin un yiu- muhe
       have a woman who have a child-woman
       'There is a woman who has a daughter'

In all cases concerned, the Action Schema is involved: in the case of English-based creoles it is the verb *get* and in the Romance-based creoles the verb *tenere* that serves as the predicate nucleus. That this generalization is not coincidental is suggested by data from some other creoles, which show a similar convergence. In the Arabic-derived Nubi of Kenya, for example, the locative verb *fii* 'be at' is also used for both existential and 'have'-constructions, as can be seen below:

(157) Nubi (Arabic Creole; Heine 1982:41, 43)
       (a) ákil fíi   náa? áá, ákil fíi   (náá).
           food be.at there yes food be.at there
           'Is there food? Yes, there is food.'

       (b) áána fíí   ma   yalá   tinín.
           I   be.at with children two
           'I have two children.'

138   *The process*

This convergence is remarkable insofar as the various 'have'-constructions to be found in creole languages are derived from a number of different source schemas: Bickerton's examples all involve the Action Schema, Nubi uses the Companion Schema (*X is with Y*), and some other creoles have the Goal Schema typically involving a benefactive preposition ('for') as a source (*Y exists for/to X*). That one and the same form is used for the expression of both predicative possession and (nuclear) existence is, however, neither confined to creole languages nor uncommon in the languages of the world; as we will see in chapter 4 (4.4), a development from 'have'-constructions to existential constructions is hardly unusual; it constitutes a highly common pattern in the development of existential expressions.

Another factor shaping the structure of 'have'-constructions appears to be contact and its possible consequence: areal spread. While there is no reliable information on the areal distribution of 'have'-constructions in the languages of the world, the little information that exists would seem to suggest that contact plays no insignificant rôle in the spread of certain source schemas. For example, as we will see below in more detail, the spread of the Action Schema and the evolution of 'have'-verbs in the languages of Europe are likely to have been motivated to some extent by contact across language boundaries (Isačenko 1974b). Similarly, the geographical distribution of the Companion Schema as a source for 'have'-constructions in central and southern Africa might be indicative of an areal expansion from Bantu to some neighbouring non-Bantu languages (cf. Otten 1992).

Another factor that has been held responsible for shaping the structure of predicative possession concerns the evolution of language. Earlier generations of mankind, it is argued, had a different notion of possession, if they had such a notion at all, be it a social or a legal one. The question as to which of the many possessive constructions attested to in earlier or present stages of Indo-European languages can be reconstructed back to the proto-language has aroused some degree of scholarly attention. This is not the place to review the discussion that has been taking place, nor to evaluate the various positions that have been maintained on this issue (see Löfstedt 1963; Isačenko 1974b; Orr 1992). What we want to achieve here is to add a few observations that might be of use for future work in historical reconstruction.

A major theme that emerged in the course of this century, if not earlier, is that 'have'-constructions, as we find them in English and most other European languages, are in no way representative of Indo-European in particular and of the languages outside the Indo-European world in general. As early as 1923, Meillet summarizes this position thus:

> Et en effet l'indo-européen n'avait pas de verbe 'avoir', pas même pour indiquer la possession sans insister, et à plus forte raison, pas pour indiquer un rapport. (Meillet 1923:9)

What Meillet wants to convey with this assertion is that Proto-Indo-European was much less grammaticalized than the modern languages derived from it are: 'chaque mot indo-européen avait son autonomie et pouvait se suffire à lui-même' (Meillet 1923:12). This means that there was no grammaticalized expression for possession; he concedes, however, that, nevertheless, possession could be expressed by means of the Goal Schema ('quelque chose est à moi'; ibid.).

While this claim was supported later by a number of other Indo-Europeanists, it was done so for other reasons than those put forward by Meillet. Isačenko (1974) distinguishes between 'have'-languages, or H-languages, and 'be'-languages, called B-languages by him, where the former have 'have' and the latter 'be' as their nucleus of verbal possessive syntax. With reference to the situation in Indo-European, he notes:

> It is well known that Indo-European was a B-language and that the verbal stems *es- and *bhū- very early merged into a suppletive paradigm preserved in most historically attested IE idioms. It is also known that verbs meaning 'have' are secondary acquisitions in all IE languages and that such verbs stem from transitive verbs with the general meaning 'to hold, to grasp'. (Isačenko 1974b:44)

Locker (1954:505) suspected that 'have'-constructions, as they are found in modern European languages, might ultimately be traced back to Basque, while Isačenko (1974b:45) says that the first European language to have introduced the verb 'have' was Greek (but see below). The corresponding position held by many contemporary students of this subject area is summarized in the following way by Lyons:

> relatively few languages exhibit what we may call 'have-sentences': i.e. possessive sentences in which the 'possessor' is the surface-structure subject of a 'verb to have' and the 'possessed object' the surface-structure object of this verb. Even in the Indo-European languages, 'have-sentences' are of relatively late and restricted development: they are not found in all the Slavonic and Celtic languages. Moreover, in the Indo-European languages in which 'have-sentences' occur (Latin, Greek, Germanic, etc.) they would appear to have developed independently. In many cases (both in the Indo-European languages and in other languages with a 'verb to have') the

140 *The process*

> possessive use of the verb seems to have developed from sentences in which it originally meant 'grasp' or 'hold (in the hand)'. (Lyons 1967:392)

Rather than the structure found in English, German, or French, it is the pattern found in some Celtic, Slavic, or Indic languages which can be claimed to reflect the situation to be reconstructed for Proto-Indo-European – in short, at the earliest stage of Indo-European, predicative possession is claimed to have involved the use of the Goal Schema (*Y exists to/for X*), and possibly also the Location Schema (*Y is located at X*). Orr (1992) claims that Slavic and Celtic share a number of historical similarities. For example, both are said to preserve some archaisms that are presumed to have their source in Proto-Indo-European, and both are said to have experienced an early replacement of the Goal by the Location Schema. The Romance and Germanic languages, on the other hand, constitute a centre of innovation and dispersal of 'have'-constructions based on the Action Schema. This dispersal has reached some Slavic and some Celtic languages but not others. In each of the two branches of Indo-European there are what Orr (1992:265) calls 'peripheral languages', which are Russian in the case of Slavic and Goidelic in the case of Celtic.

The evidence adduced in favour of the innovation thesis is remarkable (see Löfstedt 1963; Isačenko 1974b; Orr 1992); nevertheless, this thesis is not shared by all students of the subject-matter concerned (cf. Demiraj 1985). Note that the innovation thesis is not always free from extra-linguistic considerations of doubtful value. Such considerations include the claim that the notion of possession, presumed to be expressed most clearly by means of 'have'-verbs, is a recent acquisition of mankind and that schemas such as Goal or Location (usually, no distinction is made between the two) express more primitive modes of what corresponds to modern ideas of possession. We have met this view already in Meillet's (1923) work (cf. Creissels 1996:150–1); the following statement by Löfstedt summarizes this line of reasoning:

> Der Eigentumsbegriff war in der primitiven Gemeinschaftskultur der alten Indogermanen wahrscheinlich schwach entwickelt. Es gab auch kein allgemeines besitzangebendes Verbum, das dem dt. 'haben' entspräche. Man kam mit dem verbum substantivum in Verbindung mit einem Gen. oder einem Dat. aus, also den lat. Typen *alqd alcs est* oder *alqd alci est*, je nachdem der Besitzer oder der Gegenstand des Besitzes hervorgehoben werden sollte. (Löfstedt 1963:76)

In a similar vein, Isačenko (1974b:64) justifies his claim that Indo-European did not have a 'have'-verb with the assumption that 'possession

2.7 Further issues

proper' or ownership appeared in societies only after 'they have reached a certain stage of development'.

On the basis of the evidence that has become available so far, the Dative hypothesis may be said to be a respectable one; nevertheless, this evidence is not sufficient to allow for a reliable reconstruction, in particular for the following reasons. First, there is the internal Indo-European evidence which is not entirely in favour of such a hypothesis. Hittite may be a possible stumbling block: this language has a verb *har-mi* 'have', which can even be used to form a perfect and a pluperfect and thus is strikingly similar to 'have'-verbs in the modern Romance and Germanic languages (see Vendryes 1937:88; Orr 1992:249); note that Hittite is taken to represent one of the most 'archaic' branches of Indo-European.

Second, the evidence adduced so far is essentially typological; it is not based on formal (sound–meaning) reconstructions. In his pioneering studies, for example, Löfstedt (1963:70–71) observes that inalienable (social) possession of the type 'to me is a son' is attested for Gothic, Old English, Old High German, Greek (Homeric), Hittite, and Latin, while for abstract possession of the type 'to me is the name' he finds evidence in Greek, Latin, Armenian, and Slavic languages. He therefore considers it to be proven that already at the stage of Proto-Indo-European, the Goal Schema had been used. While being based on classical modes of syntactic reconstruction (Paul J. Hopper, p.c.), it hardly need be mentioned that linguistic reconstructions based exclusively on typological considerations are of limited historical significance.

Third, predicative possession belongs to those parts of grammar that tend to be renewed relatively quickly. Romance languages such as Spanish or Portuguese have renewed their major 'have'-construction twice within less than two millennia: from the Goal Schema of Latin (*mihi est* 'to me is') to the Action Schema of the *habeo*-type, to a second instance of this schema based on *tener/ter*. The possibility that the early history of Indo-European was similarly characterized by repeated renewal processes cannot entirely be ruled out.

Fourth, both the Goal and the Action Schemas are commonly found in the languages of the world, and neither can be assumed to be more strongly associated with earlier stages of human evolution than any other. The claim made in some way or other by Indo-Europeanists that the Action Schema reflects a more recent mode of expressing possession (see Isačenko 1974b; Orr 1992) has never been substantiated with evidence from languages other than Indo-European ones.

Fifth, there are a couple of major problems with this general claim. One is diachronic in nature. For example, as we saw in 2.5.3, until the nineteenth century, Hungarian had a 'have'-construction derived from the Action Schema, involving the transitive verb *bír-* 'rule' as a predicate nucleus, while modern Hungarian has the Goal Schema as its major pattern of expressing predicative possession. Furthermore, as we will see in section 5.4, the Action Schema in Bulgarian, based on the verb *imam* as a predicate nucleus, is much older than previously thought, conceivably antedating the earlier Location Schema.

A final problem relates to linguistic geography: the use of the Action Schema is far from being geographically limited. This schema constitutes a source for 'have'-constructions in a number of languages across the world, in particular in languages where a recent innovation would seem to be unlikely, as in some Khoisan languages of southern Africa. In Nama (Khoekhoe), for example, the major 'have'-construction uses the Action Schema, where the main verb is *'uu* 'take', as illustrated in (158).

(158)   Nama (Khoekhoe, Khoisan; Heinz Roberg, p.c.)
          //nâà saaro.   p   ke   /am tara.ra   'uu hâá.
          that small:bushman.M TOP two wife.DUAL:F take PERF
          'That little bushman has two wives.'

But even the construction that can be assumed to have preceded the Nama pattern exemplified in (158) must have been built on the Action Schema involving the verb //'*aî* 'take into possession, own', which is still attested as a possessive verb in nineteenth-century writings.

What the above discussion would seem to suggest is that there is no linguistic evidence to show that the modes of conceptualizing and/or encoding possession were different at any time in empirically reconstructible human history. Attempts made by Meillet and others to establish that Proto-Indo-European did not have a grammaticalized category of possession, or that earlier generations of mankind had different modes for expressing possession, have hardly been successful.

The whole issue is associated with yet another problem, namely the fact that 'have'-constructions in European languages in particular and Indo-European languages in general exhibit some striking correlations with other grammatical categories, especially with distinctions of tense, aspect, and modality. We will turn to this problem in chapter 4.

3 On attributive possession

Predicative possession belongs to the most complex phenomena in the grammar of many languages; we therefore decided to make it the main topic of this book. Compared to it, attributive possession (or nominal, or phrasal possession) appears to present a relatively simple structure: it consists essentially of two noun phrases linked to one another in a specific way. Accordingly, work on attributive possession has focussed mostly on the way the two noun phrases are linked, e.g. whether the possessee (=the head) precedes or follows the possessor (=the dependent, or genitive, or modifier), or whether the link is marked on the possessee (=head-marking), on the possessor (=dependent-marking), on both, or on neither (cf. Ultan 1978; Nichols 1988; 1992).

A detailed treatment of attributive possession would be beyond the scope of this work; nevertheless, in the paragraphs to follow we shall try to relate the findings made in the course of the preceding chapter to the structure of attributive possession, that is, we will attempt to determine how constructions of the type *Peter has a new car* differ from constructions having the form *Peter's new car*. The issue is a popular one, and it is an old one; quite a number of studies have been devoted to it in the course of recent decades.

Predicative and attributive possession resemble one another in a number of ways; some of the similarities were pointed out in Chapter 1 (section 1.2.3). Nevertheless, attributive possession was found to differ from predicative possession in the following way:

(a) it presents typically presupposed rather than asserted information;
(b) it involves object-like, time-stable contents rather than event-like contents; and
(c) it involves phrasal rather than clausal syntax.

A number of additional differences have been mentioned (see chapter 1.2 for details). In the following paragraphs we will confine ourselves to explaining some structural properties of attributive possession, more

Table 3.1. *A formulaic description of source schemas used for the expression of attributive possession.*

Formula	Label of event schema
Y at X	Location
Y from X	Source
Y for/to X	Goal
X with Y	Companion
(As for) X, X's Y	Topic

specifically, we will look at the genesis and further development of this type of construction which, like predicative possession, appears to be of universal significance. There is, however, one problem that we will not tackle here, viz. the semantics of attributive possession. As we will see below (3.2), this is a complex issue that would seem to require a more comprehensive analysis for which an adequate foundation has not yet been laid.

3.1   From source to target

Perhaps the main observation to be made in this chapter is that both predicative and attributive possession are built on the same general cognitive pattern. This means in particular that the sources from which they are derived are largely the same. The main sources for attributive possession are listed in Table 3.1.

Ignoring the basic difference between object-like and proposition-like concepts, the schemas listed in Table 3.1 can be said to be precisely the ones that we are already familiar with. (See Table 2.1). Only three do not appear here, among them the Action Schema, and there is an obvious reason for this fact: actions (or events) typically involve propositional syntax, while attributive possession is not propositional but phrasal. On the other hand, there is also one schema that has figured only marginally in the preceding discussion, viz. the Source Schema: it appears to be virtually irrelevant in the case of predicative possession (see 2.1 above), for no apparent reason.

Even if the schemas used for attributive and predicative possession are essentially the same, it rarely happens that exactly the same schema is used in one and the same language. Nevertheless, there are a few languages where the same schema is employed for both kinds of possession. In Hungarian, for example, the Goal Schema has been grammaticalized for both, as we saw in 1.2 (example (21)); we will return to this point below. Right now, each of the main schemas for attributive possession is looked at in turn.

The Location Schema forms one of the most frequently employed templates for expressing attributive possession: The possessor is conceptualized as the place where the possessee is located. The following is an example from Maninka (Malinke), where the locative postposition *lá* (*ná* after nasals) 'at' appears to have been grammaticalized to a marker of typically alienable possession.

(1)   Maninka (Mande, Niger-Congo; Friedländer 1992:60)
        Mamadu lá báara
        Mamadu at work
        'Mamadu's work.' (Historically: 'The work at the place where Mamadu is.')

Oceanic languages such as Babatana, Roviana, and Maewo use an attributive construction involving the preposition **ta*. This preposition, which has been reconstructed by Pawley (1973) for Proto-Oceanic, marks spatial relations. An example of its possessive use is the following:

(2)   Maewo (Oceanic, Austronesian; Lichtenberk 1985:121)
        laqana   ta Maewo
        language of Maewo
        'language of Maewo' (Historically: 'The language at Maewo's place.')

A more detailed treatment of Location as a source for attributive possession in African languages is found in Claudi and Heine (1989). What these authors observe is that, when the Location Schema is grammaticalized to a kind of genitive construction, it is initially confined to the expression of alienable possession, with the effect that the existing pattern of attributive possession becomes reserved for inalienable possession. We shall return to this issue in 3.4.

The formal exponent of the Source Schema is the use of ablative or related morphology for encoding the possessor, the function of this marker expressing any of the notions 'from', 'away from', 'out of', etc. The possessor may be said to be conceived of as a source figure *vis-à-vis* the possessee, which is presented as the conceptual ground.

Instances of the Source Schema are not difficult to come by; common examples can be found in European languages, including the English *of*-Genitive, the German *von*-Genitive, or the Romance *de*-Genitives, all of which may be said to be derived from a structure where the prepositional element had an ablative or source function ('(away) from' or 'out of') as its focal, or one of its focal, senses. In the following example of the English item *of* figuring in the Source Schema, the (a)-sentence is suggestive of a less grammaticalized meaning, where *of* can still be paraphrased by *out of*, while in the (b)-sentence, *of* is now almost exclusively a genitive case marker:

(3) English
    (a) two of my brothers
    (b) two cups of coffee

Note that the notion 'Source Schema' must not be confused with 'source schema'; with the latter term we refer to any schema that may serve as a structural template, and as the historical source, for a grammatical construction.

In the case of the Goal Schema, the possessor is introduced by means of some directional marker, usually an allative, dative, or benefactive adposition or case inflection. While this schema is a frequent source for predicative possession (see 2.1 above), it appears to be less common as a source of attributive possession. The following examples are taken from West African Pidgin English, involving the benefactive preposition *fo* (<English *for*), Baka, where the benefactive/dative preposition *pe* 'for, to' appears to have been grammaticalized to an attributive possession marker, and Diyari, which uses the Dative inflection for this purpose. Diyari has a morphological distinction between alienable and inalienable possession, and the Goal Schema is used for both, as can be seen in (4c) and (4d), respectively, while in Aranda, another Australian language, the Goal Schema appears to be confined to kinship and related roles as possessors, as exemplified in (4e).

(4)   (a) West African Pidgin English (Schneider 1966:92)
            apránticici fo kápenta   wok-tíng fo mésan
            'an apprentice of the carpenter'   'tools of/for the mason'

    (b) Baka (Ubangi, Niger-Congo; Christa Kilian-Hatz, p.c.)
        pe   díndó bɔ̀ngɔ̀ a   kà?
        to/POSS baby dress LOC where
        'Where are the clothes of the children?'

    (c) Diyari (Pama-Nyungan; Austin 1981:137)
        nhulu kuḍu   paku-yi   wilha- ya   wana-   li
        he.A hole.ABS dig- PRES woman-DAT digging.stick-ERG
        'He is digging a hole with a woman's digging stick'

(d) yini   thika- Ø-   mayi   nhuwa yiŋkaṛa- ya
    you.S return-IMP-EMPH spouse 2.SG.DAT-ALL
    'You go back to your husband'

(e) Aranda (Pama-Nyungan; Wilkins 1989:135, 179)
    Toby-ke   alere
    Toby-DAT   child
    'Toby's child.'

The Goal Schema occurs in some Germanic languages, particularly in Swedish, for example *vänen till mig* ('friend to me') 'my friend' (Thomas Stolz, p.c.). While the Goal Schema is not a very common source, it may nevertheless be found as a minor schema e.g. in idiomatically restricted frames, cf. English *Secretary to the President*.

The Goal Schema also appears to be present in what Campbell (1985:118) refers to as the '*pal* periphrastic possessive', illustrated in (5). Pipil *pal* is a preposition whose functions are translated by means of 'for, in order to', that is, an item that appears to include benefactive and purpose among its case functions, as is the case with many instances of the Goal Schema.

(5)   Pipil (Aztecan, Uto-Aztecan; Campbell 1985:118)
       ne ihyak   naka-t   pal ne masa:-t
       the stinking meat-ABSOL of the deer
       'the stinking meat of the deer'

An instance of the Companion Schema is found in Turkana, even if confined to contexts where a kinship term (excluding *itòò* 'mother') functions as a possessor, as in the following examples:

(6)   Turkana (Eastern Nilotic, Nilo-Saharan; Dimmendaal 1983:340)
       è- ya`   kɛŋ` kà   à-pa`    kaŋ`
       M-aunt his with F-father my
       'my father's aunt'

       a-mòtį̀ kà   è-ya`   kaŋ`
       F-pot with M-aunt my
       'my aunt's pot'

As we would predict, the Turkana possessive marker *kà* precedes the possessor, since Turkana uses prepositions rather than postpositions. In a postpositional language on the other hand, one would expect that the possessive marker follows the possessor.

We noted above that apart from Source, all schemas have immediate parallels in predicative possession, even though their relative frequency may differ. The Topic Schema is not very widespread as a source for 'have'-constructions (see 2.1 above). As a source for attributive possession, however, it provides one of the most common templates. It is responsible for a couple of properties that attributive constructions derived from it exhibit; for more details, see 3.4 below. Examples of this schema are found in (7).

(7) Afrikaans (Germanic, Indo-European)
 die boer se huis
 the farmer his house
 'the farmer's house'

 Kairiru (Oceanic, Austronesian; Lichtenberk 1985:99)
 Nur yaqal qajuo -ny
 Nur he   cousin-his
 'Nur's cousin'

Occasionally the Topic Schema leads to what Nichols (1988) calls double marking in that the possessor phrase has a specific case marking on it (Martin Haspelmath, p.c.). Thus the possessor appears in the Dative case in (8a) and in the Genitive case in (8b). It remains to be investigated how these structures are to be accounted for (but see 3.5 below).

(8) (a) Colloquial German
  dem Ahmed sein   Haus
  DAT Ahmed 3.M.SG.POSS house
  'Ahmed's house' (Lit.: 'to the Ahmed his house')

 (b) Turkish (Turkic, Altaic; Haspelmath, p.c.)
  Ahmed-in   ev- i
  Ahmed-GEN house-3.SG.POSS
  'Ahmed's house' (Lit.: 'Ahmed's his house')

Whenever the Topic Schema is used, we expect the topic, that is, the possessor, to precede the possessee, as illustrated in the above examples. There are, however, a number of Amerindian languages where the opposite order obtains; an example is provided in (9). It remains to be investigated how this situation is to be accounted for. For the time being we shall assume that we are dealing with a special case of the Topic Schema, but to distinguish constructions of the kind illustrated in (9) nomenclaturally we will refer to them as the Anti-topic sub-schema.

(9) Pipil (Aztecan, Uto-Aztecan; Campbell 1985:117)
 i- ih- i:x ne siwa:pil
 her-PL-eye the girl
 'the girl's eyes'

In the above examples of the Topic Schema, the possessor is 'cross-referenced', that is, it is pronominally repeated on the possessee, as can be seen in all the preceding examples. This, however, is not always the case; rather, the possessee may simply be juxtaposed as a specifier of the possessor. This confirms Stassen's observation according to which

> cross-reference is not a distinguishing factor in the typology of predicative possession. It is an 'intervening' phenomenon, which does not have to be accounted for in our typology. (Stassen 1995:4)

As is obvious from this discussion, we are assuming that the Topic Schema is the same irrespective of whether it serves the expression of predicative or of attributive possession: in both cases we are dealing with the schematic structure *As for X, X's Y*, where X stands for the possessor and Y for the possessee, and X presents a thematic constituent while Y adds some information on X. But there is also a difference. In predicative possession, Y is more basic: it is likely to trigger verbal agreement and X can be interpreted as a pragmatic extension of Y. In attributive possession on the other hand, it is X that tends to trigger agreement, if at all verbal agreement exists, and Y constitutes a specifying extension of X. We shall have more to say about the Topic Schema in section 3.2.

The catalogue just presented does not exhaust the list of sources for attributive possession. One might mention, for example, that in a number of languages in different parts of the world genitive markers are etymologically related to relative clause markers (Aristar 1991; Claudi 1995). Further, there is a schema, occurring in a number of genetically unrelated languages, which can be sketched roughly as *X's Y, the one of X*, where a nominal possessee has the possessor as a pronominal modifier (*X's Y*) and adds the nominal possessor as a kind of afterthought in the form of an appositional constituent; one might therefore refer to this structure as the Afterthought Schema. Diem (1986:238ff.) describes patterns of attributive possession in two Semitic languages, Aramaic and Akkadian, and he reconstructs such a schema for these languages, arguing that a structure like (10a) is historically derived from (10b). Conceivably, both the Topic and the Afterthought Schemas can be treated as varieties of one and the same more general structure (Nigel Vincent, p.c.).

(10) Aramaic (Semitic, Afroasiatic; Diem 1986:236–9)
 (a) barṯ   -eh d-   malkā
     daughter-his GEN-king
     'the king's daughter'

(b) *bart -eh, dī malkā
    daughter-his that.of king
    'his daughter, that of the king'

There is also something that appears to be a reversal of the Topic Schema: a construction of the form *the Y, that (of) X*, which gives rise to a pattern of attributive possession of the form *X's Y*. Martin Haspelmath (p.c.) finds evidence for such a schema in Chadic languages; a perhaps related schema leading to the rise of constructions of attributive possession has the form *Y, possession of X* (Haspelmath, p.c.).

Finally, patterns of marking attributive possession may go back to constructions used for predicative possession. While this is not normally the case, still, it does happen; we will return to this issue in 3.5.

As in the case of predicative possession, several schemas may occur within a given language, either in synchronic variation or in a diachronic sequence. Two examples may suffice to illustrate the kind of variation patterns that one might expect to find.

The first example concerns Old French, as summarized by Hawkins (1981:266-9). The transition from Latin to Modern French is usually portrayed as one leading from a synthetic pattern of case inflection to an analytic one involving the preposition *de*. Such an account, however, is somewhat simplified. At the stage of Old French, three patterns of attributive possession appear to have existed: one involving the preposition *a* (<Latin *ad* 'to, towards'), which is suggestive of the Goal Schema, another one involving the preposition *de* (<Latin *de* 'down from'), which is suggestive of the Source Schema, and a third one lacking a preposition. These patterns are exemplified in (11a), (11b), and (11c), respectively.

(11) Old French (Hawkins 1981:266-7)
      (a) la chambre a la pucele
          'the maiden's bedroom'

      (b) les cols de lor chevaus
          'the necks of their horses'

      (c) le filz sainte Marie
          'the son of Saint Marie'

The Source Schema was employed where the possessors were animals or objects, the Goal Schema for social rôles of more inferior standing, and the pattern without preposition was reserved mainly for proper nouns, kinship terms, social rôles of high standing, and the beings of the supernatural world. Subsequently, this variation was eliminated and only the Source Schema involving *de* survived.

But the Goal Schema has not been eliminated entirely: In accordance with the layering principle of Hopper (1991), the schema survives in contextually restricted environments. First, it has been confined largely to inanimate possession and, second, it excludes most kinds of nominal modification (Borillo 1996). But, even in those cases where human possessors and possessees are admitted, there are serious restrictions on the use of this schema. Consider the following modern French examples:

(12) Modern French (Bonneau and Pica 1995)
    (a) la belle mère à Jean
        the pretty mother to Jean
        (i) 'the mother-in-law of Jean'
        (ii) *'the beautiful mother of Jean'

    (b) le bel ami à Marie
        the pretty friend to Marie
        (i) 'the dear-friend of Marie'
        (ii) *'the beautiful friend of Marie'

The (i)-readings in (12) are suggestive of uses of the Goal Schema, where *bel(le)* is not an adjectival modifier but part of a lexicalized form, which is *belle mère* 'mother-in-law' in (12a) and *belle ami* 'dear-friend' in (12b). Whenever *belle* 'beautiful' acts as a nominal modifier, then the use of the Goal Schema is ruled out. The Source Schema is not subject to such constraints; it provides a productive pattern both for lexicalized compounds, as in the (i)-sentences in (13), and for modifier-noun constructions, as in the (ii)-sentences of (13).

(13) Modern French (Bonneau and Pica 1995)
    (a) la belle mère de Jean
        the pretty mother of Jean
        (i) 'the mother-in-law of Jean', or
        (ii) 'the beautiful mother of Jean'

    (b) le bel ami de Marie
        the pretty friend of Marie
        (i) 'the dear-friend of Marie', or
        (ii) 'the beautiful friend of Marie'

Whenever there exists an option between the two schemas, the Goal Schema turns out to be more restricted in meaning than the Source

Schema. Accordingly, (14a) has only what Bonneau and Pica (1995) call a 'group reading' while (14b) has a 'quantificational reading' in addition.

(14) Modern French (Bonneau & Pica 1995)
    (a) le   pays   à   chacun/tous
        the country to everyone/all
        'the country for everyone'
    (b) le   pays   de   chacun/tous
        the country of everyone/all
        'the country of everyone'

The second example is taken from Bulgarian, which has experienced a repeated change in schema choice (Duridanov 1956; Tania Kuteva, Ivan Duridanov, p.c.). The whole issue has been the subject of extensive controversy (cf. Qvonje 1980). Old Bulgarian had a Genitive construction whose conceptual source is no longer recoverable; the type of construction involved is illustrated in (15a). By the twelfth century, this etymologically opaque schema had been superseded by the Goal Schema, where instead of the Genitive, it was the Dative case inflection that was used to encode the possessor, as in (15b). Between the thirteenth and the fifteenth centuries, the Goal Schema was increasingly replaced by the Location Schema, where the possessor was introduced by the preposition *na* 'on', as in (15c) (due to substantial changes in the overall case system of the language the possessor was first inflected in the Locative, later in the Accusative and nowadays in a common case form).

(15) Bulgarian (Tania Kouteva, Ivan Duridanov, p.c.)
    (a) kniga   ženy
        book   woman.GEN
        'the woman's book'
    (b) kniga   žene
        book   woman.DAT
        'the woman's book'
    (c) knigata   na   deteto
        book.the on child.the
        'the child's book'

In modern Bulgarian, the Location Schema has been generalized, but the Genitive pattern has survived mainly with personal nouns as possessors, whereby the earlier Genitive inflections were replaced by special Genitive suffixes. In certain very restricted contexts, for example with the short form of personal possessive pronouns, the Dative-based pattern, too, has been preserved.

3.1 From source to target

To conclude, the patterns used for the development of attributive possession are similar to the ones to be observed in predicative possession, and both show a similar variability, as we will see in the next chapter.

A knowledge of the schemas involved in the rise of possession may be helpful for understanding why a given possessive construction exhibits the kind of morphosyntactic peculiarities it does. In many languages, for example, there is a structural correlation between the syntactic factor of word order and the morphological factor of marking agreement. On the one hand, we find that the possessor is encoded twice, as a nominal marker and as a pronominal marker on the possessee. On the other hand, we find a consistent word order pattern, where the (nominal) possessor invariably precedes the possessee. Such a morphosyntactic pattern is strongly suggestive of the Topic Schema (*As for X, X's Y*) and these, as well as other properties of the constructions concerned, can be predicted once we know which source schema is to be reconstructed for possession.

As we observed when discussing predicative possession, the reconstruction of event schemas leading to the development of possessive constructions is not always possible without a more detailed analysis of the relevant language. The following example is typical of the problems that are likely to arise in the course of reconstruction. O'Connor (1992:258) observes, for example, that alienable possession in Northern Pomo, a Hokan language of northern California, is expressed by means of a construction sketched in (16) and exemplified in (17a). As the grammatical analysis volunteered by O'Connor suggests, the primary function of the Oblique case form (OBL) of Northern Pomo is that of a benefactive marker: 'In all instances, the Oblique form of the nominal is used to indicate the role of the Beneficiary' (O'Connor 1992:182). An example of the benefactive use of the Oblique form is found in (17b). Now, as we saw above, whenever possessors are encoded by means of allative, dative, or benefactive markers we are likely to be dealing with instances of the Goal Schema. This is corroborated by the fact that Northern Pomo uses postpositions and that the Oblique form *yaču* in (17) can be interpreted diachronically as a postposition on the preceding noun phrase.

(16)   Possessor+Oblique case form – possessee

(17)   Northern Pomo (Hokan; O'Connor 1992:183, 258)
    (a) hayu-nam   yaču   ʔya:-nam
        dog- SPCF   OBL   bone-SPCF
        'the dog's bone'

(b) dakosa?- nam- yaču? man mul dod- e
youngman-SPCF-OBL she DEM make-PRES
'She made it for the young man.'

To summarize, reconstructing source schemas may sometimes be time-consuming; but in most cases there are some clues that make it possible to trace the event schema that can be held responsible for the possessive construction concerned.

We observed in the preceding chapter that it is not unusual that in a given language two or even more source schemas can be found to have developed into constructions of predicative possession (see especially 2.6). The same applies to attributive possession: one should not be surprised to find languages where three or even more schemas have given rise to patterns of nominal possession. Norwegian appears to be such a language: among the various constructions used for attributive possession in some way or other there are the ones listed in (18), which are suggestive of the Topic (18a), the Goal (18b), and the Source Schema (18c), respectively. Not all these constructions are grammaticalized to the same extent, and each of them retains some properties of its respective source structure.

(18)   Norwegian (Peter Trudgill, Elisabeth Weise, p.c.)
    (a) Per   sin hatt
        Peter his hat
        'Peter's hat'
    (b) hatt-en   til Per
        hat- DEF to Peter
        'Peter's hat'
    (c) eier-en   av hus-et
        owner-DEF.M off house-DEF.NEU
        'the owner of the house'

In chapter 1.3, a range of seven salient possessive notions was proposed and most uses of expressions for predicative possession can be described with reference to these notions. The situation is different in the case of expressions for attributive possession: while they are likely to also cover the functions expressed by 'have'-constructions, they tend to be associated with a much larger range of functions, to the extent that the term 'possession' becomes virtually meaningless (cf. chapter 5.3). A number of authors therefore argue that attributive possession, irrespective of whether it is encoded by means of independent words, clitics, case inflections, or zero, simply serves to establish a relationship between two entities.

In spite of the many treatments that are available on attributive possession (see e.g. Langacker 1993; 1995), not much is known about its semantics. We believe that this semantics, rather than being 'amorphous' or 'empty', is clearly delineated, and that it has internal structure. This structure is characterized, first, by the presence of asymmetry between possessor and possessee, which means, for example, that a reversal of the two would either yield a different meaning or result in a nonsensical utterance. Second, the various meanings or functions that constructions of attributive possession usually exhibit can be described and accounted for to a large extent with reference to the discourse contexts in which these constructions occur. Swahili, like most Bantu languages, has a construction of attributive possession that is particularly rich in functions. As Hawkinson (1979) has shown convincingly, most of these functions are predictable once appropriate contextual information is available.

In more general terms one may say that the extension patterns characterizing attributive possession lead from a conceptual relationship [possessor–possessee] to a pattern [qualifier–qualified], where the possessor comes to express a quality or property of the 'possessee' (cf. Takizala 1974; Chappell and McGregor 1989). Rather than to the question *Whose Y?*, 'qualitative possession' responds to the question: *What kind of Y?*

This extension pattern is not confined to attributive possession, it is to some extent relevant to predicative possession as well; it appears to be a characteristic of most instances of what we proposed to call abstract possession in section 1.3. For example, if one says in English that *X has no manners/feeling/guts/brain*, etc. then the message conveyed is more likely to be understood as one relating to qualities rather than to possessions of X.

That the semantics of constructions for attributive possession is not empty and/or unlimited has been claimed by a number of authors; it is suggested, for example, by the following observation made by Seiler (1977c:224–5). A German phrase like (19a) is multiply ambiguous since it includes meanings such as the ones rendered by the English translations in (19b); one could in fact conceive of many more meanings that are, or may be, associated with (19a). Nevertheless, the meaning of (19a) is not unlimited; Seiler claims, for example, that meanings such as the ones conveyed by (19c) are not part of the construction of (19a): in Seiler's wording, 'expressions containing a semantic element NEGATIVE' would not qualify for being included in (19b).

(19) German
    (a) Karls Haus
        'Karl's house'

On attributive possession

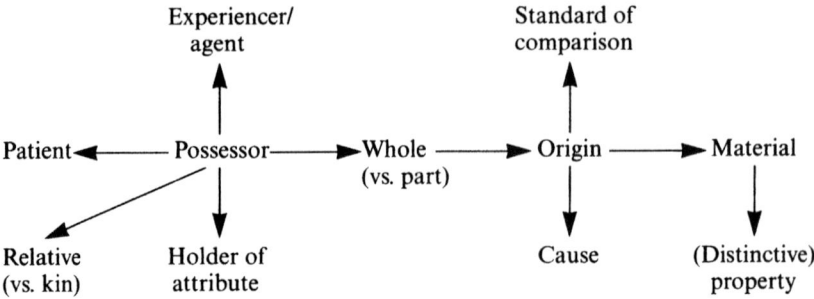

Figure 3.1. A radial network of genitival meanings (based on Nikiforidou 1991).

(b) 'the house that Karl has/owns'
'the house that Karl has built'
'the house that pleases Karl'
'the house in which Karl has lived'

(c) ? 'the house that Karl hates'
? 'the house that Karl did not buy'

Most importantly, however, it is the work of Nikiforidou (1991) which has shown that genitives, representing the paradigm form of attributive possession, have an internal semantic structure. Her findings agree with the ones made here, especially in the following points:

(a) The meanings (or functions) of genitives are motivated rather than arbitrary.
(b) They are limited in number and are part of a network of conceptual relationships, described by her as a single polysemous category.
(c) This network is similar across languages.
(d) There are significant correlations between the synchronic structure and the diachronic development of genitives.

Using a metaphor approach of the Lakoffian kind (Lakoff and Johnson 1980; Lakoff 1987) and based on the analysis of languages like Greek, Latin, French, and English, she proposes a radial network of genitival meanings which is sketched in simplified form in Figure 3.1.

3.2 Specification

In a number of languages a communicative strategy appears to be at work whereby a noun phrase is extended by juxtaposing a second noun phrase

3.2 Specification

whose main function it is to 'specify' the preceding phrase; let us call the former phrase the specified and the latter the specifier. The specifier has the following properties (or part thereof):

(a) It refers to the same general entity as the specified (even if the two are different entities, as in the case of a part-whole relations where, say, the specified refers to the whole and the specifier to a part of it).

(b) It further characterizes the specified by narrowing down the range of possible referents that may qualify as the specified. This may be achieved by (i) providing more information on the specified, (ii) making clear which of the alternatives available qualifies as the specified, (iii) and/or making clear that, rather than the specified itself, it is actually a part of it that is being referred to.

(c) It lays emphasis on the specified (e.g. by referring to it a second time by means of a different expression).

(d) It makes the specified more easily recoverable in subsequent discourse.

(e) Typically, the specifier follows the specified, although in some languages the order of the two appears to be reversed.

At the initial stage, the specifier is a *pragmatically motivated* constituent that is not necessarily part of the canonical syntactic patterns of the language concerned; it may even be of restricted grammatical acceptability. Subsequently, the specifier is increasingly conventionalized as a syntactic constituent, eventually turning into an adnominal modifier of the specified. While specification is not confined to it, possession constitutes a paradigm target area of specification: perhaps the majority of genitives (or constructions of attributive possession) owe their existence in some way or other to specification.

There are two contrasting structures, which we will refer to, respectively, as possessee specification and possessor specification. Whenever *possessee specification* is involved, at the initial stage there is a noun phrase which is specified by an adpositional phrase, as in *my friend in Australia*, or *the beer in the fridge*. At Stage II, the adpositional phrase can be understood alternatively as an adverbial phrase or as a kind of possessive modifier. Once that stage has been reached in a given language, there is only a small range of adpositions that can be employed in specifier phrases. At the final stage, III, only one adposition or case marker survives which is now interpreted as a marker of attributive possession. In more general terms, the three stages can be characterized in the following way:

Stage I: A new nominal constituent Y, for example a prepositional phrase, is added appositionally to an existing noun phrase X to further specify X. The two form neither a syntactic nor a phonological unit. Typically they are separated by a short pause (not infrequently marked in western writing systems by means of a comma) and each has an intonation peak of its own.

Stage II: Y comes to be interpreted with reference to a grammatical function other than the one for which it was introduced, that is, it is interpreted as a genitive marker, while still retaining its earlier function, for example that of a preposition. The pragmatic link gradually turns into a syntactic one in that Y is reinterpreted as a genitival modifier of X.

Stage III: X and Y form a conventionalized syntactic construction which is now interpreted exclusively with reference to its new function. X and Y are no longer separated by a break and share one and the same intonation peak.

Stage III has been reached, for example, in many European languages. In these languages, the Source Schema was introduced in the course of the last two millennia to give rise to a new pattern of attributive possession. In this way, ablative prepositions developed into genitive particles, such as *of* in English, *von* in German, or *de* in French. This process, whereby adpositional phrases turn into possessive constructions, is presented schematically in (20).

(20)   A scenario of possessee specification
Stage I   N−ADP+N   Specification
      II   N−ADP+N *or* N+GEN+N   Overlap between specification and genitival modification
      III   N+GEN+N   Genitival modification

The adpositions employed in the European languages just cited are ablative prepositions expressing the notion '(away) from', '(down) from'. Outside Europe, the Source Schema is less commonly used than alternative schemas, especially Location and Goal (for examples, see 3.1 above).

Whenever, instead of the schemas mentioned in the previous section, the Topic Schema is involved, then the result is *possessor specification*. The structure of the process from pragmatic marking to attributive possession is sketched below (as elsewhere, X stands for the possessor and Y for the possessee; see 3.1 above):

(21)   (As for) X, X's Y>X's Y

The Topic Schema is responsible for a couple of properties that attributive constructions derived from it exhibit. First, it entails that the possessor, that

3.2 Specification

is, the participant that is presented as the topic or theme, precedes the possessee. Second, it is associated with 'cross-referencing': the possessee shows agreement with the possessor, that is, the latter is encoded twice: as a nominal constituent and as a pronominal modifier (but see below). Third, the possessor and the possessee have the same general referent, at least in the early development of the construction. Most clearly, this is the case when the possessee is controlled by or is a part of the possessor. Body-parts are therefore likely to be the first to be affected by possessor specification. Examples of the latter are presented below (see also under 3.1 above).

(22) Motu (Oceanic, Austronesian; Lichtenberk 1985:99)
      boroma kwara-na
      pig   head- its
      'the pig's head'

      West African Pidgin English (Schneider 1966:93)
      kíng, i hét   ján, i dók, dem pikín
      king his head   John his dog their pup
      'the king's head' 'John's dogs' pups'

Occasionally, however, there is no modifier on the possessee; rather, the possessor and the possessee are simply juxtaposed, as in (23).

(23) Yanomama (Macro-Chibwa; Migliazza 1972:124)
      kamaca poko
      I   arm
      'my arm'

The resulting constructions are occasionally described as instances of possessor–possessee apposition. Now, in languages having a system of overt case marking, such constructions are likely to be characterized by case agreement in that the possessee (=the specifier) receives the same case marking as the possessor (=the specified). Such a situation appears to obtain, for example, in many Australian languages (cf. Dixon 1980:293), even if possessor specification of this type tends to be confined to 'inalienable' possession. In Djaru, for example, a language of western Australia, possessor and possessee are described as being in apposition, both agreeing with each other in case, which in (24) is the Absolutive (ABS). This construction is used only when the possessee is a body-part or an attribute of the possessor.

(24) Djaru (Pama-Nyungan; Tsunoda 1996:597)
      ngatyu-ngku nga=rna   mawun-Ø langka-Ø pung-an
      I-   ERG   CAR=1.SG.NOM   man- ABS head- ABS hit- PRES
      'I hit the man's head'

In chapter 2 we drew attention to what was referred to there as 'double subject marking' – a phenomenon that may arise when the Topic Schema develops into a 'have'-construction (2.1; 2.5.3). A similar phenomenon can be observed occasionally in the development from Topic Schema to attributive possession. What has been called the 'multiple' or 'double subject construction' or the 'double nominative' in various languages of eastern Asia (Kuno 1973:62–78; Teng 1974; Chappell 1996:466ff.; Tsunoda 1996:593–9) illustrates the process we have in mind: the subject (X) of an intransitive clause is further specified, where the specifier (Y) consists as a rule of a body-part of X. In such a case, Y may adopt some of the subject properties associated with X, thereby creating the impression that one is dealing with two juxtaposed subjects. An example of a resulting construction is presented in (25).

(25) Mandarin Chinese (Sino-Tibetan; Chappell 1996:484)
      #Tā- bízi tiē- zài chuanghu-shang
      3.SG nose press-at window- on
      'Her nose was pressed against the window.'

Typically, one might expect these constructions to have most or all of the following properties:

(a) The two noun phrases (X and Y) are simply juxtaposed in clause-initial position.
(b) Both exhibit some semantic and syntactic subject properties.
(c) The two noun phrases can be said to be in an inalienable relationship, where X denotes a person and Y a body-part.
(d) The predicate consists of an intransitive or stative verb.
(e) The main function of the 'double subject construction' is to describe 'a person's physical or psychological condition through a related part of the body or aspect of the personality' (Chappell 1996:507).

What distinguishes such cases from the ones discussed in chapter 2 is mainly the fact that the latter have existential verbs or copula-type elements as a predicate whereas the former use fully lexical verbs instead.

The use of possessor specification has a number of implications for the resulting possessive construction. First, it introduces a word order structure where the possessor precedes the possessee. Second, it is typically confined to human possessors. Only at a more advanced stage of grammaticalization, to be observed in relatively few languages, non-human possessors are admitted. Third, except in a few cases like (23), it implies that the possessor is encoded twice: in a nominal form as the first constituent, and in a pronominalized form as a modifier on the second constituent.

Possessee specification has fewer impacts on the morphosyntax of attributive possession. While it is likely to impose the word order pattern [possessee–possessor], in accordance with the source pattern of specification, nevertheless the reverse order may be found. Both patterns of specification appear to have in common that initially they tend to be confined to *nominal* possessors, and it is only at a more advanced stage in their development that they come to be associated with pronominal possessors.

The different effects of the two types of specification can be illustrated with an example from Pitjantjatjara, a Pama-Nyungan language of central Australia. This language has what Bowe (1990) calls a distinction between an alienable and an inalienable category. The former appears to be derived from the Goal Schema: it uses the suffix *-kul-mpa* (marked PURP) on the possessor noun phrase. This suffix also serves to encode purpose and benefactive arguments, as many instances of the Goal Schema do. The inalienable category is obviously an instance of the Topic Schema, that is, of possessor specification: It is formed by juxtaposing the possessor and the possessee in apposition, both having the same case marking. The two categories are illustrated in (26), where (26a) exemplifies the alienable and (26b) the inalienable category.

(26)   Pitjantjatjara (Pama-Nyungan; Bowe 1990:39, 54)
    (a) Kungkawara-ku   ngunytju a- nu
        girl-   PURP   mother   go-PAST
        'The girl's mother left.'

    (b) Paluṟu   minyma-ngka tjunta-ngka iti   tju-nu
        3.SG.NOM woman- LOC lap- LOC baby put-PAST
        'She put the baby on the woman's lap.'

While the inalienable category is confined to body-parts as possessees, all other nouns seem to be construed alienably. Both constructions have possessor–possessee as their basic order, but, while the alienable construction has the reverse order as a pragmatically marked alternative (Bowe 1990:39–40), the inalienable construction does not seem to allow for alternative arrangements of constituents.

Such structural characteristics are in line with the properties associated with the two types of specification: in the case of possessee specification, word order is not crucial, especially since there is a case marker (*-kul-mpa*) to serve disambiguation if need should arise. In the case of possessor specification, word order appears to be fixed, as one might predict. Furthermore, as one might also expect, possessor specification involves nouns that are in a part–whole relationship with, or controlled by, the possessor: the most likely category of nouns to be affected first are body-parts, as is the case in Pitjantjatjara.

Pitjantjatjara has no cross-referencing on the possessee, unlike most other languages using possessor specification. There is a possible explanation for this: possessor specification and inalienability are confined to body-parts, and, in quite a number of languages, terms for body-parts may not take possessive modifiers whenever the possessor is overtly expressed in the same clause, a phenomenon that has been treated in the relevant literature as 'possessor deletion' (see 1.2, 3.3). To summarize, Pitjantjatjara exhibits both patterns of specification, and attributive possession in this language can be explained with reference to these patterns.

As we noted in chapter 1 (section 1.2), Chappell and McGregor (1989) propose a kind of construction that can be related in some way or other to attributive possession: in addition to the dichotomy alienable vs. inalienable, they describe a third construction type which they call 'classification'. With this term they refer to a phenomenon 'whereby the dependent nominal indicates the type of entity that is being referred to by the head noun' (Chappell and McGregor 1989:28). We listed (1.2.2) a catalogue of six properties that are associated with this construction type. These properties include apposition, that is, the juxtaposition of a dependent noun and its head, in that order, where the head is referential while the dependent is a non-referential noun which specifies the class or type to which the head noun belongs.

Both the description and the exemplification provided by Chappell and McGregor (1989) suggest that we are dealing essentially with instances of possessor specification. More specifically, most examples of 'classification' appear to be instances of the Topic Schema, which we have described in Table 3.1 by means of the formula *(As for) X, X's Y*. In a number of examples provided by Chappell and McGregor, however, there is no 'cross-referencing', that is, the 'possessor' is not repeated pronominally on the 'possessee', as, for example, in (27). As we observed above, this feature is quite compatible with the structure of the Topic Schema.

(27)   Gooniyandi (Australian; Chappell and McGregor 1989:29)
         girili mandaadda
         tree Leichhardt:tree
         'Leichhardt tree'

3.3 On 'possessor ascension'

Specification is a ubiquitous strategy, its effects can be observed in all languages known to us, and in many different kinds of construction. And it can be held responsible for a variety of different grammatical structures. Consider the following English examples:

(28)   English
         (a) The dog bit Cliff.
         (b) The dog bit Cliff on the ankle.
         (c) The dog bit Cliff's ankle.

(28a) is a canonical transitive English sentence. (28b) and (28c) on the other hand, have a third participant in addition, namely *ankle*. This participant is encoded in different ways: it appears as a prepositional phrase in (28b) but as the head noun of a genitive construction in (28c). The difference between the last two sentences in (28) has been described as one where (28c) is more basic while (28b) is derived from (28c) by means of an operation variously dubbed 'possessor ascension', 'possessor raising', or 'possessor promotion'; we mentioned this operation briefly in the introductory chapter (section 1.2), for a critical appraisal of it, see, for example, Blake (1984:438; 1990:102), Chappell and McGregor (1996b). Within the transformational paradigm, for example, possessor ascension (or possessor raising in the terminology of that paradigm) is based on the assumption that (28b) and (28c) have the same meaning. The authors just mentioned argue, however, that such an assumption is wrong, mainly for the following reasons:

(i)   In (28b) the action is represented as more intimately affecting the person than in (28c).
(ii)   The body-part is represented in (28c) as though it were disembodied from the person, that is, as though it were a separate entity.
(iii)   Furthermore, in (28b), the action is viewed as being directed at the person whereas in (28c) the action is viewed as being directed at the part to the exclusion of the person.
(iv)   What all this amounts to, Chappell and McGregor (1996b) argue,

is that the body-part 'ankle' is treated as a part of Cliff's personal domain in (28b) but not in (28c).

One may wonder how such differences in meaning arise. It seems that in order to answer this question, one needs to consider the patterns of grammaticalization which are responsible for the development of the relevant constructions. In accordance with such an account, (28a) would be said to represent the most basic structure, both diachronically and synchronically. (28b) can be said to be historically derived from (28a), by adding a specifying locative adjunct whereby a predication of the type (28a) came to be further specified by the post-modifying adverbial phrase *on the ankle*. The original semantics of this structure appears to be still present to some extent, in that the target of the action in (28b) is the person, and the action thus affects the person more intimately than the body-part, while the specifier (*on the ankle*) merely presents some additional information on the person, by localizing the region affected by the action of the dog. All this does not apply to (28c), where the body-part is the target and the person is mentioned merely in the form of a genitival modifier.

Cross-linguistically, example (28b) appears to be an instance of a more general structure. On the basis of a larger sample of languages it would seem that (28b) represents one out of four widespread patterns or construction types. In English, only two of these are represented; the following examples are therefore taken from German, where instances of all four patterns can be found (cf. König and Haspelmath 1995 for a more detailed discussion):

(29) German
    (a) Paula ist am Bein verletzt
        Paula is at.the leg wounded
        'Paula is wounded on the leg.'

    (b) Der Hund hat Paula ins Bein gebissen
        the dog has Paula in.the leg bitten
        'The dog bit Paula on the leg.'

    (c) Paula tut das Bein weh
        Paula.DAT does the leg pain
        'Paula has pain on the leg.'

    (d) Der Arzt hat Paula das Bein gerettet
        the doctor has Paula.DAT the leg saved
        'The doctor saved Paula's leg.'

What the four sentences in (29) have in common is that they each contain a case expression that is not necessarily associated with the case frame of the main verb. This expression is a prepositional phrase (*am Bein* and *ins Bein*, respectively) in (29a) and (29b), and a Dative phrase (*Paula*) in (29c) and (29d); it further specifies the core argument, which is the sentence subject in (29a) (=*Paula*) and (29c) (=*das Bein*), and the direct object in (29b) (=*Paula*) and (29d) (=*das Bein*). Thus, (29) can be said to represent specifying constructions *vis-à-vis* the corresponding non-extended constructions in (30). Specification introduces either a possessor, as in (29c) and (29d), or a possessee, as in (29a) and (29b).

(30) German
    (a) Paula ist verletzt
        Paula is wounded
        'Paula is wounded.'

    (b) Der Hund hat Paula gebissen
        the dog has Paula bitten
        'The dog bit Paula.'

    (c) Das Bein tut weh
        the leg does pain
        'The leg has pain.'

    (d) Der Arzt   hat das Bein gerettet
        the doctor has the leg saved
        'The doctor saved the leg.'

Thus the constructions distinguished in (29) are each suggestive of a different pattern of encoding. These patterns can be characterized schematically as in (31).

(31) The main patterns of possessive specification (the specifier is presented in the right-hand column)

I	X is affected	at body-part Y
II	Z affects X	at body-part Y
III	Body-part Y is affected	at/to/for possessor X
IV	Z affects body-part Y	at/to/for possessor X

Patterns I and III differ from II and IV essentially only in the fact that they lack an agent (Z) that is present in the latter. I and II on the other hand, differ from III and IV in that the specifier is a body-part (Y) in the former and its possessor (X) in the latter patterns. There is some variation in the way these patterns are encoded. On the whole, however, the morphosyntax associated with each pattern tends to be the same across languages, at least in all those cases where possessive specification is in fact involved in the genesis of inalienable possession. Each of these patterns is now looked at briefly in turn.

Pattern I is characterized by the fact that the possessor (X) is encoded typically as the clausal subject while the body-part (Y) is introduced by means of the Location Schema (*at Y*), that is, the body-part is encoded as a locative adjunct, as in (29a). Instead of Location, the Source Schema (*from Y*) appears to be used in the French example in (32), involving the preposition *de*.

(32) French (König & Haspelmath 1995:29)
Sylvie est noire de   cheveux
Sylvie is   black from hair
'Sylvia has black hair.'

Pattern II differs from I most of all in that there is an agent (Z), typically encoded as the clausal subject, while the possessor (X) appears as the complement. The body-part is also encoded as a locative adjunct, as can be seen in (29b), but there is a second alternative according to which the body-part appears as a specifier, having the same case encoding as the possessor but lacking the categorial properties associated with the morphosyntax of the possessor. The schematic structure of such instances of possessor specification is illustrated in (33).

(33) Kalkatungu (Paman, Pama-Nyungan; Blake 1990:102)
Ithi ngai-ngu thapantu-thi   thuna malhtha
ant me- LOC foot-   LOC   run   mob
'A mob of ants is running over my foot.'

Pattern III typically has the body-part (Y) as the subject while the possessor is added by using the Location Schema, as in (34), or the Goal Schema, as in (29c). Accordingly, the possessor is likely to appear either as a locative or else as a directional, benefactive, or dative case expression. König and Haspelmath (1995) observe that the structure represented by (29c), introducing the possessor in the Dative, is by far the most common in Europe but uncommon outside Europe. It may therefore be described as an areal property of Europe.

(34) Irish (König and Haspelmath 1995:27)
Bhí an lámh ar crith   aige.
was the hand on tremble at.him
'His hand was trembling.'

Pattern IV has the body-part (Y) as a complement while the possessor appears either as a locative or a directional, benefactive or dative expression. Thus, as in the case of III, possessive specification involves adding the possessor (X) via either the Location Schema, as in (35), or the Goal Schema, as in (29d).

(35)   Russian (König and Haspelmath 1995:27)
       Traube xotel   osmotret' u Bestuževa pravuju ruku.
       Traube wanted look   at Bestužev right   hand
       'Traube wanted to look at the right hand of Bestužev.'

In the tradition of relational grammar, 'possessor ascension' means that the possessor ascends out of the possessor phrase to become a dependent of the verb. Such an analysis, even if supported by synchronic observations, is at variance with diachronic evidence. On the basis of the approach sketched here, terms like 'possessor ascension', 'possessor promotion', etc. are redundant, perhaps even misleading. König and Haspelmath (1995:4) therefore use 'external possessor construction' as an alternative term. While this label is more appropriate than all previous ones, nevertheless it is not entirely satisfactory for our purposes. First, it is not applicable to all patterns that we are concerned with here: as we saw above, the possessor is external in III and IV but not in I and II, where one might talk of 'external possessee constructions'. Second, the term does not reflect the fact that we are dealing with a process leading from a more basic structure, exemplified in (30), to an extended structure, as illustrated in (29), where the extension mechanism involved is specification. Instead of 'external possessor' we shall therefore use the term *possessive specification*, introduced in 3.2, which applies to all four patterns sketched in (31) above. Thus, patterns I and II are suggestive of possessor specification, where the possessor is specified by mentioning the body-part affected, while III and IV represent a kind of possessee (=body-part) specification by mentioning the person to whom the body-part belongs.

A large range of alternative labels is in use in the various philological traditions. Frequently, these terms highlight properties that are characteristic of the patterns to be found in the languages concerned. In the German tradition, for example, terms like *dativus sympathicus* (Havers 1911) and *Pertinenzdativ* (Isačenko 1965) have been proposed, highlighting the fact that it is the Dative case of patterns III and IV that has been employed for possessive specification, as illustrated in (29d) above.

That we are dealing here with the results of a process rather than with a state is suggested by the following: when comparing the basic structure, illustrated, for example, in (36a), with the extended structure, as in (36b), one may say the following:

(i)   (36b) contains a Dative constituent (*mir*) for which there is no equivalent in (36a).

(ii)   This constituent further specifies the subject (*das Gesicht*) by naming its possessor.

(iii) (36b) is an instance of pattern III which occurs in a limited set of contexts only, typically involving a human being and his or her body-part; (36a) is not constrained in this way.

On the basis of such observations one may say that unextended structures, as illustrated in (36a), are basic, while corresponding extended structures, as in (36b), are derived.

(36)   German (König and Haspelmath 1995:2)
    (a) Das Feuer brennt.
        the fire   burns
        'The fire is burning.'

    (b) Mir   brennt das Gesicht.
        me.DAT burns the face
        'My face is burning.'

Derived (or extended) structures contain a constituent that is not an obligatory part of the clause, and it does not occur in the corresponding basic structure. It may happen, however, that that constituent becomes conventionalized to the extent that it is no longer an adjunct but develops into an obligatory participant in contexts where body-parts are involved.

In a number of languages, possessor specification is not confined to human possessors and body-parts. Rather there can be inanimate instead of human participants, or events that seemingly do not affect the possessor. Consider the following examples from Maasai (the gloss '3:1' stands for an inverse prefix where the subject is a third-person and the object a first-person pronoun):

(37)   Maasai (Ilkeekonyokie dialect; Eastern Nilotic, Nilo-Saharan; cf. Payne & Barshi 1995)
    (a) áa- duŋ   Stage A
        3:1-cut
        'He cut me'

    (b) áa- duŋ ɛn-káíná   Stage B
        3:1-cut F- arm.ACC
        'He cut my arm' (Lit: 'He cut me, the arm.')

    (c) áa- yyɛ́t im- beníá [. . .]   Stage C
        3:1-search F.PL-bag.ACC
        'He searched my pockets' (Lit.: 'He searched me, the pockets.')

(d) áa- duŋ en-kíné   Stage D
    3:1-cut F- goat.ACC
    'He cut my goat.' (Lit.: 'He cut me, the goat.')

It would seem that these examples are each suggestive of a different stage of evolution. This evolution can be sketched in the following way:

Stage A: There is a person (X) who is affected by a certain process; (37a) is an example of such a situation.
Stage B: Rather than X as a whole, it is actually a body-part (Y) of X that is affected. The speaker expresses this by adding the specifying information regarding Y. We are now dealing with an instance of pattern II.
Stage C: Instead of a body-part, the specifier Y may now be an alienable item on the body, such as a piece of clothing or decoration.
Stage D: Instead of an item on the body, Y may now be an item close to X, such as a relative, or a personal belonging like a domestic animal or a utensil.

The order in which conceptual transfer proceeds is largely in accordance with what Tsunoda (1996:576) calls the *possession cline* (more precisely, it should be called the possessee cline of attributive possession). According to the structure proposed by him on the basis of evidence from Japanese and a few other languages, nouns are most likely to be acceptable as possessees if they belong to a category located at the left end of the scale (38), and increasingly less acceptable the more one moves toward the right end of the scale.

(38)   body-part > inherent attribute > clothing (> kin)
       > pet animal > product > other possessee

Note, however, that neither our four-stage scenario nor Tsunoda's possession cline tell the whole story, for example, since both take care of the possessee only. Thus, Stage D, for example, may involve a part–whole relationship where both possessor and possessee are characterized by inanimate inalienable possession (see section 1.3 above). Swahili appears to have conventionalized Stages A, B, and C, as illustrated in (39a) through (39c), but at Stage D, in (39d), there is an inanimate part–whole relationship.

(39)   Swahili (Bantu, Niger-Congo; cf. Kwon 1995:120ff.)
        (a) a- li-   ni-kata.   Stage A
            he-PAST-me-cut
            'He cut me.'

(b) a- li-   ni-vunja mkono.   Stage B
    he-PAST-me-break arm
    'He broke my arm.'

(c) a- li-   ni-tatua shati.   Stage C
    he-PAST-me-tear shirt
    'He tore my shirt.'

(d) a- li-   shona koti mkono.   Stage D
    he-PAST-sew   coat arm
    'He sewed the sleeve of the coat.'

Languages differ with regard to the number of stages they have grammaticalized. Many languages have not gone beyond Stage B, that is, possessive specification is confined to body-parts as possessees. Northern Pomo, as described by O'Connor (1992:262ff.) is one out of many examples: possessees figuring in possessor specification appear to be associated invariably with body-parts (see (40, 41) below).

Northern Pomo also illustrates another feature that makes it a special case of possessor specification. While the possessee is likely to appear as a kind of appendix on the possessor, it may also come to be more closely associated with the verb. The development in Northern Pomo can be described in the following way: at Stage A there is an ordinary transitive structure, typically consisting of an 'agentive subject' (A) and a 'patientive object' (P), as exemplified in (40a). When the speaker wishes to specify that the action concerns not the object as a whole (=the possessor) but rather a body-part (=the possessee) of the object, s/he can add the body-part noun, as in (40b). In a similar way as we saw above, the possessee lacks some properties of a full clausal participant: It is not case-marked and may not receive the determiner (SPCF) -*nam*. Furthermore, the possessee is always placed adjacent to the verb and O'Connor (1992:262–3) observes that 'it appears to verge on being incorporated into the verb'.

(40)   Northern Pomo (Hokan; O'Connor 1992:168, 263)
        (a) hayu-nam- yaʔ   moːw-al kane
            dog- SPCF-A him- P bite
            'The dog bit him.'
        (b) Mary tuh ʔaː ʔuymo dikel-ye
            Mary P   I.A face wipe-PERF
            'I wiped Mary's face.'

Northern Pomo is in no way exceptional: König and Haspelmath (1995:30–31) mention similar instances of possessee incorporation from Chukchi and Acehnese (Achinese).

3.3 On 'possessor ascension'

Possessor specification in Northern Pomo now competes with the canonical pattern of attributive possession, which is based on the Goal Schema, as we saw in 3.1 above. But a semantic distinction is consistently maintained, and this is in accordance with the grammaticalization patterns involved. Thus, whenever 'the effect on the possessor is deemed to be more important than that on the body part', possessor specification is favoured (O'Connor 1992:271). That the degree of the possessor's affectedness is indeed stronger whenever possessor specification is involved can be demonstrated with the following example, where (41a) illustrates the canonical construction based on the Goal Schema and (41b) the construction involving possessor specification.

(41)   Northern Pomo (Hokan; O'Connor 1992:275)
    (a) hayu yaču?   ʔuy mo:w xabe wih   baneh
        dog OBL   eye he.A rock INSTR   hit
        'He hit the dog's eye with a rock.'

    (b) hayu yačul mo:w xabe wih   ʔuy baneh
        dog P   he.A rock INSTR   eye hit
        'He smashed the dog's eye with a rock.' (=The eye was destroyed.)

This section was not meant to prove accounts based on the notion 'possessor ascension' wrong. We were dealing with only one of a number of quite different morphosyntactic structures that have been subsumed under this label. Our main goal was to demonstrate that there is an alternative approach, offering explanations of 'possessor ascension' which are outside the scope of earlier approaches. Such explanations have to do with a pragmatic strategy, viz. specification, and account for phenomena such as double case marking, or what has been described as 'body-part syntax', *chômeur* (='item without employment'), and the like.

In a similar fashion, it would seem that other terms that have been proposed in works on the syntax of possession may profitably be reconsidered. What has been said about 'possessor ascension', for example, also applies to 'possessor deletion': as we observed in chapter 1 (1.2.1), it presupposes that in the constructions concerned there was a possessor that is deleted. Thus, examples like the following have been cited as instances of 'possessor deletion' since there is no overt possessor (as the translation shows, English does require an explicit possessor in this case):

(42)   French
    Il ferme les yeux
    he closes the eyes
    'He closes his eyes'

There is no justification for using the term 'possessor deletion' within our framework since there is no evidence that there ever was a possessor in the construction concerned. Following König and Haspelmath (1995), we therefore propose to talk of an implicit rather than a 'deleted' possessor in such cases.

3.4 On inalienability

In chapter 1 we drew attention to the distinction between two salient kinds of possession, viz. alienable and inalienable possession, in short, to inalienability as a grammatical category. There are quite a number of languages, spoken in all major parts of the world, that mark such a category. This category tends to involve the following properties (see especially Nichols 1988; 1992:116ff.; Chappell and McGregor 1996b):

(a) It is confined to attributive possession.
(b) It is likely to be associated with a number of marking features. For example, alienable nouns can be described as being marked and inalienable ones as unmarked. This means, for example, that, as a rule, more phonological and/or morphological expenditure is employed to encode alienable, as opposed to inalienable, possession.
(c) Inalienable possession involves a tighter structural bond between possessee and possessor (Nichols 1992:117).
(d) Possessive markers on inalienable nouns are more 'archaic', that is, they look etymologically older than those used on alienable nouns (Nichols 1992:117).
(e) The nouns belonging to the inalienable category include kin terms, body-part terms, or both, usually also some other groups of nouns.
(f) The inalienable category consists of a closed set of nouns, while alienability is an open-class category; its membership is described by Nichols (1988:562) as 'infinite'.

This does not exhaust the list of properties associated with inalienability. A number of additional characteristics have been pointed out by Nichols (1988; 1992:116–23). On the basis of a survey of North American and other languages she finds that there is a small range of main patterns for marking inalienability. The criterion employed by her is morphosyntactic in nature: languages which have the grammatical element used for signalling a possessive relation placed on the head noun (=the possessee)

3.4 On inalienability

are called head-marking (also called head-marked by the author) while in dependent-marking (or dependent-marked) languages the possession marker is found on the dependent noun (=the possessor). Rather than being head- or dependent-marked, languages may be double-marked (=having both kinds of marking in the same construction), or they may have no marking at all, or else they may have split patterns. Perhaps more importantly, Nichols discovered that the distinction head-marked vs. dependent-marked correlates positively with presence vs. absence of inalienability morphology: inalienable possession almost always involves head-marking. In her words,

> the inalienables take marking which is more nearly head-marking or less dependent-marking than the marking of alienables; inalienable possession is head-marked while alienable possession is dependent-marked. (Nichols 1992:117)

In languages having a split pattern (i.e. where two marking structures exist, correlating with the distinction 'inalienable' vs. 'alienable'), two possibilities exist, namely:

(43)   (a) The alienable (=open) set is dependent-marked where the inalienable set is not.
          (b) The inalienable (=closed) set is head-marked where the alienable set is not (Nichols 1988:578).

Nichols does not offer an explanation for this correlation; she is satisfied to argue in favour of a causal relationship leading from form to meaning: the presence of inalienability can immediately be related to formal structure; it is the structural fact of head-marking possession that gives rise to the grammatical category of inalienability (Nichols 1988:582–3). Thus, she concludes, we are dealing with an example where 'form determines the possibility of occurrence of a grammatical category', that is, with a development as sketched in (44).

(44)   Grammatical form > grammatical meaning

Nichols' conclusion, if it were correct, would have remarkable implications, in particular since she maintains that her findings prove the 'Saussurean dogma' wrong; according to this dogma, there is no connection between form and content (Nichols 1988:557, 583).

The problem raised by Nichols (1988; 1992) is a complex one; an appropriate solution would seem to require a more detailed analysis of the synchronic and diachronic situation of all individual languages figuring in her sample. On the basis of the findings that we presented in chapter 2 and the preceding sections of the present chapter, a few more general observations seem possible that may be helpful to account for some of the structural characteristics described by Nichols. What these observations suggest is that, rather than linguistic form, it is meaning or, more generally, the cognitive source structures that can be held responsible for the morphosyntactic characteristics of attributive possession.

As Nichols demonstrates, in addition to head/dependent-marking there are other factors that are involved in the process. First, she observes that there is no invariant semantic content to inalienability. The second factor has to do with the pragmatic factor of frequency of use. As we just saw, nouns treated as inalienable are the ones most frequently associated with the explicit marking of a possessor. Third, there is a phonetic correlation: inalienable expressions are phonetically simpler and/or shorter than alienable ones (1992:117). And, finally, she also draws attention to a temporal correlation in that inalienable possession tends to exhibit the more archaic morphology.

It would seem that the structure of inalienability as described by Nichols is due to the effect of several different patterns of conceptualization. Perhaps the most common one has to do with the way new forms of attributive possession arise. Once the situation in a given language has reached a stage where the morphology used for encoding attributive possession is 'worn out', that is, has been eroded to the extent that juxtaposition is the only means left for marking a possessive relationship, one may expect a new marking pattern to emerge. This new pattern is likely to involve a locative marker (translatable as 'at, in, on, by', etc.) if the Location Schema is chosen, or an ablative ('from'), an allative ('to'), or a comitative marker ('with') in the case of the Source, the Goal, and the Companion Schema, respectively.

The need for introducing such a new pattern is most pronounced in contexts where it is least obvious that a possessive relation exists. Introducing a new pattern appears to be least compelling in the case of possessees which can be predicted to be associated with a 'possessor', that is, in the case of body-parts or kin terms. Thus, it is the latter items, that is, items typically associated with 'inalienability', that are most likely to be ignored when a new pattern of marking attributive possession is created. Accordingly, whenever such a situation arises, we are confronted with a structure of possession marking having the following properties:

3.4 On inalienability

(a) The old pattern of attributive possession consists of a juxtaposition of the possessor and the possessee noun phrases without any marking, or marked with a minimum of phonological material.

(b) The old pattern involves possessee nouns that are inherently associated with a possessor and/or require the possessor to be obligatorily expressed. Such possessee nouns include body-parts and/or kin terms as well as other items typically dubbed 'inalienable', 'inherent', and the like.

(c) Since the new pattern is likely to be built on either the Location, the Source, the Goal, or the Companion Schema, the resulting morphosyntactic structure will have a form roughly as sketched in (45a).

(d) Since the relational marker, irrespective of whether it is an adposition or an inflectional affix, is part of the same constituent as the possessor, the resulting morphosyntactic structure is one as sketched in (45b), where the possessee is unmarked while the possessor is associated with a locative, comitative, or related morphology.

(45) (a) Possessee {at, from, to, with} + possessor
(b) Possessee [possessive marker + possessor]

Depending on basic word order constraints obtaining in the language in question, the possessee and/or the relational marker may follow rather than precede the possessor. Thus, in what has been referred to as 'rigid' verb-final languages, like Japanese or Nama, one might expect the possessor to precede the possessee and the relational morphology ('at, from, to, with') to follow the possessor, that is, in such languages one is more likely to meet a mirror-image of (45), that is, a situation as sketched in (46).

(46) (a) Possessor + {at, from, to, with} possessee
(b) [Possessor + possessive marker] possessee

(e) In constructions of attributive possession, possessees are commonly described as syntactic heads and possessors as dependents (or modifiers). In accordance with this terminology, the old pattern is associated with no marking at all while the new pattern is a dependent-marked one.

(f) Since the old pattern is associated with those nouns that are most likely to correspond to the notion of 'inalienability', however that notion is to be defined, that pattern tends to be described as the inalienable category. Accordingly, all other nouns of the language concerned are said to belong to the 'alienable' category.

Thus, we are faced with a structure of 'inalienability' that is in fact in line with the cross-linguistic generalizations proposed above, that is, (i) the inalienable category is morphologically unmarked while the alienable category has the features of a marked category; (ii) the inalienable category is older, and it is likely to be suggestive of a tighter structural bond between possessee and possessor; (iii) the nouns belonging to the inalienable category are the ones that one would not expect to occur without formal mention of their 'possessor', be they nouns referring to kin relations, body-parts, or relational concepts.

Situations as the one just sketched have been described by Claudi and Heine (1989) and the reader is referred to that paper. Suffice it to mention the following example from Kabiye. Kabiye is a Gur language spoken in northern Togo, which has introduced the Location Schema to create an inalienability category. Accordingly, the erstwhile locative noun *té* 'home' was grammaticalized to a marker of alienable attributive possession, while the older pattern without a formal expression of possession is largely confined to terms for kinship, body-parts, and relational nouns.

In a similar way as in Kabiye, an alienable category was introduced by means of the Location Schema in other languages, like Ewe, a Kwa language of eastern Ghana and southern Togo, and Acholi, a Nilotic language of northern Uganda (Claudi and Heine 1989). In his account of inalienability in Creek, Martin describes a similar situation in some detail, where the 'inalienable' category retains the older 'Class II' prefixes while the 'alienable' category uses the 'Class D' (= dative-marked) prefixes, which are a result of the use of the Goal Schema. Martin concludes:

> On this approach, nouns that are obligatorily 'possessed' are viewed as one fortified position on the battleground between the older II prefixes and the innovative D prefixes. Hence, it is possible that 'relationship', 'inalienability', and even 'possession' are constructs resulting from overzealous synchronic analysis. (Martin 1993:443)

The emergence of inalienability may be the terminal stage in the rise of a new grammatical category, but it can also be a transient stage in the evolution from the old to the new pattern of marking attributive possession. Such a stage would then be characterized by the fact that the new pattern has not yet affected a smaller number of nouns (that is, those that tend to be labelled 'inalienable'). The next stage would be one where the new ('alienable')

3.4 On inalienability

pattern extends to *all* nouns of the language, thereby eliminating the alienability category. Whenever that happens we will expect the new pattern to be used initially as a highly marked, and more expressive alternative to the old pattern, before it is generalized as the only means of marking attributive possession.

This is what appears to be happening in Ewe. As we just observed, this language has grammaticalized the Location Schema to an alienable construction of the type illustrated in (46). The old pattern, consisting of the juxtaposition of possessor and possessee, has become restricted to spatial relations, kinship terms, and a few other items, that is, to a class of nouns that can be, and has been called, the inalienability category (Claudi and Heine 1989). But this category is in danger of being eliminated in that it is now possible to use the new ('alienable') pattern also for inalienable nouns. So far, this is done only in clearly marked and emphatic contexts (Ameka 1996:800), but it is conceivable that, in the end, this marked use will become the normal way in which attributive possession is expressed in Ewe.

While many languages have drawn on the Location Schema, other languages have favoured alternative schemas instead. Thus, Creek, or Choctaw, a Muskogean language (Davies 1984), and Pitjantjatjara, a Pama-Nyungan language of central Australia (Bowe 1990) appear to have recruited the Goal Schema. There is also at least one example where the Source Schema appears to have been involved. Nichols (1988:566) provides the following data from Eastern Pomo as an instance of a structure where a closed set of kin terms takes head-marked possession, as in (47a), while most nouns take the dependent-marked pattern, with a Genitive-marked possessor, as in (47b).

(47)   Eastern Pomo (Pomoan, Hokan; McLendon 1975:92, 108)
     (a) wí- bayle
         1.SG-husband
         'my husband'

     (b) wáx   šá.ri
         my:GEN basket
         'my basket'

Now, the Eastern Pomo marker *wáx* is composed of the first person singular object (oblique) pronoun *wí* 'me' plus the suffix *-bax*, which indicates possession, origin, composition, as well as a number of other functions; the evidence provided by McLendon (1975:153–5) would seem to suggest that expressing the notion 'from' is one of its earliest functions, which again would suggest that (47b) originally meant roughly 'the basket from me'. This would mean that Eastern Pomo, like English and a number of other European languages (see 3.1 above), has grammaticalized the Source Schema to a construction of attributive possession. What would distinguish Eastern Pomo from these languages is that its earlier construction, exemplified by (47a), survives with a restricted set of nouns, thereby giving rise to a split pattern of marking for attributive possession.

To conclude, many of the formal correlations pointed out by Nichols and others can be accounted for with reference to the event schemas from which the relevant constructions of attributive possession are derived. In languages that have undergone the evolution sketched above we will expect the 'inalienable' category to form the older, unmarked, and morphosyntactically tighter construction. But there are alternative ways in which a language may acquire a category of inalienability. Nichols (1988:564–5; 1992:120–1) discusses the situation in Navajo which has a small set of inalienable nouns, called bound nouns by her. These nouns cannot stand by themselves but must take a possessive prefix, as in (48a). When used without a possessor, the marker '*a*-, standing for an unspecified third-person possessor (UNSP), must be used, as in (48b). In order to encode nouns other than inalienable (or bound) ones, a strategy referred to as 'secondary possession' is used. The effect of this strategy is that the unspecified possessor marker '*a*- loses its third person reference and is reinterpreted as a new base for encoding alienable nouns, as illustrated in (48c). For a similar example see Thompson (1996:656–68) on Koyukon Athabaskan, where the bound indefinite pronoun *k'e*- 'something' (*denaa*- in the case of human body-parts) has largely assumed the role played by '*a*- in Navajo, assuming the function of an 'alienation marker'.

It would seem that Navajo has recruited the Topic Schema (*(As for) X, [X's] Y*) for alienable possession, as is suggested most clearly by (48d). And the same schema appears to have been drawn on to graft the 'secondary possession' construction onto the inalienable one: the possessor appears to be presented as a thematic constituent, followed by the possessee. There is cross-referencing in the case of nominal possessors though not when pronominal possessors are involved, as in (48c).

(48) Navajo (Athapaskan, Na-Dene; Nichols 1988:564–5)
    (a) bi- be'
        3.SG-milk
        'her (own) milk'

(b) 'a-   be'
    3.UNSP-milk
    '(someone's, something's) milk'

(c) be- 'a- be'
    3.SG-UNSP-milk
    'her milk, e.g. the cow's milk that she bought at the store'

(d) 'ashkii bi-   deeshí
    boy   3.SG-younger.sister
    'the boy's younger sister' (lit.: 'the boy his younger sister')

The outcome of this process is similar to the one sketched above and can be described exhaustively with reference to the parameters defined by Nichols: the older construction, being phonologically shorter, morphologically unmarked, and confined to a limited set of possessee nouns, survives as an inalienable category, while the more recent construction develops into an alienable category having an 'infinite' membership of possessee nouns.

To conclude, the fact that there exist correlations between morphological marking on the one hand, and presence vs. absence of an inalienability category on the other, can be accounted for with reference to the way these constructions evolve. For example, it would seem that the Navajo pattern of marking 'alienability' is triggered by the Topic Schema. There is an established pattern for encoding nouns that can be expected to have an overtly marked possessor on them. Now, (48c) provides a way of using that pattern to further specify the relevant information: you just need to introduce a thematic participant that is likely to be understood as the possessor of the item presented in (48b).

The limitations inherent in form-based approaches become apparent when one compares the Navajo situation with that found in the Mayan Tzutujil language. Nichols (1988:563ff.) assigns Navajo and Tzutujil to the same type of marking as regards inalienability (=her pattern 1): both are head-marked, that is, it is the possessee that receives the morphological marking, and both have a limited set of nouns (called bound nouns by her) that must be formally possessed.

But there are also remarkable differences, and these differences appear to be due to the contrasting genesis of the two constructions. We noted above that the Navajo construction is an example where the Topic Schema has been grafted onto a construction that originally was confined to inalienably possessed nouns. In the Tzutujil example, the alienable/inalienable distinction is not the result of the grammaticalization of the Topic Schema, nor of any other event schema, rather the distinction appears to be the result of a morphological process of derivation. By contrast with the Navajo situation, we are dealing with a process leading in the opposite direction: nouns in Tzutujil are normally alienable, i.e. expressions like *nuu-b'aaq* 'my bone' or *nuu-kiik*' 'my blood' are understood to denote alienability, i.e. 'my bone to make an awl with' and 'my blood to make blood sausages with', respectively. In order to introduce the notion of inalienable possession, the nouns concerned have to take a suffix -VVl (having the allomorphs *-aal, eel, -iil,* and *-uul*), which almost invariably co-occurs with a formal marker denoting the possessor. The use patterns of this suffix are far from clear. Its functions include that (a) of forming abstract nouns, (b) of expressing the taxonomic notion 'a kind of X'; accordingly, its use is required on nouns in questions like (49). (c) Furthermore, it is used 'when a human possesses something that is normally alienable, but possesses it in an inalienable way' (Dayley 1985:146) and Dayley refers to this function as 'abnormal' possession. In its latter use, the suffix behaves like a derivational morpheme, even if Dayley observes that it also has inflectional properties (cf. Dayley 1985:146, 150). An example of 'normal' (=alienable) possession is provided in (50a) and of 'abnormal' (=inalienable) possession in (50b).

(49)   Tzutujil (Mayan, Penutian; Dayley 1985:150)
       naq   chi   chee7-aal
       what at/to   tree- ness
       'What kind of tree is it?'

(50)   Tzutujil (Mayan, Penutian; Dayley 1985:147)
       (a) nuu-muuj ('Normal' possession)
           my- shadow
           'my shade' [e.g. of a tree that I am sitting in]

       (b) n- muuj- aal ('Abnormal' possession)
           my-shadow-aal
           'my shadow'

In accordance with their different genesis, the structure of inalienability differs considerably between Navajo and Tzutujil: the morphological material employed for expressing the inalienable/alienable distinction is entirely different, as we saw above, and so is the structure of marking. In Navajo, inalienable nouns are morphologically unmarked and alienable ones marked, while in Tzutujil it is the other way round.

While it is easy to characterize the notion inalienability (see especially Haiman 1985a:130; Nichols 1988:568), it is much more difficult to define it. As we saw in the introductory chapter (1.2.1), quite a number of attempts have been made, but none has really been successful. Take the following

Table 3.2. *The distribution of inalienable and alienable nouns in Pima-Papago (Source: Bahr 1986:165).*

Classes of nouns	Previous unowned state	Sequential ownership	Alienable noun (=use of -*ga*)
Natural resources	+	+	+
Domesticated plants	+	+	+
Domesticated animals	+	+	+
Old man, old woman	+	−	+
Kinfolk	−	−	−
Body-parts	−	−	−
Most artifacts	−	−	−
Some artifacts	−	+	+

formulaic characterization proposed by Ameka on the basis of Wierzbicka's semantic primitives approach:

(51)　One can think of X and Y like this:
　　　they are like parts of the same thing:
　　　When one thinks of Y
　　　　one cannot not think of X
　　　X cannot do with Y anything X wants to (Ameka 1996:786)

In some way or other, (51) takes care of perhaps most instances of inalienability. Still it is very general, to the extent that it applies also to situations that are not normally treated as inalienable in the languages of the world. If we know, for example, that Peter loves Joan dearly and cannot think of anything but marrying her, then one might say that (51) does apply (where Peter=Y and Joan=X), but one will hardly talk of an inalienable possessive relationship, even if Peter wished that it were one.

In his study of Pima-Papago of northern Sonora, Mexico and southern Arizona, Bahr (1986) claims that two parameters are sufficient to define inalienability: (a) previous unowned state, and (b) sequential human ownership. Bahr's generalizations on the semantic distinction between the two classes are presented in Table 3.2.

The two parameters distinguished in Table 3.2 are said to be sufficient to define the category of inalienability: whenever there is a '+' in Table 3.2 we are dealing with alienability, that is, the use of the suffix -*ga* is obligatory and, conversely, whenever there is no '+', as is the case in the 'kinfolk-', 'body-parts-', and 'most artifacts'-classes, we are dealing with inalienable nouns. Bahr (1986:163) adds that being possessable is a prior condition for being alienable and it would seem that whenever a temporally unlimited ownership or relationship is involved, we are likely to be dealing with the inalienable category, while the alienable category appears to imply that ownership can be discontinued.

Bahr is not the only one to propose a semantic account for why certain nouns in a given language are treated as inalienable; concerning other remarkable attempts, see Crowley (1996) on Paamese, or Ameka (1996) on Ewe. On the whole, these proposals are not entirely satisfactory, since on a closer look there remain various exceptions to the rules proposed. The observations made in this section suggest that, rather than being a semantically defined category, inalienability is more likely to constitute a morphosyntactic or morphophonological entity, one that owes its existence to the fact that certain nouns happened to be left out when a new pattern for marking attributive possession arose. Accordingly, we find a wide range of variation in the way inalienability is encoded; it is associated e.g. in Pitjantjatjara with body-parts only, in Choctaw with body-parts and kin terms, in Ewe with kin terms and relational concepts but not with body-parts, and in Kabiye with body-parts, kin terms, and relational concepts (cf. Chappell and McGregor 1996b). It would seem that in many instances of inalienability in the languages of the world, the following observation by Nichols applies:

> There is no invariant semantic content to 'alienability'. It is simply a formal split in the marking of adnominal constructions, with the more fused or archaic of the two marking types associated with exactly those nouns that are most often possessed'. (Nichols 1988:582)

There is no evidence either to suggest that inalienability constitutes a notional category of any kind; the following observation made by Bahr on Pima-Papago would seem to apply also to other languages having an inalienability category:

> there is no native-made commentary that says that -*ga* 'means' alienable and no-*ga* means inalienable. In fact, I have not learned a way to say 'alienable' and 'inalienable' in Pima-Papago. If there is a way, it certainly is not on everyone's lips, not even on the lips of the elderly arbiters of the language. (Bahr 1986:162)

It is hoped that the preceding paragraphs have shown that 'inalienability' refers to a number of different phenomena, and that trying to understand and explain its cross-linguistic meaning without reference to time is unlikely to yield meaningful results: which shape 'inalienability' exactly takes in a given language is to a large extent dependent on the pragmatics of its genesis and further evolution.

3.5 Attributive and predicative possession

A common theme in works of the past decades is that predicative possession is basic/underived or underlying while attributive possession is derived from the former by means of a specific set of rules. One thread of reasoning underlying this thesis is that the two are semantically similar and that attributive possession is highly general in meaning whereas predicative possession is more specific. The problem is a complex one and we will not attempt to solve it. Nevertheless, a few observations from the perspective of grammaticalization theory may be appropriate.

There are in fact examples to suggest that a clausal or propositional morphosyntax can give rise to a nominal morphosyntax and, more specifically, that patterns of predicative possession occasionally give rise to attributive possession. Ultan (1978:15), cites Cocopa, a Yuman language of Arizona and California, as an example. Frequently, this process involves the use of a nominalizing/gerundival morphology (e.g. *a woman having five children*) or a relative clause morphology (*a woman who has five children*). Second, there appear to be cases where predicative possession serves as a straightforward model for attributive possession. Tok Pisin (Melanesian Pidgin English) might be an example, where the English verb *belong* developed into a marker of attributive possession ('of'), for example *papa bilong papa bilong mi* ('father of father of me') 'my grandfather' (cf. Watkins 1967:2196).

Another kind of process whereby a clausal syntax gives rise to a pattern of attributive possession can be illustrated with the following German example (see Fritze 1976 and Agel 1993:41–53 for details). In colloquial German there is a construction of attributive possession based on what grammarians call the adnominal possessive Dative. (52) is an example of it:

(52) German
dem Bürgermeister seine Briefmarken
the.DAT mayor his stamps
'the mayor's stamps'

The pattern is probably relatively recent. Although it is occasionally observed in Old High German (Lockwood 1968:21), clear instances of it appear in the course of the fifteenth century; during the initial phase (AD 1470–1530), the pattern was confined to animate possessors before its use was extended to inanimate possession. In accordance with the Overlap

Model mentioned above (Figure 2.1), the transition from predicative to adnominal case marking can be described with the following examples, where (53a) illustrates the source structure of clausal syntax, (53b) the overlap structure, which can be interpreted with reference both to the source (i) and the target structure (ii), and (53c) the target structure, which can be interpreted only with reference to adnominal case marking.

(53) Colloquial German
    (a) Er hat dem Bürgermeister seine Briefmarken geschenkt.
        he has to.the mayor his stamps donated
        'He gave his stamps to the mayor.'

    (b) Er hat dem Bürgermeister seine Briefmarken verkauft.
        he has to.the mayor his stamps sold
        (i) 'He sold his stamps to the mayor.'
        (ii) 'He sold the mayor's stamps.'

    (c) Dem Bürgermeister seine Briefmarken sind gestohlen worden.
        to.the mayor his stamps are stolen become
        'The mayor's stamps have been stolen.'

To summarize, the emergence of this construction appears to be due to the reinterpretation of a sequence of a Dative and an Accusative case expression as an attributive possessor–possessee construction (cf. Burridge 1990:42). According to Stassen (1995), such a general process is not uncommon in the genesis of attributive possession. As an intermediate stage in the evolution from predicative to attributive possession, he argues, there is the Genitive Schema (*X's Y exists*). Originally, the possessor (*X*) and the possessee (*Y*) are distinct participants in the clause. Due to their syntactic contiguity they gradually come to be reinterpreted as forming one single constituent (*X's Y*). This constituent then becomes a construction for attributive possession. Thus, the following Toradja example (54a) of predicative possession is said to have been grammaticalized to the attributive pattern of (54b).

(54) Toradja (East Indonesian, Austronesian; Stassen 1995)
    (a) Taoe se'e re'e kodjo baoela -nja
        people these exist really buffalo-their
        'These people really have buffaloes.'

    (b) Taoe baoela -nja
        people buffalo-their
        'The buffaloes of the people'

In a similar fashion, the evolution of the Source Schema in Romance appears to have entailed a development from an adverbial morphosyntax,

3.5 Attributive and predicative possession

involving the Latin preposition *de-* 'from', to a nominal morphosyntax, giving rise to such markers of attributive possession as French *de*, Spanish *de*, Italian *di*, etc.

What these examples suggest is, first, that specification is not the only strategy employed for developing patterns of attributive possession (see 3.2 above). Second, it also suggests that the phrasal syntax of attributive possession can be traced back in some cases to a clausal syntax of case marking.

It is, however, equally possible that, at least in cases like the following, we are witnessing a development in the opposite direction: rather than the Genitive Schema giving rise to attributive possession, we would be dealing with an evolution where a verb of existence is added to a genitive construction, thereby creating the Genitive Schema. At the initial stage there is a pattern of nominal possession as in (55a) which provides the template for the Genitive Schema, exemplified in (55b). Possible examples of such an evolution are (56) and (57).

(55)   (a) X's Y
           (b) X's Y exists>X has Y

(56)   Urubu-Kaapor (Tupi-Guarani; Stassen 1995)
           (a) Maneru rok
               Maneru house
               'Maneru's house'
           (b) Maneru rok   ym
               Maneru house exist
               'Maneru has a house.'

(57)   Tzutujil (Mayan; Stassen 1995)
           (a) Jun run-keej n- ata?
               one his-horse my-father
               'My father's horse.'
           (b) K'o jun run-keej n- ata?
               exist one his-horse my-father
               'My father has a horse.'

At the present stage of research such hypotheses remain conjectural; what is required is further evidence which would allow us to decide whether we are in fact dealing with an overall evolution from predicative to attributive possession, or an evolution in the opposite direction, or else a development that proceeded from predicative syntax to attributive possession in languages like German and Toradja, but from attributive to predicative possession in languages like Urubu-Kaapor and Tzutujil.

3.6 Conclusions

Two main claims are made in this chapter. First, predicative and attributive possession are built on essentially the same conceptual templates. Nevertheless, the two are kept apart in most languages, that is, the two types of possession are usually developed independently of one another. The second claim is a strong one: many constructions used for attributive possession, it is argued, can be traced back to specification, a pragmatic strategy whereby a nominal constituent is extended by adding another constituent whose main function is to specify and/or emphasize the preceding one. The range of constructions that appear to be based on specification is considerable and it is important to keep the various uses of this strategy apart. As we saw in the preceding paragraphs, for example, whether we are dealing with possessee specification or with possessor specification is essential for describing and accounting for the structural characteristics of possessive constructions.

The above discussion has done little more than to point out where future explanations for certain linguistic facts must be sought. We were dealing with such notions as specification, possessor ascension, and inalienability. Our knowledge of these phenomena in particular and the development and structure of attributive possession in general is still in its infancy stage, which means that generalizations on either of these issues must of necessity remain preliminary. The observations made in the preceding paragraphs were simply meant to demonstrate that grammaticalization theory offers a new perspective for describing and understanding these phenomena.

An area which urgently requires further study concerns the relationship between predicative and attributive possession. We found some evidence to suggest that a clausal morphosyntax may give rise to nominal morphosyntax; adpositions, for example, commonly develop into genitive markers. At the same time, however, we also drew attention to the fact that nominal morphosyntax can form the basis for the evolution of predicative possession, as appears to be the case when the Genitive and the Topic Schemas are involved (see especially section 2.1).

This chapter was concerned mainly with what happens when a given event schema gives rise to patterns of attributive possession. As in chapter 2, we were looking at the evolution from non-possessive to possessive constructions. Our attention will now shift to processes whereby possession itself gives rise to non-possessive grammatical categories.

4 *From possession to aspect*

Possessive constructions frequently resemble constructions serving the expression of other semantic contents. This may be coincidental in a given case; usually, however, it is not: as we saw in the preceding chapters, there are some conceptual domains that appear to be systematically related to possession. The present chapter provides a number of additional examples, though of a different kind.

Once a source schema has given rise to an expression for predicative possession, the latter itself may be the source of more abstract concepts, in particular of grammatial functions such as (a) markers of conditional protasis, (b) markers of deontic modality, (c) aspect markers, (d) tense markers, especially future tense markers (Fleischman 1982a, 1982b), (e) existential markers and copulas. In addition, 'have'-verbs also occur as 'links for addition' in cardinal numerals, as e.g. in Quechua or the Nilo-Saharan language Mountain Nubian, which both have a construction of the type 'ten one-having' to denote 'eleven' (Greenberg 1978c:265). Furthermore, a number of authors (e.g. Locker 1954; Allen 1964; Benveniste 1960; Isačenko 1974b) have drawn attention to structural parallels that can be observed across languages between the morphosyntax of predicative possession on the one hand, and that of perfect aspects and other grammatical categories on the other.

A discussion of all these developments would exceed the scope of this book; the reader is referred to the relevant works (especially Bybee and Pagliuca 1985:73ff.; Bybee, Perkins, and Pagliuca 1994; Claudi 1994; Heine 1993, 1994c; Heine et al. 1993). To illustrate the kind of development that leads from possession to grammatical concepts, we will look at one of these functions in more detail. This function, or functional domain, is aspect. Note, however, that aspect is not a properly delineated conceptual domain; rather aspectual categories overlap with or give rise to categories commonly classified as belonging to tense or modality (cf. Bybee and Dahl 1989). What we have to say therefore relates to some alternative domains as well; we will have to say more about this issue in 4.3 and 4.4.

188   *From possession to aspect*

Aspect has been discussed in a variety of different works. One of the most seminal works, if not the most seminal one, is that by Bybee, Perkins, and Pagliuca (1994), which, like the present one, is written in the framework of grammaticalization theory. What distinguishes the present study from that by Bybee, Perkins, and Pagliuca (1994) is that the goal is much more limited. I want to demonstrate, first, that the evolution of aspectual categories is described most profitably in terms of propositional structures, that is, of event schemas, rather than in terms of lexical items developing into grammatical forms. Second, as we saw in the preceding chapters, the ontological status of possession is far from clear. A number of other domains have been named as being related to possession in some way or other, the domains perhaps most frequently mentioned being location, existence, equation, and identification. Another objective of the present chapter, therefore, is to look into the question of how possession is related to these domains in general and to verbal aspect in particular.

4.1   Parallels

There is in fact a striking parallel between the marking of verbal possession and that of verbal aspect, to the effect that in many languages roughly the same morphology is used for 'have'-constructions and for certain aspect categories. Consider the following examples, where the (a) utterances express verbal possession and the (b) utterances a progressive aspect (in the interlinear glosses of (1), (2), and (3), the copula elements in the (a)-sentences are glossed as progressive markers (PROG) in the (b)-sentences. This is due to the different morphosyntactic behaviour these items exhibit in the two types of sentences):

(1)   Swahili (Bantu, Niger-Congo)
        (a) wa- na   pesa.
            they- be.with money
            'They have money.'

        (b) wa- na-   ku- la.
            they-PROG-INF-eat
            'They are eating.'

(2)   Hausa (Chadic, Afro-Asiatic; Kraft and Kirk-Greene 1973:93ff.)
        (a) mu-nàa dà   aikìi.
            we-be   with work
            'We have work.'

(b) mu-nàa aikìi.
we-PROG work(ing)
'We are working.'

(3) Ewe (Kwa, Niger-Congo)
(a) ga le wó- sí.
money be.at their-hand
'They have money.'

(b) wó- le é- ɖu-ḿ.
they-PROG it-eat-PROG
'They are eating it.'

That the occurrence of the item *le* in both (3a) and (3b) is not coincidental can be seen when these utterances are used in the past tense, where *le* is replaced by *nɔ* in both cases, as shown in (4).

(4) Ewe (Kwa, Niger-Congo)
(a) ga nɔ wó- sí.
money sit their-hand
'They had money.'

(b) wó- nɔ é- ɖu-ḿ.
they- sit it-eat-PROG
'They were eating it.'

Similarly, in Yaqui, the same morpheme *-ek*, described by Jelinek and Escalante (1988) as a Perfective aspect marker (PERF in these authors' glosses) is employed to mark both possession and aspect, as can be seen in (5a). Different morphemes are used when other TAM categories are employed but in each case they are shared by the verbal TAM expression and the possessive construction, as illustrated in (5b).

(5) Yaqui (Uto-Aztecan; Jelinek and Escalante 1988:414)
(a) Peo kar- ek   Peo vuit- ek
    Pete house-PERF   Pete run- PERF
    'Pete has house(s).'   'Pete ran.'

(b) Peo kari- ne   Peo vuiti-ne
    Pete house-FUT   Pete run- FUT
    'Pete will have house(s).' 'Pete will run.'

Note also that in many European languages, including English, constructions using 'have' as their predicate base have given rise to both expressions of verbal possession and of perfect aspect. Such constructions involve the items 'be' or 'have' as auxiliaries, and the main verb is encoded as a past or passive participle, rather than a gerundial or infinitival main verb (see chapter 2). Some examples are presented in (6) to illustrate the formal similarities involved across languages.

(6)   English   (a) I have a house.   (b) I have eaten.
        German   Ich habe ein Haus.   Ich habe gegessen.
        French   J' ai une maison.   J' ai mangé.

Benveniste (1960:128) records a similar distinction in Ancient Egyptian, the example he gives is presented in (7) below.

(7)   Ancient Egyptian (Benveniste 1960:128)
        (a) nb   n- j
            gold to-me
            'I have gold.'

        (b) mr   n -j śn
            loved to-me brother
            'I have loved my brother.'

Such a parallelism is also found in Classical Armenian, even though the structures involved are rather different than the ones looked at above:

(8)   Classical Armenian (Benveniste 1960:127–8)
        (a) nora tun   ē   (b) nora teseal ē
            of.his house is   of.his seen   is
            'He has a house.'   'He has seen.'

What makes Ancient Egyptian, or Armenian for that matter, a special case is simply the fact that its transitive 'have'-construction is based on a source schema other than the Location, the Companion, or the Action Schema. Rather, Armenian uses what Benveniste (1960:127) calls the *être+génitif prédicat* as its equivalent for 'have', that is, it appears to have derived that 'have'-construction from the Genitive Schema (*X's Y exists*). Accordingly, the perfect construction has the morphosyntactic properties associated with this schema, viz. the encoding of the possessor as a genitival constituent and of the possessee as the clausal subject. Similarly, Ancient Egyptian uses the Goal Schema for both possessive and aspect constructions.

4.2   Specifying possession

That possessive constructions are exploited for a large range of functions other than possession has been pointed out in many works on the subject; the reader is referred, for example, to Brugman (1988) for a survey of the remarkable expansion patterns that the English 'have'-construction has experienced.

One major driving force in the conceptual expansion of possession can be seen in what we will call here specifying possession (cf. 3.2). With this term we refer to a widespread mechanism whereby a canonical construction of the type *X has Y* takes an attributival constituent modifying or qualifying the possessee (*Y*). One effect this force may have is to turn a possessive expression virtually into its contrary, viz. 'non-possession', as is suggested by the following English examples from Brugman (1988):

(9)   I had to wait in line for a half hour because they *had three sick tellers*.
        Becker *has a missing finger*.

While specification in (9) consists of an adjectival attribute on the possessee, perhaps a more common strategy is to use adverbial modifiers. The effect such modifiers may have, at least in English and a number of other languages, is to turn an expression for permanent possession, as in (10a), into one for physical possession, as in (10b).

(10)   (a) Do you have a passport?
            He has a pink shirt.

        (b) Do you have your passport with you?
            He has a pink shirt on him.

Another function specifying possession has in English is to form expressions for inanimate alienable possession (see 1.3 above). The English have-construction is used for inanimate inalienable possesesion (e.g. *That table has three legs*) but not normally for inanimate alienable possession (*?That table has three books*). The latter notion can, nevertheless, be expressed by means of the 'have'-construction if a locative prepositional phrase coreferential with the subject is added, as in (11).

(11)   That table has three books on it.

But perhaps the most remarkable contribution of specifying possession lies in the creation of new grammatical constructions, such as perfect categories in European and other languages.

The evolution from 'have'-construction to perfect aspect has received some scholarly attention in Indo-European linguistics, and a number of contrasting hypotheses have been put forward. According to one thesis, this evolution is closely associated with one particular source schema, viz. the Action Schema (see especially Isačenko 1974b). It is widely held that both 'have'-constructions and perfects in many Indo-European languages are part of a more general semantic evolution involving the following stages in particular: 'Take, take hold of, receive' > 'hold, keep' > 'own, occupy' > 'have' (transitive verb) > 'have' (auxiliary) (cf. Meillet 1923; Vendryes 1937; van Ginneken 1939). While some argue that the shift from 'have'-construction to perfect started in Latin or the early Romance languages (Meillet 1923; 1926:142f.), others claim that it happened independently in various Indo-European languages (Vendryes 1937; Demiraj 1985). However that may be, while the co-occurrence of the Action Schema and of 'have'-perfects appears in fact to be areally biassed, there is massive evidence to suggest that this co-occurrence is not confined to the Action Schema. In Armenian, for example, it involves the Genitive Schema, in Irish the Location Schema, and in Persian the Goal Schema (see Vendryes 1937; Anderson 1973). What this suggests is that the shift from possession to aspect is relatively independent of the way in which the relevant expression of possession has evolved; we will return to this issue in Section 4.3.

The development from possession to perfect aspect has been accounted for with reference to a kind of metaphorical process, whereby the possessor of an object is used as a vehicle to express the agent of an action (cf. Seiler 1977b; see below). While this might be suggestive of a straightforward transfer pattern, it actually is not (see 4.3 below): the evidence available suggests that more often than not, this process was triggered by specifying possession, roughly as sketched in (12) (see Fleischman 1982a):

(12)   A   He has a letter
           B   He has a letter # (a) written (one)
           C   He has written # a letter
           D   He has written
           E   He has gone

At Stage A, we are dealing with a transitive structure, where the subject refers to the possessor and the object to the possessee. At Stage B, the possessee is further specified by means of a restrictive modifier or afterthought encoded by a transitive verb in a participial form or as a verbal adjective; let us call this the 'specifying possession stage'. At Stage C, the modifier is reinterpreted as the main verb, and, at Stage D, the new main verb can now occur without an object, i.e., as a transitive verb 'in absolute use', as Bybee and Dahl (1989:71) put it. Finally, at Stage E, the class of new main verbs is extended to include intransitive verbs. This development entails a number of additional reinterpretations, in that erstwhile main verbs assume the function of auxiliary verbs, the proposition turns from a static into a dynamic one, and the possessor into an agent. Examples of this diachronic

4.2 Specifying possession

evolution have been presented, for example, for Latin and the Romance languages (Harris 1982:47), and for Middle High German (Dal 1952:128; Bybee and Dahl 1989:71–3).

A more detailed description of such an evolution can be found in Vincent (1982:79–85). Vincent is able to demonstrate that the transition from possession to 'have'-perfect in Latin crucially involved a shift in the identification of the subject from the erstwhile main verb *habere* to the verb encoded as a past participle form, that is, to the subsequently emerging new main verb.

That such an evolution is of a more general significance is suggested by the following observations. First, it can also be reconstructed on the basis of synchronic states, as illustrated with the following example from Bulgarian (where PART = perfective past passive participle): (13a) is suggestive of Stage A, (13b) of Stage B, (13c) of Stage C, and (13d) of Stage D above.

(13) Bulgarian (Tania Kouteva, p.c.)
    (a) Imam tezi lekcii.
        have.I these lectures
        'I have these lectures.'

    (b) Imam gi napisani.
        have.I them write.PART.PL
        'I have them written.'

    (c) Imam napisani tezi lekcii.
        have.I write.PART.PL these lectures
        'I have written these lectures.'

    (d) Imame sgotveno.
        have.we cook.PART
        'We have cooked.'

Second, it is not confined to conceptual chains leading from the expression of possession to aspectual constructions: it appears to be the same if, instead of aspectual contours, notions of tense or modality are involved. The English *have to*-construction, for example, which has given rise to expressions for deontic modality of obligation and, to a minor degree, also for epistemic modality, appears to have undergone a similar development (cf. Plank 1984). Specifying possession in this case consisted of an infinitive functioning as an adverbial adjunct of purpose.

Now, if we ignore the intermediate stage B in cases like (12) or (13) and simply compare Stages A and C, the impression may arise that we are dealing with a metaphorical transfer from possession (*X has item Y*) to aspect (*X has (done) action Y*), modality (*X has to do action Y*), or any other more abstract notion. We will return to this issue in section 4.3.

The evolution from possession to aspect is likely to have an impact on the morphosyntax of the languages concerned. In some languages it has given rise to an ergative syntax. Trask (1979) distinguishes between two basic kinds of ergative structures, referred to by him as A and B ergativity. While Type A ergativity derives 'from a passive made obligatory', B ergativity has a possessive source. Our interest here is exclusively with the latter, which he finds, for example, in Indo-European languages like Kurdish or Old Persian, as well as in Tibetan, Eskimo-Aleut, the ergative languages of Polynesia, and the South Caucasian languages.

Type B ergativity is said to develop typically in languages that have grammaticalized a possessive schema to a perfect or perfective aspect, but only in those that encode the possessor as an oblique case expression. The oblique cases concerned are almost invariably locative, dative, or genitive case forms, that is, they belong to possessive constructions derived from either the Location, the Goal, or the Genitive Schema. This means that ergativity does not arise if the Action or Companion Schemas are involved, since, in these schemas, the possessor appears as the clausal subject. Accordingly, Type B ergativity did not arise in the Romance or Germanic languages, which are characterized by the use of the Action Schema: in these languages, the process leading from possession to perfect construction had the effect that the possessor was reanalysed as the agent; at the same time it retained its subject function in the nominative case. In Type B languages like the ones listed above, however, reanalysis of the possessor as an agent was a source for ergativity; Trask describes the development involved thus:

> Now in a language lacking a verb 'have', possessive predications are commonly made by putting the possessor into an oblique case, most often the dative, locative or genitive – carrying an overt mark. And re-interpretation of such a possessor as an agent would automatically bring about ergative case-marking. Thus, a sentence of the general form *To me/Of me/At me (is) a window broken*, on being re-interpreted to mean 'I have broken a window', would yield a typical Type B pattern, with the agent overtly marked, the patient unmarked, the verb agreeing with the patient in number and gender but not in person, the verb not agreeing with the agent at all, and the whole thing confined to the perfect. (Trask 1979:398)

The evolution from possession to aspect may give rise to what are called 'hybrid forms' by Heine, Claudi, and Hünnemeyer (1991:231–3), that is, to structures that combine properties of their possessive source with properties acquired in the course of their development towards aspect. Hagège (1993:63–4) discusses the case of Classical Armenian, whose major 'have'-construction is derived from the Genitive Schema: in this language, a structure of the form *X's Y exists* gave rise to a possessive construction of the form *X has Y*. As we saw earlier in this chapter, the latter construction again provided the conceptual template for the perfect. Now, the patient noun in transitive perfect forms receives the accusative prefix *z*-. This fact is interpreted by Hagège as being suggestive of a development from what he calls a 'be structure' to a 'have structure', where the Genitive-marked agent is a relic of the earlier possessive schema (and ultimately of the Genitive Schema) and the Accusative-marked patient represents the new construction type.

4.3 Patterns of shift

What the research summarized above appears to suggest is that there is a unidirectional development from possession to aspect; no instances have been reported so far that would suggest that aspect constructions may give rise to possessive constructions. The questions that remain to be answered include the following:

(a) Are aspectual constructions derived from all the various source schemas involved in this process?
(b) Which aspectual notions may arise in this way?
(c) What accounts for the process, that is, what forces can be held responsible for the fact that time and again, possession serves as a structural template for aspectual concepts?

Question (a) can be answered in the affirmative: it seems that the correlation extends to all the schemas distinguished. Instances of the Action Schema are provided by European languages mentioned above, such as English, German, or French; we also came across instances of the Location, the Goal, and the Genitive Schemas (see section 4.1 above), and the Swahili example (1) in 4.1 may be said to illustrate the Companion Schema. A more complex situation is found in Luiseño, where the Topic Schema can be held responsible for the rise of what appears to be a present tense. Consider example (14) (see also 3.2 above):

(14) Luiseño (Takic, Uto-Aztecan; Steele 1977:121)
 noo=p   ?oy   noma?max
 I   =UP you:object my:liking
 'I like you.'

196   *From possession to aspect*

The symbol 'UP' stands for the clitic *up* (shortened to *-p* after vowels), whose functions include that of a topic marker but which has acquired some subject properties in examples like (14). (14) is derived from the Topic sub-schema of Existence, its literal meaning may be paraphrased as something like 'As for me, my liking you (exists).' There is, however, evidence to suggest that (14) is not immediately derived from Existence but rather from a possession schema. The major 'have'-construction in Luiseño is in fact historically an instance of the Topic Schema, having the structure $X+up - X$'s Y exists, where $X+up$ and X's Y are both subjects (see 2.5.3 above). An instantiation of this structure is presented in (15):

(15)   Luiseño (Takic, Uto-Aztecan; Steele 1977:114)
       noo=p   notoonav   qala
       I=   UP   my:basket   is
       'I have a basket.'

This means that the tense construction in (14) has all the main properties associated with the 'have'-construction, that is, it requires the presence of the clitic *up* and of two subjects. The fact that there is no inflected verbal element in (14) while there is one (*qala*) in (15), does not seem to constitute a problem for this interpretation. First, such a verbal element is not necessarily present in 'have'-constructions, as example (16a) shows; second, such a verbal element is also present when (14) is used in other tenses, as can be seen in (16b).

(16)   Luiseño (Takic, Uto-Aztecan; Steele 1977:121, 124)
       (a) noo=p   nopuuš   konokniš.
           I   =UP my:eye   green
           'I have green eyes.'

       (b) noo=p   ?oy   noma?max   miyxlowut
           I   =UP you   my:liking   FUT
           'I'm going to like you.'

As a final example one might cite the case of Latin, which, as we observed in preceding chapters, has experienced a replacement of the Goal by the Action Schema in expressing predicative possession: a structure of the form (17a) was gradually replaced by (17b). Van Ginneken (1939:87) observes that, from the third century AD onward, this replacement was paralleled by a corresponding shift in aspect marking, whereby a structure like (18a) gave way to one like (18b).

(17)   Latin (van Ginneken 1939:87)
       (a) mihi   est   liber
           to.me   is   book

(b) librum habeo
    book   have.I
    'I have a book'

(18) Latin
(a) mihi illud factum est
    to.me that done   is

(b) habeo illud factum
    have.I that done
    'I have done it.'

To conclude, it appears that the nature of the source schema is of secondary import to the issue concerned. Question (b) can be answered in the following way: there are essentially two kinds of aspectual concepts that tend to be derived from possession. On the one hand, there are the perfect/terminative categories characteristic of European languages. On the other hand, we find progressive/continuous categories and, since these are likely to be further grammaticalized, also imperfectives and present tenses (Bybee, Perkins, and Pagliuca 1994).

It would seem that there is no immediate correlation between the type of source schema and the aspectual notion concerned. For example, while in Ewe the development was one from Location to progressive construction, as we saw above, in Irish, as well as some North Russian dialects, the Location Schema gave rise to perfect or perfective categories, as exemplified in (19).

(19) Irish (Orr 1992:254)
tá sé déanta agam
is it done   at:me
'I have done it.'

'Northern Russian dialects' (Orr 1992:254)
U menja bylo telenka zarezano
at me   was calf   slaughtered
'I have slaughtered a calf.'

Which of the two aspectual notions is involved can be derived from the respective morphological makeup of the main verb: if the main verb is presented as a time-stable or static concept, typically encoded by means of a participial morphology, the grammatical category involved is that of a perfect/resultative. Conversely, if the verb is dynamic, referring to events rather than states and being marked by infinitival or gerundival morphology, the resulting categories are likely to denote progressive and related notions.

There appears to be a second distinguishing characteristic in addition: whenever perfect/perfective categories are present, the diachronic pathway appears to have involved what we referred to above (4.2) as 'specifying possession'. In the case of progressives on the other hand, there is no evidence for an intermediate stage of specifying possession.

The answer to question (c) is more complex and requires a more detailed treatment. Part of an answer has been provided in some way or other by students of Indo-European languages who have drawn attention to the formal similarities to be found in many of these languages between expressions for verbal possession and for perfect aspects. The answer given has to do with metaphorical transfer: according to these authors, the aspectual notion of perfectivity is described in terms of possession. A number of proposals for interpreting this process can be found in the relevant literature. According to Locker (1954:509), past activity is viewed 'from the perspective of present having' (*l'activité passée vue du point de vue d'un avoir actuel*'), and, for Benveniste (1960:127), the agent is presented as a possessor (*le parfait présente l'auteur comme possesseur de l'accomplissement*'.). Such views appear to be suggestive of an interpretation in terms of what is called by Heine (1994b) the metaphor model, according to which aspect, or certain instances of aspect, are expressed metaphorically in terms of the domain of possession. Possessive constructions involve possessees that are typically tangible and/or visible items. Now, when, instead of a concrete item, a dynamic situation is expressed, an aspectual notion is likely to emerge. Thus, the transition from possession to aspect involves a conceptual transfer pattern that can be described by means of the following formula, where 'item Y' is encoded as a noun (plus modifiers) and 'activity Y' as a non-finite, typically nominalized verb:

(20)   X has/owns item Y > X has/owns activity Y

Formula (20), which echoes Seiler's (1977b) 'Possessor-of-an-Act' configuration, describes one relevant component in the transition from possessive to aspectual constructions. In addition, the answer to question (c) has a couple of more complex components. One has been discussed in 4.2 in connection with 'specifying possession.' Another one relates to the pragmatics of the process concerned. The transition from possession to aspect is an instance of a more general process that we may call auxiliation. This process entails a kind of reinterpretation of thing-like, time-stable concepts as dynamic situations, that is, as actions, events, etc.; the reader is referred to Heine (1993) for details of the process. More specifically, auxiliation has the effect that, instead of nominal complements, verbal complements may be used. Obviously, when such a reanalysis takes place, the meaning of the main verb will be affected as well: verbal complements tend to invite certain inferences that are not there when nominal complements are involved, and these inferences in turn may be conventionalized to grammatical functions. It is in this context that the grammaticalization of possessive expressions has to be placed: it can be interpreted as a process whereby an expression like *X has item Y* receives a verbal complement (= *X has (control over) action Y*), thereby giving rise to the inference *X is engaged in doing Y*, with the effect that a progressive construction may result.

What this interpretation would seem to suggest is an analysis not only in terms of metaphor, but also in terms of inferential processes, that is, of strategies that fall within the scope of what is described by Heine (1994b) as the context model.

To conclude, the shift from possession to aspect can be accounted for by reference to at least two contrasting models. An answer that is compatible with the metaphor model has been proposed within the paradigm of localist theory (especially Anderson 1973), according to which grammatical categories are inherently locative in nature. It is therefore to be expected that different categories within one and the same language reflect the same general pattern. Some of the above examples in fact support such an analysis: the copula verbs *naà* of Hausa and *le* of Ewe are both locative copulas, and, ultimately, both the 'have'- and the progressive constructions of these two languages, are apparently derived from Location. Such a reconstruction is also supported by recent findings on grammaticalization, according to which the Location Schema provides one of the main sources for aspect categories (Bybee, Perkins, and Pagliuca 1994; Heine 1993).

There is, however, a problem with such a generalization: it accounts for only part of the instances we are concerned with here. The structural similarities between predicative possession and aspectual categories are not confined to constructions that, either diachronically or synchronically, involve location. Take the above example from Swahili: both the 'have'-construction and the progressive are based on the use of the comitative marker *-na* '(be) with', but neither diachronically nor synchronically can this marker be associated with location; it expresses the usual functions associated with comitatives, such as accompaniment, means, or manner, but not location. To summarize, many of the structural similarities between 'have'-constructions and aspect categories are outside the scope of localism (see below).

The shift from possession to aspect in Swahili appears to have been made possible by the fact that, instead of a nominal complement, a verb nominalized by means of the infinitive prefix *ku-* could be used. Thus, the sentence *wa-na-ku-la* 'they are eating, they eat' (ex. (1b) in 4.1) can be reconstructed as **wa-na ku-la* 'They have (something) to eat.' The infinitive prefix was eroded except when followed by disyllabic verbs beginning with a vowel or by monosyllabic verbs. The overall evolution of the Swahili Progressive construction can be reconstructed as in (21) and the inferential mechanism involved roughly as in (22).

(21)   Companion > Possession > Progressive (> Present tense)

(22)   (a) X is (together) with item Y   Companion
        (b) X has item Y   Possession
        (c) X 'has' (=is engaged in) action Y
        (d) X is doing action Y   Progressive
        (e) X does action Y   Present tense

But there is yet another problem. While the straightforward shift from possession to aspect may be the expected case, it does not account for all cases where possession and aspect exhibit an obvious morphosyntactic relationship. The situation may be more complex, as we will now demonstrate. The examples are taken from Ewe and Hausa, that is, from two languages that we cited above as cases where possessive and aspect constructions exhibit a similar morphosyntax.

In Ewe, the Location Schema has been the source of both the major expression for 'have' and the Progressive aspect. Both are derived from the structure **le . . . me* 'be inside of . . .': their common source is sketched in (23a), the resulting Progressive Schema in (23b), and the Possession Schema in (23c). As the reconstruction in (23) suggests, however, possession and aspect have been grammaticalized in different ways: the postposition *me* 'in(side)' has been eliminated in the case of predicative possession and reduced to *-ḿ* in the case of the Progressive (see Heine 1993:119–26 for details).

(23)   (a) NP   *le*   'be at' NP   *me* 'inside' >
        (b) *NP   *le*   'be at' nominalized verb *me* 'inside' >
            NP   *le*   PROG nominalized verb *-ḿ* PROG
        (c) *Possessee *le* Possessor *así* 'hand'+*me* 'inside' >
            Possessee *le* Possessor *así*

4.3 Patterns of shift 201

If the Progressive structure in (23b), exemplified by (3b) in section 4.1, were derived from the possessive structure of (23c), one might have expected that the complement noun *ásì* 'hand' would have been preserved, that is, one would have to account for why *ásì* has disappeared in the course of this process. Rather it seems more plausible that the conceptual shift proceeded straight from Location to Progressive. This evolution can be sketched as in (24).

(24)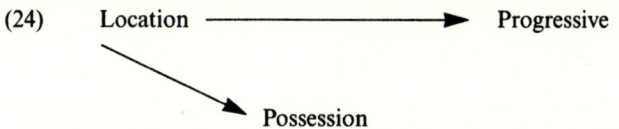

Location ⟶ Progressive
↘ Possession

The transfer pattern sketched in (24) can be held responsible for progressive/continuous constructions in quite a number of languages and, since progressives tend to develop into imperfectives and present tenses, also for imperfective and present tense categories (Bybee, Perkins, and Pagliuca 1994).

The situation in Hausa appears to be even more complex. The evolution from Location to Progressive (or Continuous or Continuative aspect, as it is also called by Hausa grammarians) is described in Heine (1991:161). It is summarized in (25), where four stages are distinguished (cf. Wolff 1993:112–13):

(25)
```
              Stage                      Example
(I)   Subject+  nàa –  Locative    ya-nàa  gidaa.
      pronoun  'be at' compl.      he-be.at home
                                   'He is at home.'

(II)  Subject+  nàa –  noun de-    ya-nàa  màganàa.
      pronoun         noting       he be.at speech
                      event        'He is talking.'

(III) Subject+  nàa –  nominal-    ya-nàa  saamù-n    kuɗii.
      pronoun         ized verb    he-be.at get-  GEN money
                                   'He is getting money.'
                                   (Lit.: 'He is at getting of money.')

(IV)  Subject+  nàa –  verb        ya-nàa  sàami kuɗii.
      pronoun                      he-be.at get    money
                                   'He is getting money.'
```

Possession appears to have taken a different course. It is also derived from Location, but in addition it uses the comitative preposition *dà* 'with', which also has a wide range of other functions, as is common with comitative markers. Consider the following examples:

(26) Hausa (Chadic, Afroasiatic)
(a) ya-nàa gidaa.
he-be.at house
'He is at home.'

(b) ya-nàa dà gidaa.
he-be.at with house
'He has a house.'

Thus, like Ewe, Hausa has a 'have'-construction that is based on the Location Schema. Unlike Ewe, however, Hausa has grafted a Companion Schema on to Location, the semantic content of this complex schema being historically something like *X is (somewhere) with Y*; concerning the notion of 'complex schema', see Heine (1993:37–43). Accordingly, the evolution of Hausa can be summarized as in (14).

(27) Location ───────────────→ Progressive
      Location+Companion→   Possession

This evolution accounts for the fact that both the progressive and the possessive construction have the morphological relic *nàa* of the Location Schema as part of their expression, and that the Possession Schema uses the comitative preposition *dà* in addition. It also accounts for the fact that, for example in relative clauses, the item *nàa* is replaced by *kè(e)* in all three constructions, that is, in locative, progressive, and possessive uses of this item (Wolff 1993:112–13, 495).

To summarize, progressive aspects, as well as some other aspectual notions, may be derived from possession. As we saw above, however, the fact that possessive and aspect constructions are etymologically related need not imply that expressions for aspect are necessarily derived from possessive constructions. Rather, as the examples from Ewe and Hausa show, both may be traced back to other schemas, that is, to schemas such as Action, Location, and Companion, from which possession itself is derived. This brings us to a much discussed issue, viz. the question of how possession is related to such notions as existence, ownership, and location.

4.4 Existence, possession, location, and other domains

Consider the utterance 'There is a bike, it is Maria's, but she doesn't have it, it is in the store.' The utterance contains four predications, and each is associated with a different concept or schema: 'There is a bike' is suggestive of what we referred to in chapter 2 as 'nuclear' existence (*Y exists* or

4.4 Existence, possession, location, and other domains

There is Y), 'it is Maria's' of our Equation (*Y is X's*), 'she doesn't have it' of Possession (*X has Y*), and 'it is in the store' of Location (*Y is at X*). That these as well as a few other schemas are interrelated in some way or other was claimed by a number of linguists and philosophers, and this claim formed the subject of a considerable body of research in the 1960s and 1970s (see e.g. Kahn 1966; Lyons 1967, 1968a, 1968b; Fillmore 1968; Christie 1970; Kuno 1971; Kimball 1973). The claims made in many of these works are:

(a) Possessive, existential and locative constructions are related to one another.
(b) That they are related is suggested by the fact that these constructions exhibit the same rule behaviour in certain uses (though not in others).
(c) All these constructions are locative in their underlying structure, that is, the relationship between all these constructions is a result of their shared underlying locative structure.

While this research has revealed a wealth of insights on the syntax of the constructions concerned, there remain a number of questions that have not been answered satisfactorily. First, it does not become entirely clear what the nature of the presumed underlying structure is, especially whether it is morphosyntactic or conceptual, synchronic or diachronic, etc. Most of the parameters employed are taken from synchronic syntax, yet there are also diachronic arguments (e.g. Lyons 1968a:390; Christie 1970:176). Second, the term 'locative' is used in a number of different ways. Although a distinction is made in some works between 'concrete locative' and 'abstract locative' (Lyons 1968a; Christie 1970), the exact significance of 'abstract locative' remains fuzzy. Third, some of the claims made by these authors are so general or vague as to be close to tautology. Consider the following statement by Kimball:

> grammatically objects are inalienably possessed by their places of location. It *follows* from this claim that any statement of existence is necessarily a locative, for inalienably possessed NP's semantically and syntactically occur only with their possessors. (Kimball 1973:268)

Assertions like 'any statement of existence is necessarily a locative' appear to be so general that they can easily be reversed without losing much of their truth value.

That the various schemas are interrelated has also been argued for by Clark (1970; 1978) and Bickerton (1981). Clark (1970) finds that in most languages her sample of roughly fifty languages, one and the same term is used for more than one schema: in some languages, two schemas are expressed by means of the same term, in others there are three, in still others, all four schemas have the same expression, and only a minority of languages have a different term for each of the four schemas (see 5.1 below). Based on Clark's findings, Bickerton (1981:244–55) argues that these four schemas, referred to by him, respectively, as the relationships of existence, ownership, possession, and location, are not only universally related to one another but that they constitute a 'semantic space', and that this space has internal structure. This structure is defined by him in terms of the notion of contiguity: he says that all four relationships are contiguous to one another, with the exception of existence and ownership, and of location and possession, which are noncontiguous. Bickerton's most important finding is contained in his 'contiguity constraint', according to which

> no language can use the same morpheme to express any two noncontiguous relationships (i.e., location and possession, or existence and ownership) unless that same morpheme is also used to express one of the intervening relationships (i.e., existence or ownership in the first case, location or possession in the second). (Bickerton 1981:245)

That this constraint is a crosslinguistically relevant one has been demonstrated with reference to both Clark's (1970) sample and an additional sample of thirty-three languages collected by Wilson (1983:9). But there are also examples that contradict the contiguity constraint. That noncontiguous schemas may be 'jointly lexicalized' without involving contiguous ones can be demonstrated with an example from Fijian, taken from Wilson (1983:9). Further examples are provided by Ewe and Hausa. In Ewe, the item *le* figures as the predicate nucleus of location and possession, as can be seen in (28a) and (28b), while *nyé* is used for ownership and *lii* (or *lee*) for existence, as shown in (28c) and (28d), respectively.

(28)   Ewe (Kwa, Niger-Congo)
    (a) é- le   xɔ- á   me.   Location
          s/he- be.at house-the in
          'He is in the house.'

    (b) ga   le   é- sí.   Possession
          money be.at his-hand
          'He has money.'

    (c) ga   sia nyé tɔ-   nye. Ownership
          money this be   property-my
          'This money is mine.'

4.4 Existence, possession, location, and other domains

(d) ga   lii.   Existence
    money be.there
    'There is money.'

Similarly, in Hausa the predicate nucleus is *nàa* in the case of location and possession, but *nee* (masculine) or *cee* (feminine) when ownership is involved, and *àkwai* (or *dà*) when existence is expressed. To summarize, Bickerton's contiguity constraint hypothesis is not without exceptions. Nevertheless, as noted already by Wilson (1983), it appears to be applicable in a more restricted form: so far, no language has been found where out of the four relationships, only ownership and existence are expressed by the same item. Whether Bickerton's (1981:246–55) attempt to account for this fact is convincing must remain doubtful (cf. Wilson 1983), but we will not pursue this question here. Rather, our concern is with the following question: how can the fact be explained that in many languages, two, three, or even all four schemas receive the same encoding?

A meaningful answer to this question, we argue, is not possible without taking the cognitive processes into consideration that are responsible for such situations. If two concepts A and B are both encoded by form X then this may be the result of any of the following processes (assuming that other possible causes such as chance, homonymic merger, etc. can be ruled out): either X denoted first A and was later extended to also denote B, or vice versa, or else X denoted originally C and later on came to be used also for the expression A and B. With reference to the present topic, all three possibilities are relevant.

Findings on regularities in conceptual shift suggest that these four schemas can be related to the following chain of grammaticalization:

(29)   A grammaticalization chain of predicate types

Postural >	Locative >	Possessive >	One-place >	Two-place
verb	verb/ copula	verb	copula of existence	copula of identity

Concerning empirical evidence on which (29) is based, the reader is referred to relevant grammaticalization studies, especially Heine and Reh (1984), Devitt (1990), Heine et al. (1993; see also Anderson 1975). As we observed in chapter 2.1, Devitt (1990:103, 113) found out that the verbal items figuring as a predicate nucleus in domains like the ones dealt with in (29) can be arranged along a scale extending from postural verbs via locative verbs, existential verbs, copulas having a temporary sense to general copulas, where postural verbs represent the least and general copulas the most strongly grammaticalized poles of the scale. Devitt's scale of grammaticalization covers all the situations described in (29) except the possession stage. That possessive verbs can be derived from locative verbs has been demonstrated in chapter 2.1 with reference to the Location Schema; one example from Finnish, which has made use of the Location Schema, may suffice to illustrate this development.

(30)   Finnish (Freeze 1992:577)
        Liisa-lla   on   mies.
        Lisa- ADESSIVE COP.LOC man
        'Lisa has a husband.' (Lit.: 'A husband is on Lisa.')

That possessive verbs may develop into existential verbs has also been demonstrated in chapter 2.1. French *il y a*, for example, is historically a possessive construction, its literal meaning being 'it has there'; in modern French, however, it is normally interpreted exclusively as an existential expression, meaning 'there is/are'. The process leading from predicative possession to existence constitutes in fact one of the most common ways in which existential expressions arise. It normally happens when instead of a human possessor there is an inanimate possessor which develops into a non-referential 'dummy participant'. The marker for that dummy participant is normally derived from a third-person singular inanimate pronoun, as in (31a); in Bantu languages it is the locative noun class markers that tend to be used for this purpose, as illustrated in (31b).

(31)   (a) Baka (Ubangi, Niger-Congo; Christa Kilian-Hatz, p.c.)
            'e   tɛ   bo   dàdì   a   bè.
            3.SG.NEU be.with   people   many   at   party
            'There are many people at the party.' (Lit.: 'It has many people at the party.')

        (b) Swahili (Bantu, Niger-Congo)
            pa-   na   wa-tu   w-engi.
            LOC16-have 2- person 2-many
            'There are many people.' (Lit.: 'There has [it] many people.')

Assuming that the predicate types figuring in (29) are representative of major conceptual domains, (29) may be taken as reflecting a conceptual transfer pattern of the kind proposed in (32). Note that postural verbs include both inactive (e.g. *to stand*) and active meanings (e.g. *to stand up*) and that the former are likely to be conceptually derived from the latter. We will therefore assume that the grouping 'postural verbs' distinguished in (29) above is suggestive of the Action Schema. Furthermore, we also include in (32) the conceptual transfer patterns outlined in 4.3, according to which possessive constructions are used for the expression of aspectual notions such as perfect or progressive, which again may develop into tense categories like past and present, respectively.

(32) Action > Location > Possession > 'Nuclear' > Identity
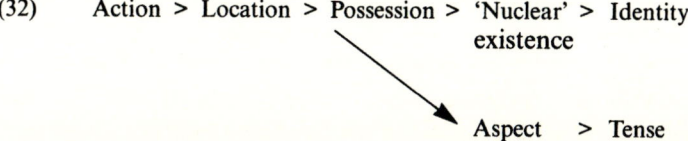
existence

Aspect > Tense

The evolutional scale proposed in (32) has a number of implications. First, it does not support the claim made by adherents of the localist paradigm and others (see above; see also 1.4) according to which location is an ontological domain that can claim conceptual, temporal, or both conceptual and temporal, priority over all other domains. Second, it allows for predictions of the following kind: If there is a linguistic expression which refers to more than one of the domains listed in (32) then that expression is likely to have been used first for the leftmost of these domains. For example, if in a given language there is a linguistic form denoting both possession and identity then we can predict with a certain degree of probability that the latter is historically derived from the former, or else, that both are derived from any of the domains further to the left (that is, from either location or action). Third, the scale proposed in (32) does not only apply to linguistic forms having to do with possession; rather it is applicable to other kinds of conceptual transfers as well. For example, locative expressions may be extended straight to identity without necessarily involving possession or (nuclear) existence.

4.5 Conclusions

In the preceding sections we have picked out a few conceptual domains that are, or are said to be, related to possession. At the same time, however, we have not been able to do justice to all the relationship patterns that possession is claimed to be associated with in the various philological traditions. In Romance languages like Spanish or French, for example, 'have'-constructions have given rise to expressions for deontic modality, and eventually to future tense markers. Much has been done to unravel the mechanism of the process involved (e.g. Fleischman 1982a, 1982b), but much more needs to be done. The main purpose of the present chapter was not only to provide new answers to old questions, but also to suggest a new perspective for relating possession to conceptual domains like the ones looked at here.

What the observations made above suggest is that the four domains discussed by Clark (1970; 1978), Bickerton (1981), and others are in fact related to one another in that they represent different stages of one and the same grammaticalization chain. This relationship accounts for the fact that expressions associated with different domains frequently have the same, or at least an etymologically related, form in a given language. At the same time, these observations also suggest that interpreting location and possession, or existence and ownership, as being 'noncontiguous' raises more problems than it solves, especially since expressions for location commonly give rise to possessive constructions and expressions for existence to constructions for equation/identity. As we saw in section 2.1, expressions for equation/identity again are responsible for paradigm patterns of 'belong'-constructions, that is, of expressions for ownership.

Our discussion in this chapter was confined to two kinds of diachronic and conceptual directionality. We saw that there is a systematic relationship between possession and verbal aspect, and that this relationship can be accounted for in terms of a unidirectional evolution from the former to the latter. But possessive constructions are involved in an even wider range of evolutional processes, as was mentioned in the introduction to this chapter. In order to study such processes in any greater detail, more information is required on domains of conceptualization other than possession.

5 Evaluation

The main claim made in this work is that possession, as it is manifested in language structure, can be traced back to other domains of human experience. This observation is not new, as we will see in the first section of this chapter, where a number of alternative approaches are briefly discussed. Some implications of the approaches used and the findings arrived at in previous chapters are reviewed and summarized in the remainder of this chapter.

5.1 Alternative approaches

The study of possession has been approached from a number of different perspectives. In the present section, the framework used in the preceding chapters is related to alternative views on the relevant subject-matter. To this end, a few salient studies that have contributed to the analysis of predicative possession in some way are briefly looked at. Selection is highly restricted; possession has been a popular topic in linguistics, and to do justice to all the studies that have been devoted to this topic in the course of this century would require a separate, book-length treatment. Priority is given to works that in some way or other contribute to solving the problems discussed in the introductory chapter (section 1.4).

That there are systematic correlations in case marking between possessive constructions, on the one hand, and the morphosyntax of transitivity, perfect or perfective forms on the other, has been demonstrated first by Allen (1964). Allen does not attempt to account for these correlations; accordingly, it remains unclear, for example, whether they are synchronic or diachronic in nature, or what they mean with reference to linguistic categorization. Ten years earlier, pioneering work on possession was published by Locker (1954). Locker sets up a typology of expressions for 'have'-constructions that is very similar to the one proposed here. Similarities relate in particular to the following points: first, he describes

Table 5.1. *Correspondences between event schemas and Locker's propositional types.*

Propositional type (according to Locker 1954:501)	Event Schema
'As far as I am concerned, it exists' (*En ce qui me concerne, il existe*)	Topic
'My X exists' (*Mon... existe*)	Genitive
'Something is where I am, is to me' (*Une chose est chez moi, à moi*)	Location, Goal
'I am with something' (*Je suis avec une chose*)	Companion
Verbal expressions for 'have' (*L'expression verbale de la notion de l'avoir*)	Action

'have'-constructions with reference to their conceptual source. Second, he characterizes the various types by means of propositional formulas that closely resemble the schematic characterizations employed here. And third, his types roughly coincide with our schemas, as can be seen in Table 5.1. Differences concern on the one hand the fact that Locker (1954:501) mentions two further types in addition (cf. chapter 2 above), and, on the other hand, that he does not distinguish between the Location and the Goal Schemas.

Regrettably, Locker's analysis did not get quite the response it deserved; with few exceptions (cf. Claudi 1986), it was ignored by subsequent research. Benveniste (1960:121), for example, does not seem to have taken notice of it and, instead, proposes a basic typology into those languages having a 'have'-verb and those using 'be to' (*être à*) instead. The former, referred to as the *habeo*-type, include *nos langues* ('our languages') and are said to be rare, a lexeme for 'have' being a late acquisition in Indo-European. The latter are called the *mihi est*-type and, wherever sufficient information is available, this type is said to have preceded the *habeo*-type in time. Although Benveniste (1960:121–2) cites a number of languages using the Location, the Companion, and the Existence Schemas, he does not subdivide his *mihi est*-type any further.

Like many other authors, Benveniste (1960:114ff.) draws a major boundary between 'be' as a copula and 'be' as a verb. The former serves to 'express identity between two nominal terms' and may have zero expression in a given language, while the latter is a full verb expressing existence. Benveniste argues that there is neither a natural nor a necessary relation

5.1 Alternative approaches 211

between the two. What such a claim would seem to ignore is that the two kinds of 'be' share an obvious relationship based on grammaticalization. Diachronically, this relationship is defined by the fact that expressions for verbal 'be' develop into expressions for copular 'be', as Benveniste himself observes. Synchronically, this process is reflected in the fact that in many languages the same expression is used for both, as is the case in English (see 4.4 above). That there are languages that formally distinguish the two does not alter this fact.

In a similar vein, Locker's typology is ignored in Isačenko's (1974b: 44–55) seminal paper on 'be' and 'have'. Isačenko proposes a twofold division of the languages of the world into what he calls H-languages (=languages making extensive use of *have*) and B-languages (=languages that either have no verb *have* or else make only restricted use of it). The former include the Germanic and the Romance languages, Czech, Slovak, Serbo-Croatian, and Lithuanian, while Estonian, Latvian, Hungarian, Finnish, and Russian are examples of the latter. The boundary between the two types cuts across the Slavic and Baltic territories. Polish, Ukrainian, and Belorussian are said to represent a transitional stage from B- to H-languages. Isačenko postulates temporal priority for B-languages; he observes, for example, that Proto-Indo-European was a B-language and that the first European language to have introduced the verb 'have' was Greek; note that Locker (1954:505) had suspected that it was Basque which was responsible for the introduction of 'have'-constructions in European languages; we have alluded to this discussion in chapter 2.7.

While Isačenko's analysis highlights an important typological contrast to be observed in European languages, it does not discriminate between the major schemas distinguished here. His notion of H-languages may be said to correspond to our category of Action Schema, but his B-languages include all other languages, that is, languages that derive their major pattern of verbal possession from either the Location, the Existence, or the Companion Schema.

Like Isačenko, Ultan (1978:33–5) proposes a binary typology of predicative possession. His primary criterion is the syntactic function associated with possessor and possessee noun phrases. The syntactic functions considered are subject and predicate and, accordingly, the two types distinguished are: (a) the possessee equals the predicate, and (b) the possessee equals the subject. Type (a) is said to be fairly rare and to be restricted to 'comitative or comitative-instrumental' predicates; it coincides with our Companion Schema. Type (b) has three subtypes, called the object-designated, the locative-designated, and the possessor-designated. The first two roughly correspond, respectively, to our Goal and Location Schemas, while the nature of possessor-designated forms does not become entirely clear on the basis of the description volunteered by Ultan. The Action Schema is not considered in Ultan's typology – a fact that has some implications for the generalizations proposed by him, as we will see below (5.5).

While most authors are satisfied with providing a description and/or classification of possessive expressions, an explanatory framework is proposed by Claudi (1986), and the present work owes much to her pioneering work. Like Locker (1954), she distinguishes between actual 'have'- constructions and their conceptual sources. She proposes three such sources, which she refers to by means of propositional formulas. Thus, our Action Schema roughly corresponds to her formula *I have what I took*, the Location and Companion Schemas to her formula *I have what exists where I am*, and the Goal Schema to her formula *I have what exists for me*. Claudi is able to demonstrate that many previous attempts at accounting for the morphosyntax and semantics of predicative possession were doomed to failure because they ignored the conceptual transfer patterns that can be held responsible for the growth of these structures. Regrettably, Claudi's work has not appeared in print and, hence, has not been considered in subsequent studies on the subject.

Another scholar who has come up with a typology related to ours is Hengeveld (1992:157–69). In his discussion of non-verbal predication, Hengeveld presents a catalogue of predication types that closely resembles the above classification. Thus, his locative predication type corresponds to our Location Schema, as can be seen in (1), and his equative predication type to our Equation Schema, as in (2).

(1)   Egyptian Arabic (Semitic, Afro-Asiatic; Hengeveld 1992:162)
      ʿand-i   ʿarabijja.   Location
      LOC-1.SG   car
      'I have a car.'

(2)   Tamil (Elamo-Dravidian; Hengeveld 1992:161)
      Inta pustakam raaman-   atu.   Equation
      this book   Raman.POSS-NOM
      'This book is the one of Raman,' 'This book is Raman's.'

Note also that Hengeveld divides the existential type into three subtypes and these subtypes correlate with our three types of Existence: his 'Possessor as Experiencer' subtype corresponds to our Goal, his 'Possessor

Table 5.2. *Correspondences between event schemas and the classifications proposed by Hengeveld (1992) and Stassen (1995).*

Predication type (Hengeveld 1992)	Types of predicative possession (Stassen 1995)	Event Schema
Lexical predication	Have-possessive	Action
Locative predication	Locative possessive	Location
Existential predication	–	(Existence)
Possessor as Experiencer	Locative possessive	Goal
Possessor as Restrictor	–	Genitive
Possessor as Theme	Topic possessive	Topic
Equative predication	–	Equation
Proprietive/privative predication	Comitative possessive	Companion

as Restrictor' to our Genitive, and his 'Possessor as Theme' to our Topic Schema, as can be seen in the following examples volunteered by him:

(3) Nasioi (East Papuan, Indo-Pacific; Hengeveld 1992:163)
Danko oto- deru- mauŋ.   Goal
spear COP.3.SG-2.SG.DAT-PRES
'Do you have a spear?' (Lit.: 'A spear there-is-to-you?')

(4) Nasioi (East Papuan; Hengeveld 1992:164)
Manikuma dakana oto- mauŋ.   Genitive
woman POSS.2.SG COP.3.SG-PRES
'Do you have a wife?,' 'Does your wife exist?'

(5) Mandarin (Sinitic, Sino-Tibetan; Hengeveld 1992:165)
Tā yǒu sān- ge háizi.   Topic
3.SG COP three-CLFR children
'He has three children.' (Lit.: 'As regards him, there are three children.')

Furthermore, our Companion Schema correlates with one of the subtypes of what Hengeveld (1992:165–7) calls the 'proprietive/privative predication type'. Finally, what Hengeveld (1992:157–60) calls the 'lexical predication type' is structurally similar to our Action Schema. Another classification has been proposed recently by Stassen (1995), who distinguishes four types of predicative possession, more precisely of 'have'-constructions: the locative possessive, the topic possessive, the comitative possessive, and the 'have'-possessive. The main correspondences between Hengeveld's, Stassen's, and our classification are summarized in Table 5.2.

The correspondences pointed out in Table 5.2 are crude ones and they have to be seen in the light of the different frameworks adopted by the authors concerned. What we wish to emphasize is that event schemas, or predication types or types of predicative possession for that matter, must not be equated with the resulting possessive schemas. First, the relationship between the two is a diachronic one: possession can be traced back historically to these source schemas via the grammaticalization processes outlined in 2.2 above. Second, the two are also conceptually different. For example, a possessive construction derived from the Location Schema is no longer synchronically a locative predication: it is likely to have been grammaticalized to the extent that it has lost its locative meaning and, even if it still has a locative morphosyntax, it serves primarily or exclusively the expression of possession. In short, an understanding of the relationship between source and target schemas would seem to require some knowledge of the grammaticalization processes linking the two – an observation that has been ignored in most of the works reviewed above.

And the same also applies to other kinds of approaches, especially those written in or influenced by the localism paradigm, where possession is treated as locative in nature. For Clark (1978), for example, all four sentences in (6) below are 'locational': 'I argue that the possessor in the two possessive constructions is simply an animate *place*. The object possessed is located in space, just as the object designated in existential or locative sentences. In possessive constructions, the place happens to be an animate being, such that +Animate Loc becomes a Pr [=possessor]' (Clark 1978:89).

(6)   (a) There is a book on the table.
        (b) The book is on the table.
        (c) Tom has a book.
        (d) The book is Tom's.

To consider possessive sentences as locative or locational would either mean that we are dealing with two kinds of locative structures, one illustrated by (6a) and (6b) and the other by (6c) and (6d), or else that the term 'locative' is used in such a wide sense that it becomes virtually vacuous. When Ramos and Ceña (1980) for example, tried to apply the localist approach as used by Lyons (1967), Clark (1970), Christie (1970), and others to Tagalog, they were disappointed. Neither did they find any evidence that location and possession were interrelated, nor any support for the thesis that the latter is derived in some way or other from the former. None the less, work on possession done within the framework of localism has

5.1 Alternative approaches

contributed tremendously to our knowledge of possession and its relationship to other domains of conceptualization.

Among the many recent treatments that have been proposed to deal with predicative possession, perhaps the majority fall within what may loosely be called the formal paradigm, where 'formal' includes, but is not confined to, works written within the tradition of generative grammar. Such treatments include in particular Bendix (1966:37–115) on English, Hindi, and Japanese, Fillmore's (1968:61–81) pioneering work on English and some other languages, Langacker (1968) on French, and Freeze (1992) on a worldwide sample of languages. Underlying these treatments there appear to be assumptions of the following kind:

(a)   There are a number of different constructions in a given language that serve the same purpose, viz. that convey roughly the same meaning. In our case, this meaning has to do with possession.

(b)   The differences observed between these constructions are not accidental, rather they are suggestive of morphosyntactic regularities that can be described by means of a restricted set of rules.

(c)   Underlying these differences there is unity: all constructions can be derived in a principled way from one and the same underlying structure. This structure may be identical with or similar to one of the various constructions, but it need not bear any formal resemblance to any of them.

(d)   The more different constructions there are that can be derived from that underlying structure, the more advantageous or successful the approach adopted by the linguist is.

One of the central notions of this paradigm is that of an underlying, basic, or 'underived' structure. The shape that this structure takes differs from one author to another. For Langacker (1968), Fillmore (1968), or Kayne (1993) it closely resembles our Goal Schema. Thus, according to Fillmore's approach, inalienable possessor noun phrases derive from a deep structure Dative case role. Similarly, Langacker (1968:67) proposes the structure *être+Obj+NP+Dat+NP* as underlying possessive sentences in French, where the phrase *Dat+NP* corresponds to the possessor and *Obj+NP* to the possessee. Accordingly, a French sentence like (7b) is said to be derived by means of a set of rules from structure (7a). The latter structure closely resembles one of the surface constructions to be found in French, exemplified by *Le livre est à moi* 'The book is mine', which is a straightforward instance of the Goal Schema. For Freeze (1992) again, the universal structure underlying possession has the features characteristic of the Location Schema; we will return to that structure below.

(7)   French (Langacker 1968:68)
      (a) *est* Obj *le livre* Dat *moi* →
      (b) *J'ai le livre*

Although not adhering to the generative tradition, the approach developed by Bendix (1966) follows the overall guidelines just sketched. Like Fillmore (1968), Bendix argues, however, that it is not possible to reduce all instances of possession to a single structure. Rather, what is required are two separate underlying structures or 'submeanings' for what he calls 'A has B' constructions: one called general and the other called inherent. The former largely corresponds to Fillmore's notion of alienable and the latter to his notion of inalienable possession. The two underlying constructions and the structures derived from them are printed in (8) below (where A=possessor, B=possessee, C=B, X stands typically for *with*, *for*, *to* or a locative preposition, and Y may be null; see 2.1 above for more details).

(8)   General: B is X A Y → A has B
      Inherent: C is A's B → A has B

The strategy employed by Bendix for setting up a general formula ('A has B') on the one hand, and the general and inherent sub-formulas on the other, is based on paraphrase, whereby different constructions expressing the same meaning are allocated to the same category if they exhibit a systematic paraphrasis relationship (cf. Bendix 1966:38).

The treatments sketched above, as well as other works on possession based on the formal paradigm, differ in a fundamental way from the approach employed here. Differences concern first of all methodology: while the former attempt to establish regularities, systematic similarities, or presumed identity between different construction types, we are concerned with variation within one and the same elementary structure, more precisely, with the different uses of the same event schema.

Second, this methodological discrepancy affects the results obtained in a crucial way: While formal approaches lead to generalizations holding between different construction types, approaches based on grammaticalization theory like the present one lead to generalizations about both the evolution and the synchronic status of a given construction.

Third, while both kinds of approach have to do with reconstruction in a wider sense, the goal of reconstruction is different: the underlying entities postulated within the formal paradigm are meant to account for structural variation, while the source schemas in the grammaticalization approach are diachronic in nature and reconstruction therefore has to be in accordance with historical reality.

While the formal models address some issues that are outside the scope of our approach, there are a number of questions that cannot be answered satisfactorily on the basis of those models, such as the following:

(a) Why is it that, among the large range of morphosyntactic structures that people dispose of, it is invariably the same small pool of structures that is selected for the expression of possession? For example, why did speakers of English develop the kinds of coding options for possession and related notions they did, like the ones illustrated in (9), rather than choose among the many other conceivable patterns the language offers them?

(9) (a) Jane has a child.
    (b) Jane is with (a) child.
    (c) The child is Jane's.
    (d) The child belongs to Jane.

(b) Why are possessive constructions frequently severely constrained in their morphosyntactic behaviour? For example, why can I say (10a) but not (10b) or (10c)?

(10) (a) Jane has a cold.
    (b) ?Jane is with a cold.
    (c) ?The cold is Jane's.
    (d) ?The cold belongs to Jane.

(c) Why is each construction associated with a specific range of possessive notions?

These questions may suffice to illustrate the difference in orientation between the two kinds of approach looked at here; for a catalogue of other questions, the reader is referred to the introductory chapter (1.4; see also 5.4 below).

That 'have'-constructions, predicate locative, and existential constructions are all 'derived' from a single underlying structure which has a preposition as the head of the predicate phrase has been claimed by many linguists subscribing to the localist paradigm (cf. e.g. Lyons 1967, 1968a, 1968b; Clark 1978); more recently it has also been argued for by Freeze (1992): all three constructions are said to be members of what he calls the 'locative paradigm', in which the thematic arguments are LOCATION and

THEME. Accordingly, the three sentence structures exemplified in (11) are said to be derived from a structure where the predicate phrase is prepositional (PP), the theme argument is the specifier of the predicate phrase, and the location is the complement (Freeze 1992:558).

(11) (a) The book is on the bench.   (Predicate locative)
      (b) There is a book on the bench. (Existential)
      (c) Lupe has a book.   ('Have')

Freeze's goal is ambitious. Not unlike localists like Clark (1970), he claims that formal differences among the three kinds of construction are cross-linguistically very restricted and highly predictable, and he undertakes to reveal the relations between these constructions in 'universal grammar' (Freeze 1992:554). The difference between (11a) and (11b) is accounted for in terms of movement: 'The movement of either the theme or the location to the subject position is governed by the [±definite] feature of the theme: a definite theme may move to the subject position, yielding the predicate locative. Alternatively, an indefinite theme may stay in place while the location moves to the subject position, yielding the existential' (Freeze 1992:559). 'Have'-constructions are accounted for in the same way as existential constructions in that in a structure [theme – copula – locative argument], the locative argument moves to the subject position. The 'have predication' is interpreted as a locative predication, and the subject of 'have' as a location (ibid., pp. 578, 580). 'Have' copulas, he says, differ from 'be' copulas in that they are 'basically existentials with a [+human] locative argument' (p. 592). With regard to the status of items denoting 'have', he decides (p. 589) that 'have' and 'be' are copula forms that are not lexical, but rather should be analysed 'as features of Infl'.

Freeze's analysis is probabilistic in nature, as can be illustrated by such notions as 'restricted differences', 'undeniable similarities', 'high predictability', 'tendencies' figuring prominently in the generalizations proposed. The first issue that is relevant here concerns cross-linguistic comparison. First, he observes that in Hindi, Tagalog, Yucatec, Russian, and Finnish, both existential and 'have' predications have a locative subject and a Theme+copula in the predicate. Note that all examples presented are suggestive of our Location Schema, but Freeze (1992:577) claims that these examples represent cross-linguistically the 'default' or 'normal' relationship between the existential and the 'have' predication. No mention is made of alternative schemas, for example of other scholars who, using formal approaches like Freeze, had decided on a structure akin to the Goal rather than the Location Schema (see above).

Yucatec Maya, for example, has three different constructions for possessive predication, being derived, respectively, from the Location, the Equation, and the Existence Schemas. The Yucatec examples provided by Freeze (1992:577, 586), however, are confined to the Location Schema, which, as we observed above, is most easy to reconcile with his notion of a 'locative paradigm'. It would seem that Freeze would have more difficulty in accounting for the two other schemas, which both have the effect that the possessor is encoded as a nominal modifier.

Second, in addition to this syntactic evidence, Freeze also uses morphological evidence: existential and 'have' predications, he argues, share the same copula form, not only in the above languages but also in languages like Mandarin Chinese (*you*), Shanghainese (*yu*), Hebrew (*yeš*), French (*avoir*), Portuguese (*ter*), Modern Greek (*echei*), Quechua (*tiya*), Trukese (*mei*), Yosondua Mixtec (*yo*), and Turkish (*var*). No attempt is made, however, to account for the fact that quite a different situation obtains in many other languages, as the data presented, for example by Clark (1978) and Wilson (1983) show; these, as well as other seminal works on the relationship between existential constructions and 'have'-constructions, or on possession in general, are missing in Freeze's references. Note further that the author does not comment on the fact that for many of the copula forms presented it would be hard, if not impossible, to establish a meaningful connection between existential and 'have'-constructions.

His third piece of evidence concerns the claim that, universally, the subject of 'have' predications is a location. In addition to languages like Gaelic, that have grammaticalized the Location Schema, English and German are cited as examples, where a locative adverbial agreeing with the possessor is said to be required in certain contexts. It remains unclear, however, how such a situation is relevant to the issue under consideration. Take the following example cited by Freeze:

(12)   German (Freeze 1992:582)
    (a) Hans   hat ein Taschenmesser.
        Hans   has a   pocket-knife
        'Hans has a pocket knife.'

    (b) Hans   hat ein Taschenmesser dabei.
        Hans   has a   pocket-knife   there.on
        'Hans has a pocket knife on him.'

Both utterances in (12) are in fact instances of possessive expressions, even though they are suggestive of different possssive notions. (12a) is most likely to be interpreted as an instance of permanent, and (12b) of physical posssession: (12b) does not mean that the pocket knife 'belongs' to Hans but rather that it is 'locally associated' with Hans. What the locative adverb *dabei* in (12b) appears to achieve is that it turns an expression for permanent possession, which is the most prototypical of all possessive notions, into one that is more marginally associated with possession, that is, one for physical possession. That a locative adverbial agreeing with the possessor does not contribute to the possessive meaning of the utterance concerned can be seen in (13), where the locative preposition *über* 'over' appears to be responsible for the fact that (13) is likely to receive a non-possessive interpretation: (13) may be uttered, for example, in a situation where someone is threatening to kill Hans with a knife.

(13) German
Hans hat ein Messer über sich.
Hans has a knife over himself
'Hans is faced with a situation where there is a knife above him.'

There is a fourth piece of evidence presented by Freeze that appears to be more intriguing: he draws attention to the fact that in some languages, existentials and 'have'-constructions tend to be in complementary distribution in that the former have inanimate subjects and the latter human subjects (1992:584). He concludes that 'the [±human] feature of the location is responsible for many superficial differences between the existential and the "have" structures' (Freeze 1992:585). He does not, however, endeavour to explore the explanatory potential underlying this observation, namely the fact that the grammaticalization of the Location Schema entails a stage where a human participant encoded as a locative argument ceases to be a locative argument and comes to be reinterpreted as a possessor (see chapter 2).

Another problem that arises in the course of Freeze's analysis can be seen in his use of terms like 'similarity' and 'unity/identity'. For example, he observes that there are 'undeniable similarities' between the existential and the 'have' predication, and he concludes that therefore there is 'unity' between the two and that 'the "have" predication *is* the existential' (Freeze 1992:576). Throughout the paper it remains unclear what the significance of his notion 'similarity' is. This would not be a serious issue if Freeze had decided on a theoretical framework that takes such notions as similarity or graded membership of a category for granted. Such notions, however, are hard to reconcile with a framework based on discrete categorization, as the one adopted by Freeze appears to be.

5.1 Alternative approaches 221

We have picked out but a few topics figuring in Freeze's discussion. There remain a number of other problems that his analysis raises, and that make an evaluation of his analysis a difficult exercise. The main shortcoming in his approach can in fact be seen in his insistence on one universal underlying structure for all 'have'-constructions in all languages. The alleged underlying structure selected by him corresponds closely to a more grammaticalized stage of the Location Schema, and it is therefore not surprising that most of the languages cited by him are those that have made use of this schema. Quite naturally, he concludes that the absence of a (locative) preposition in English 'have'-constructions constitutes a seeming 'mystery' (Freeze 1992:587).

Freeze claims that his treatment is explanatory: 'I have opted for the analysis that seems most explanatory' (Freeze 1992:589). But it remains unclear what is explanatory about this analysis. A number of essential questions that arise when one is dealing with such constructions either receive an inadequate answer or else remain unanswered altogether. Such questions are in particular: (a) Why are 'have'-constructions in a number of languages related to locative/existential constructions in the first place? (b) Like Bach (1967), Freeze (1992:576) observes that the fact that English has different copulas in 'be' predications and 'have' predications is seemingly 'pathological' when so many languages do not. Why do such 'pathological' situations nevertheless exist? (c) Freeze (1992:580) claims that 'the subject of "have" is universally a location'. Why is it in fact that in a number of languages the subject of 'have'-constructions has the properties of a locative constituent, and why does this not apply to other languages? The kind of explanation that Freeze proposes can be illustrated with the following quotation:

> 'Have' predications of various kinds, including those with 'have' copulas, were then shown to be basically existentials with a [+human] locative argument – thus explaining the distinction between 'have' copulas and 'be' copulas. (Freeze 1992:592)

Although the generalization contained in this statement applies only to a limited number of languages, it is nevertheless an important one. Whether in fact it constitutes an explanation, as the author claims, must remain controversial.

It would seem that what Freeze presents is hardly more than an observation on the complementary distribution of 'have' copulas and 'be' copulas. In order to turn this observation into an explanatory account, the following question needs to be answered: why is it that 'have'-constructions, at least in some languages, can be 'shown to be basically existentials with a [+human] locative argument'? We have volunteered an answer in chapter 2: in languages that have grammaticalized the Location Schema to a 'have'-construction, a cognitive process has taken place whereby a possessor has been metaphorically conceptualized in terms of a location – in a similar way as had already been argued for by Lyons (1967). Thus, the noun phrase used for the expression of the possessor is encoded as a locative complement. In other cases again, Freeze avoids explanatory accounts even though such accounts would seem to offer themselves.

To summarize, an account like the one proposed by Freeze (1992) does not seem to be appropriate for explaining the cross-linguistic structure of possession, its main shortcoming being, first, that it ignores the dynamics underlying the use of possessive constructions. Second, treatments of the kind presented by Freeze (1992) or Kayne (1993) also ignore the fact that possessive constructions derive from a small range of quite different conceptual sources. Any attempts at reducing these sources to one, be that within a diachronic or a synchronic framework, are likely to result in an inadequate analysis.

5.2 Event schemas

One of the main concerns of this work is with event schemas. The schemas of conceptual transfer outlined in chapter 2 (2.1) relate to elementary ways of expressing experience; they refer to basic situations, such as what one does (Action Schema), where something is located (Location Schema), who one is accompanied with (Companion Schema), or what exists (Existence Schema). Event schemas are propositional in structure, that is, they are encoded by means of a clausal syntax, and in that respect they differ from other kinds of concepts that have been drawn on to deal with grammaticalization, such as objects and activities. That they are not relevant only to the analysis of phenomena like the ones looked at here has been argued for in Heine (1993).

Event schemas are in fact not isolated phenomena, and their relevance is not confined to accounting for language structure: they appear to be but one manifestation of a more general cognitive mechanism that is recruited for understanding and transmitting experience. Another manifestation of this mechanism can be illustrated with reference to a notion that has found some currency in cognitive anthropology and ethnology. That there exists a limited pool of propositional structures that can be held responsible for

Table 5.3. *Semantic relationships according to Casagrande and Hale (1967:167).*

1	Attribute:	X is defined with respect to one or more attributes of Y.
2	Contingency:	X is defined with relation to an antecedent or concomitant of Y.
3	Function:	X is defined as the means of effecting Y.
4	Spatial:	X is oriented spatially with respect to Y.
5	Operational:	X is defined with respect to an action Y of which it is a goal or recipient.
6	Comparison:	X is defined in terms of its similarity and/or contrast with Y.
7	Exemplification:	X is defined by citing an appropriate co-occurrent Y.
8	Class inclusion:	X is defined with respect to its membership in a hierarchical class Y.
9	Synonymy:	X is defined as an equivalent to Y.
10	Antonymy:	X is defined as the negative of Y, its opposite.
11	Provenience:	X is defined with respect to its source Y.
12	Grading:	X is defined with respect to its placement in a series or spectrum that also includes Y.
13	Circularity:	X is defined as X.

structuring experience in general and for expressing abstract concepts has been established independently by several different lines of research. One of the first systematic treatments to demonstrate the significance of semantic relationships in shaping meaning was presented by Casagrande and Hale (1967). They set out to study about 800 Papago folk definitions for objects, events, processes, qualities, and actions. All the definitions linked two or more folk terms together by means of a semantic relationship: 'a definition can be regarded as a statement of a semantic relationship between a concept being defined and one or more concepts' (Casagrande and Hale 1967:167). They discovered 13 types of semantic relationships from which all 800 definitions were constructed. These types are summarized in Table 5.3.

Semantic relationships can be characterized in the following way:

(a) They have a basic structure consisting of two terms and a relationship holding between them.
(b) Their number in any culture is quite small.
(c) They appear to be universal.
(d) People almost always express themselves by using terms that are linked together by means of semantic relationships.

(e) Semantic relationships are a means of reconstructing 'most of a culture's principles for organizing symbols into domains' and of decoding the meaning of these symbols (Spradley 1979:107).

What distinguishes event schemas from semantic relationships is the fact that the latter can be described as an analytic tool available to the anthropologist for studying symbolic organization, while event schemas represent a set of structural templates that are available to human beings for the expression of more abstract concepts. What the two have in common in particular is, first, that they typically have a structure consisting of two arguments and a predicate; second, that their number is limited; and, third, that they are the same across cultures and may be described as universal primitives.

Some of these similarities are straightforward. For example, the semantic relationship 'Action X is characteristic of Y' of Colby, Fernandez and Kronenfeld (1981) is suggestive of our Action Schema, or their 'X is the usual location of Y' relationship of our Location Schema. In other cases, the parallels are less obvious, and in a few cases no immediate parallels exist; for the majority of semantic relationships, however, correlations of some kind can be found.

5.3 On categories and universals

What the above discussion has hopefully shown is that any attempt at defining possession universally on the basis of similarities in linguistic form is not very likely to be met with success. The diversity in morphosyntactic and morphophonological structures used for encoding possession is enormous and makes it difficult for the student of universal linguistics to come up with cross-linguistic generalizations. We observed above, for example, that possessor encoding may involve virtually any of the morphological means commonly encountered in case paradigms: the possessor may appear as the subject, the direct or the indirect object, as an oblique case expression, as an ergative, or as a non-ergative participant (cf. Clasen 1981). And the same applies to the possessee: it may be encoded as a subject in the nominative case in one language and as an oblique case expression in another. In a similar way, the predicate nucleus of possessive expressions may be a lexical verb, a verb exhibiting a reduced verbal behaviour, a copula, or even zero. Furthermore, the possessor–possessee relation may have the characteristics of a topic–comment or a comment–topic structure, or neither of these structures.

5.3 On categories and universals 225

Much of this diversity becomes predictable once we look at the conceptual nature of possession, at the way it evolves and the way it is synchronically structured: both the source schemas described in chapter 2 and the seven notions that appear to form reference points in structuring the domain of possession, we argue, are part of a universal inventory of cognitive options available to humans. Such options may, but need not, be exploited by a given speech community, a local community, or an individual in a given situation, they may provide an occasional means for expressing thought, or they may develop into conventionalized patterns of linguistic usage.

The problem of what is universal about predicative possession thus might seem to be a complex one. But there are some recurrent phenomena in the cross-linguistic expression of possession that one feels entitled to call 'universal', even though they relate to linguistic, rather than to conceptual, structures. First, as has also been observed by other authors (e.g. Langacker 1994:43–4), all human languages can be expected to have conventionalized forms regularly employed for the expression of possession.

Second, all human languages can also be expected to discriminate between different types of possessive predications. In the introductory chapter (1.2) we made a distinction between attributive and predicative possession, and the latter was further divided into 'have'- and 'belong'-constructions. It seems that these three kinds of constructions are consistently distinguished in the languages of the world, a distinction that relates to the respective genesis and evolution on the one hand, and to the synchronic pragmatics and syntax of these constructions on the other. But perhaps the most striking difference exists in semantics. Consider the following examples, which are representative of the three kinds of construction. (14a) is a 'belong'-construction, it is confined to the expression of permanent possession. (14b) is a 'have'-construction, and it also has permanent possession as one of its meanings (e.g. *Suzanne has a car, that is, it belongs to her*). But the 'have'-construction exemplified by (14b) is also used for other possessive notions such as temporary possession (e.g. *Suzanne has a car but it doesn't belong to her*). The attributive construction in (14c) includes all these meanings plus a number of additional ones; it may refer, for example, to a car that Suzanne wanted to buy but never did, or to a car that she sold, or to a car that she saw, mentioned, etc., in short, it may denote possession, but it may also stand for meanings that bear no discernible relationship to possession.

(14) (a) The car belongs to Suzanne.
      (b) Suzanne has a car.
      (c) (It is) Suzanne's car.

The difference between these three kinds of construction is not confined to English; it can be observed in many areally and genetically unrelated languages. What this suggests is that, cross-linguistically, three different kinds of possessive categories can be distinguished. One corresponds to the English construction exemplified in (14a): It is essentially 'monosemous', and it is a 'belong'-construction. The second, corresponding to (14b), is a 'have'-construction and has a 'polysemous' structure in that it is used to refer to two or more different possessive notions. The third, corresponding to (14c), is an instance of attributive possession. It is likely to express all seven possessive notions distinguished in section 1.3 plus a number of others; it tends to be 'polysemous' to the extent that in some of its uses it no longer bears any relationship to possession (cf. 2.5 above).

If constructions of type (14c) 'tend to be polysemous' then this does not mean that they are so in all their uses. Depending on the context in which they are used, they may be open to various interpretations, but in other uses they may be like 'belong'-constructions of type (14a), that is, they are confined essentially to one interpretation only, as in (15) which cannot refer, say, to the married man Suzanne is always talking about, but rather denotes unambiguously the man related to Suzanne by marriage (Taylor 1989a:669).

(15) Suzanne's husband.

We will assume that the threefold distinction just sketched is of universal significance. There are, however, a number of other generalizations that appear to have universal status as well. On the basis of the foregoing we may propose, for example, the following universal statements:

(i)   If we find an expression for predicative possession in a given language, then that expression is likely to be derived from one of the source schemas described in chapter 2.
(ii) Such expressions are the result of grammaticalization, i.e. of a process whereby a concrete schematic content is employed for the expression of a more abstract function.

According to these statements, possession is a derived concept, one that requires other concepts for its expression. This raises a more general question alluded to repeatedly in the course of this work: In which sense can possession be said to be 'universal?' The term 'universal' has received a variety of different interpretations. It has been applied, for example, to situations such as the ones listed in (16) (cf. Heine 1993:10–11):

(16) Notions of universality

    (a) There is a category or property X and all languages have it and/or consistently mark it.
    (b) While all languages have X, it need not be consistently marked; for example, it may have 'zero expression' in certain environments.
    (c) While all languages have it, there are languages that have no formal expression for it.
    (d) The majority of languages worldwide have X.
    (e) X is found in a number of languages across genetic and areal boundaries.
    (f) If a language has category or property X then it also has Y (implicational universal).
    (g) Languages or categories of type X are significantly more frequent than languages/categories of type Y (distributional universals).
    (h) My theory postulates X to be universal and whenever the theory is contradicted then I have to account for that in a principled way.

No evaluation of these universal notions is attempted here. In previous accounts, virtually any of these situations was taken as a starting-point for generalizations on possession.

As we observed in chapter 3, some Indo-Europeanists argue that possession is not a 'universal' phenomenon, but that its emergence constitutes a recent acquisition of mankind, due to developments that must have taken place in the course of Indo-European history. This position was echoed by students of 'primitive societies', who argued that, traditionally, these societies have no concept of possession. Steere (1933:113–14), for example, concludes that 'in the Bantu mind there is no mental concept of *possession*' and that, if we ignore his claim, we are in danger of grafting the European idea of possession on to the 'Bantu mind'.

Our observations suggest that such claims are unfounded, since all languages that we came across have conventionalized expressions for possession and, hence, possession is a linguistic phenomenon that might qualify as a universal in the sense of (16a) above. Such observations also appear to be supported by indirect evidence, for example, by the widespread occurrence both of linguistic items for 'steal' and of the cross-cultural legal relevance of theft.

Among the phenomena that have been named frequently in connection with universal properties of possession, the use of 'be'-verbs or copula elements deserves particular mention. These elements, it is argued, are universally associated with possessive constructions (cf. Isačenko 1974a; Clark 1978) and, no doubt, we are dealing with a universal in the sense of (16e) above. One may wonder, however, what the significance of this observation may be. As the discussion in the preceding chapters suggests, the presence of such elements can be described as epiphenomenal, and is largely predictable on the basis of the source structures described in chapter 2: schemas such as Location, Goal, or Equation, for example, can be expected to have 'be'-type predicates as part of their encoding.

5.4 On explanation

The explanations proposed here are essentially extra-linguistic in nature. They relate to the way we experience the world around us and use these experiences in communicating with other members of our species. Event schemas provide a convenient way of conceptualizing recurrent types of experiences – experiences that have to do with ontological distinctions between action, location, existence, etc. But event schemas are also extremely useful for communication: they are ideal for expressing what we think, feel, and want. Most of all, they provide convenient templates for describing abstract contents, and possession is a relatively abstract concept.

In chapter 1 (1.4) we raised a number of questions regarding the structure of predicative possession. On the basis of the observations made in the course of this book we are now in a position to answer those questions:

(a) The question of why expressions for predicative possession frequently resemble expressions for existence, location, and the like can be answered in the following way: the majority of schemas employed for the grammaticalization of predicative possession involve predicates whose original meaning relates to location, existence, etc.

(b) This also answers the question of why so many languages employ 'non-verbal' expressions for predicative possession, or why 'have'-constructions frequently involve verbs having what Seiler (1988:94) calls a 'marginal status', exhibiting, for example, systematic paradigmatic gaps. That there are many languages that employ 'non-verbal' expressions for 'have' may be accounted for with reference to either or both of the following observations. First, this fact has to do with the nature of verbs figuring in source schemas of 'have'-constructions: schemas such as Location, Companion, etc. frequently involve copula-like items as predicates, and

5.4 On explanation

such items naturally exhibit a reduced verbal behaviour. The second part of the answer has to do with the effects of grammaticalization. Even if the source schema involves a full-fledged verb, as is always the case when the Action Schema is recruited, that verb tends to lose verbal properties once it becomes a marker of predicative possession. Such properties include the ability to take the whole range of morphological trappings characteristic of full verbs, or to be associated with distinctions of tense, aspect, negation, person, and number.

(c) We also wondered in the introduction why predicative possession exhibits such a large variety of different encodings in the languages of the world. That the possessor in 'have'-constructions can be encoded either as a subject, an object, a locative, a comitative, or a genitival constituent, that is, that it may be associated with virtually any of the existing case markings, is due to the fact that such constructions can be traced back to a small pool of contrasting conceptual schemas and that each schema provides a specific template for the morphosyntax of the resulting possessive construction. Thus, the possessor is likely to be encoded as the sentence subject in languages that have recruited the Action or the Companion Schema, while the possessor can be predicted to be encoded as a complement in languages that have made use of the Location or the Goal Schema (cf. section 2.7, table 2.9).

(d) Another issue concerns the observation made by a number of authors that the situation found in European languages is typologically somewhat exotic (cf. Bach 1967:479; Hopper 1972:119–200; Clark 1978:111; Ultan 1978:34). There is an obvious reason for this: the linguistic structure of 'have'-constructions found in Romance and Germanic (though not necessarily in Slavic, Celtic, or Finno-Ugric) is determined primarily by the effects of one particular schema, that is, the Action Schema (even if this is no longer synchronically recoverable in most of the cases concerned). This fact accounts for a pattern of encoding verbal possession that is relatively uniform on the one hand, and 'exotic' on the other: uniform, in that the possessor is typically encoded as the sentence subject and the possessee as the object, and 'exotic' because the Action Schema is not among the most frequently employed source structures in the languages of the world.

(e) The question of why quite a number of languages employ a locative morphology for presenting 'have'-constructions can be answered in two ways. First, the Location Schema is one of the predominant sources for 'have'-constructions in the languages of the world. The second part has to do with the fact that predicates figuring in a number of schemas may historically be derived from locative predicates. Thus, even in cases where the Location Schema was not immediately involved, we should not be surprised to find 'have'-constructions that are etymologically related to locative morphology.

This brings us to perhaps the most widely discussed issue in this general debate, namely the question as to how such notions as existence, identification, and location are related to the notion of possession: are they all the same, are they different but belong to the same general ontological category, or are the structural similarities to be observed between them in many languages accidental? As we have tried to establish in chapter 4, all these questions have to be answered in the negative. Rather, these notions are conceptually distinct, but they are in a relation of conceptual and diachronic derivation, in that expressions for predicative possession are derived from expressions for action, location, etc. Thus, perhaps the most meaningful way to account for these structural similarities is with reference to the cognitive transfer patterns involved.

(f) The question of why the syntax of possessive constructions is frequently peculiar, in that it cannot be reconciled with rules operative elsewhere in the language concerned, has been dealt with in various parts of this work. In more detail, we were concerned with this question in 2.5.3, where we were looking at a couple of peculiar morphosyntactic structures that one expects to arise when, for example, the Location or the Topic Schema is grammaticalized to a 'have'-construction.

One answer to the question of why possessive sentences are frequently peculiar has been volunteered by Jelinek and Escalante (1988:411). These authors observe that such sentences, while involving a relationship between two entities, do not exhibit the kind of relationship seen in a prototypical transitive sentence, where an agent acts upon a patient. Such an answer is not entirely satisfactory, simply because possessive sentences frequently have neither a synchronic nor a diachronic relationship with transitive sentences, as we saw in the preceding chapters. Furthermore, in the case of possessive sentences derived from transitive constructions, that is, in instances of the Action Schema, transitive sentences do not consist of prototypical ones only, yet even if non-prototypical sentences are involved, they do not normally exhibit the same kind of 'marginal status' that expressions for predicative possession do. Thus, there must be other factors in addition. These factors have to do with the particular grammaticalization processes and pragmatic principles that interact in the creation of possessive

5.4 On explanation

constructions; we have looked at these factors in the preceding chapters (especially 2.2 and chapter 3).

(h) The question as to how the relationship between 'be' and 'have' in the languages of the world is to be conceived turns out to be a complex one. With reference to predicative possession, the answer may be disappointing. While expressions having 'be' as one of their constituents serve as a template for expressing possession, the opposite can also hold true: as we saw in the preceding chapters, 'have'-constructions may give rise to existential predicates, cf. French *il y a* ('it there has' >) 'there is'. Thus, the question does not seem to make much sense unless looked at with reference to the event schemas of which 'be' and/or 'have' form a part; we have discussed this issue in chapter 2.1.

As we noted there (section 2.1), in a number of instances of the Location Schema there is no verbal item corresponding to the notion *is at* in the formula proposed for this schema (*Y is at X*). There are essentially two main explanations for this fact. The first would be that, in the language concerned, the notion of a locative copula has, or may have, zero expression. The second is that, in the process of grammaticalization, complex markers, and in particular discontinuous markers, tend to be simplified in that a given grammatical category which is expressed by more than one item, tends to become reduced to one marker (see chapter 2.2). Reduction may have the effect that the item expressing *is at* is eliminated.

Perhaps the main purpose of linguistic explanation is to answer the question of why language structure is the way it is. We have presented a number of examples that suggest that the approach proposed here makes it possible to provide such answers. In concluding, we may extend this question to the English 'have'-construction: Why is it, for example, that this construction has a transitive syntax? Why is the possessor encoded as the subject and the possessee as the direct object, considering the fact that such a structure is relatively rare in the languages of the world? The answer has been provided in chapter 2 (see especially 2.4): the English 'have'-construction is derived from the Action Schema and has retained the main properties associated with this schema, namely a transitive clause structure where the possessor is encoded as the subject and the possessee as the direct object. This leaves us with the question of why English *have* is a transitive verb but at the same time lacks essential properties associated with transitive verbs, such as the ability to passivize. The answer to this question was provided in section 2.2: Grammaticalization entails decategorialization. With reference to the Action Schema, this means that the verb involved loses in properties characteristic of its category and, in the case of action verbs, the ability to passivize is one of the earliest casualities to be observed in decategorization (see Heine 1993).

Explanation is closely related to prediction, even though the relationship between the two is a complex one (cf. Lass 1980). The findings made in the preceding chapters allow for a number of predictions, where 'prediction' is used in a wider sense, relating not only to future situations but also to unknown synchronic states and reconstructed past situations, for example, when derived from regularities of diachronic evolution. The grammaticalization of possession can also shed light on this kind of prediction, as the following example may illustrate.

It is widely held that 'have'-constructions in Russian as well as other Slavic languages were originally based on Location, involving the locative preposition *u*, perhaps preceded by the Goal Schema (Orr 1992:249), and that the expansion of the Action Schema using the verb **jimeti* 'to have' as a predicate nucleus is an areal innovation triggered by developments to be traced back to Greek, Romance, and/or Germanic languages.

Bulgarian is cited as an instance of a language that has been shaped by these processes. Modern Bulgarian has a variety of different 'have'-patterns. Its major pattern is based on the Action Schema involving *imam* (< **jimeti*) 'have' as the main verb. This pattern, let us call it the *imam*-construction, is used for a wide range of possessive notions including permanent, inalienable, abstract, and inalienable inanimate possession. Additional 'have'-patterns found in Bulgarian are the *u*-construction, an instance of Location based on the locative preposition *u*, which is largely confined to the expression of physical and temporary possession, and the *săs*-construction, an instance of the Companion Schema based on the preposition *s(ăs)* 'with', which expresses a number of possessive notions but not permanent possession. In addition, there is a 'belong'-pattern based on the preposition *na* 'on' (Tania Kouteva, p.c.).

Leaving aside the latter two patterns, which are not mentioned in relevant studies, the impression conveyed in these studies is that the *u*-construction is an old one while the *imam*-construction is more recent, even though it is attested already in Old Church Slavonic Gospel texts (Isačenko 1974b; Orr 1992). Orr (1992:250) notes, for example, that the *u*-construction was more frequent in Middle Bulgarian but has since become very restricted in scope, while the *imam*-construction has been generalized.

Such an interpretation is hard to reconcile with findings made on the grammaticalization of possession (see chapter 2). A construction that includes inalienable and abstract possession among its meanings is likely to be old, since such meanings develop later than, for example, physical or temporary possession. Observations on the evolution of the Location Schema, for example, suggest that the expected direction of development is from physical via temporary to permanent and eventually to inalienable and abstract possession. Now, as noted above, the Bulgarian *u*-construction covers essentially only physical and temporary possession. We can therefore conclude that, compared to the *imam*-construction, the *u*-construction is of recent origin, at least in the form used in Modern Bulgarian.

In the light of such observations it might be worth reconsidering previous reconstructions based on written documents. It would seem that, while the *imam*-construction is widely attested at the stage of Old Church Slavonic, it must remain doubtful whether the *u*-construction did provide an established pattern for possession at that stage (cf. Orr 1992:249–51; Ivan Duridanov and Tania Kouteva, p.c.). To conclude, findings based on the methodolgy sketched in this volume might shed new light on reconstructions based on orthodox methods in historical linguistics.

A major theme of this work has been to demonstrate that extra-linguistic factors, in particular those that have to do with conceptualization and communication, can be held responsible for many of the properties commonly associated with possessive constructions. Compared to these, linguistic factors appear to be of secondary import. There is perhaps one notable exception: according to Stassen (1995), the question of which schema is employed in a given language to develop a 'have'-construction crucially depends on the way simultaneous propositional sequences are encoded in that language. Languages that have a morphosyntactic deranking of simultaneous sequences, for example, are claimed to use the Location Schema, while languages that have backgrounding of simultaneous sequences use the Topic Schema. Such correlations are remarkable; it remains to be demonstrated, however, what their explanatory significance is.

5.5 Conclusions

The main interest in the preceding chapters has been with explaining possessive constructions. This means that a number of issues that are not immediately related to this goal were not, or not appropriately, covered. That is why we have dealt, for example, with process verbs like 'take' or 'receive', but not with transaction verbs like 'give' or 'buy': whereas the former provide conceptual sources for possessive expressions, the latter do not. One might also wonder why, in a work devoted to possession, the concern has been with notions such as action, location, accompaniment, and the like. It is hoped that the preceding chapters have made it clear that possession, as we encounter it in linguistic discourse, is not an independent and self-contained domain, but rather exhibits a number of systematic relationships with other domains of human conceptualization. While it may be said to be a universal concept, in that all societies we are familiar with have conventionalized expressions for it, these expressions can universally be traced to non-possessive expressions for a small pool of concrete schematic experiences.

Discussions of possession and/or ownership have occasionally focussed on issues concerning the relationship between language structure and extra-linguistic human behaviour. One of these issues centres around the question of whether linguistics might not shed light on the evolution of mankind, for example, whether earlier generations of mankind might not have conceptualized possession differently from the way modern societies do. According to a widespread thesis expounded in established circles of Indo-Europeanists and other philological traditions, 'primitive societies' lack grammaticalized expressions for possession, or else have a different understanding of it. For Isačenko (1974b:64), for example, possession proper 'is a legal notion appearing in societies after they have reached a certain stage of development', and he is therefore not surprised that he fails to reconstruct a 'have'-verb for Proto-Indo-European.

Another, related, claim has it that the spread of the Action Schema in the languages of western societies has had to do with the development of 'active' modes of social and economic interaction, more particularly with the rise of capitalism. Finally, according to a third thesis, the development from concrete possession (e.g. *He has two cars*) to abstract possession (*He has two problems*) is a characteristic of western societies (Meillet 1923; Creissels 1996:150–1) and is indicative of the 'alienation' that these societies have experienced (Fromm 1976).

We have found no empirical substantiation for any of these theses. The grammaticalization of the Action Schema is not confined to the western world. As we saw in the preceding chapters, it is also found in other parts of the world where quite different social, economic, and technological conditions obtain. Also, abstract possession is in no way a characteristic of languages like English and German but may be found in much the same way in other languages (cf. Creissels 1996).

These, as well as many other generalizations that have been proposed on

5.5 Conclusions 235

extra-linguistic correlates of possessive constructions suffer from what one might call the 'literal meaning fallacy'. A given linguistic expression, it is argued, has a basic or literal meaning, and, whenever that expression is found to have other meanings in addition, this fact is taken as evidence for speculations on the mental, cultural, social, and other attributes presumed to be characteristic of the people using that expression. What is ignored in this kind of research in particular is, first, that in many languages worldwide abstract concepts like possession are expressed by exploiting a small pool of concrete source structures.

Second, the transfer from source structures to the target structures of possession leads to the emergence of chain-like linguistic structures: possessive constructions are part of more extensive grammaticalization chains. A simplified form of these chains is sketched in (17), where P_1, P_2, etc., stand for the various possessive notions distinguished in chapter 1.3, X for the source schemas discussed in chapter 2.1, and Y for schematic contents arising from the grammaticalization of possessive constructions, such as the existential or aspectual concepts that we discussed in chapter 4.

(17) $X > P_1 > P_2 \ldots > P_n > Y$

The grammaticalization chain associated with a given linguistic form may cover any sub-range of concepts figuring in (17). If, in addition to one or more of the possessive notions, it also includes either X or Y, as is frequently the case, then the form concerned is 'polysemous' to the extent that it has both possessive and non-possessive uses. To conclude, the fact that expressions for possession are also used to convey other meanings can be accounted for in a principled way by reference to the cognitive forces that gave rise to them; it need not, and frequently is not, suggestive of any specific mental, cultural, or other forces.

A question that may arise in this connection is whether possession belongs to, or should be treated within, the domain of the lexicon or that of grammar. Closely related to this issue is the following question that we alluded to in the introductory chapter (1.2): are verbs meaning 'have' less meaningful than other verbs? Is English *have* meaningless, as Bach (1967:476–7) claims, or is its semantic content comparable to that of other verbs, as others have argued (see Brugman 1988:41ff.)? An answer to this question crucially depends on the theoretical framework one adopts. On the basis of the present framework one may say that possession is located along a conceptual chain that is lexical at one end and grammatical at the other. With reference to the chain in (17), this means that X is located at the lexical end, and the further one moves towards Y the more one approaches the grammatical end of the chain. The English item *have* covers a wide spectrum of uses along the chain in (17). In utterances like *He has two cars* its use is located somewhere in the center of the chain, while in utterances like *He has left* or *He has to leave* it is located in the Y region.

In chapter 1 we mentioned the view expressed by Bickerton (1990:56–7) according to which English *have* is an odd verb since it can appear in a wide variety of contexts, and express a variety of very different relations. We tried to account for this 'oddness' with reference to some basic principles of grammaticalization. In a simplified manner one could say this 'oddness' is due to the fact that, rather than having been invented by modern speakers of English, the verb *have* and its various use patterns are the historical product of cognitive forces that are the same across languages, and that are by no means confined to this verb, or to the domain of possession as a whole for that matter (see Heine, Claudi, and Hünnemeyer 1991).

A number of detailed treatments have become available on the subject-matter discussed here (see especially Locker 1954, Benveniste 1960, Ultan 1978, Clark 1978, Seiler 1983, Wilson 1983, Hengeveld 1992) and in most of these studies, the relationship between 'be'- and 'have'-constructions was an issue of major concern. With few exceptions, such as Locker (1954) and Claudi (1986), no attempt has been made in those studies to account for this relationship in terms of conceptual transfer patterns, in short, with reference to grammaticalization. As we tried to demonstrate in chapter 2.7, these patterns are diachronic in nature, but, since diachronic processes tend to be retained in the synchronic state of a given language in the form of contextually defined variation, they are in much the same way an issue of synchronic description. This fact has been ignored in much of the literature of mainstream structural linguistics, be it Bloomfieldian or Chomskyan.

Our main interest in this work has been with cross-linguistic generalizations relating to a fairly complex subject area. It goes without saying that a number of questions could not be addressed, such as the following: What makes schema X, rather than Y, eligible for a specific grammatical concept? Are there any correlations between a given source schema and a specific kind of possessive concept? For example, how does the distinction between alienable and inalienable possession relate to the distinction between source schemas? A few generalizations were proposed in chapter 2.3, but a more extensive treatment is urgently required. Furthermore, no attempt was made to deal with the question of what our findings mean with reference to the distinction made by earlier generative grammarians between surface structure and deep/underlying structure. Whether 'have'-verbs, or 'be'-verbs for that matter, are deep-structural entities, as some have claimed, or else must be introduced as formatives via transformations or any other operations, is an issue that is outside the scope of this work.

Another issue concerns the question of why the source schemas discussed in chapter 2 are grammaticalized exactly the way they are. For example, with regard to the Companion Schema, why is it normally the case that the structure *X is with Y* turns into the structure *Possessor is with Possessee* rather than *Possessee is with Possessor*? Conversely, why does the use of the Location Schema inevitably lead to a development from *Y is located at X* to *Possessee is located where the Possessor is*, rather than to *Possessor is located where the Possessee is*? There are possible answers, still, a more comprehensive understanding of these patterns of grammaticalization, especially of the expectation norms associated with situations such as those described by these source schemas, is urgently required.

We have confined ourselves mainly to one type of category, viz. predicative possession. But many of the generalizations made also hold true for other kinds of categories. For example, as we have shown elsewhere, four different event schemas can be held responsible for the structure of comparative constructions in the vast majority of languages (Heine 1994a), and most of the auxiliaries used for the expression of aspect and tense in the languages of the world can be traced back to ten basic event schemas (Heine 1993). What is perhaps even more noteworthy is that it is always the same concrete source schemas that are recruited as structural templates for the expression of more abstract meanings. Thus, schemas like Action (what one does), Location (where one is located), Motion (where one moves from/to), or Companion (who one is accompanied by or associated with), can be expected to provide the most convenient and the most frequently employed templates – not only for the expression of possession but also for expressing grammatical categories like perfect/anterior, or progressive, or for comparative concepts. And it is always the same linguistic process that is triggered. One characteristic of this process can be seen in the fact that it involves an overlap stage, where the expression concerned can be interpreted simultaneously with reference to both the source meaning and the target meaning, that is, where there is ambiguity between the two meanings. Thus, rather than being unusual or abnormal, ambiguity constitutes a predictable component in the development and uses of 'have'-constructions.

The observations just made are also relevant in a number of ways for diachronic reconstruction. On the one hand, they provide new insights for evaluating previous reconstructions. A common assumption made, for example, in some of the Indo-European works cited in the preceding chapters is that if one finds neighbouring languages or language groups sharing some structural property then the most obvious explanation for this fact would be in terms of a historical relationship, be that areal or genetic relationship. Our findings on grammaticalization suggest that such an assumption has to be taken with care. If, for example, two areally and/or genetically related languages both use a 'have'-construction derived from Location, then such a structural similarity need not be due to historical relationship. Rather, the speakers of these two languages may have chosen one and the same conceptual source independent of each other. The pool of sources serving the development of a given grammatical category is fairly small and, hence, there is a certain degree of probability that the same sources are recruited independently of one another.

Another point may be illustrated with an example from Oceanic linguistics. Lynch (1982) argues that the present-day constructions of attributive possession to be found in Oceanic languages derive historically from verbal structures in Proto-Oceanic, which is the hypothetical ancestor of this group of the Austronesian family. For example, the origin of modern patterns of general possession is claimed to have involved a clausal structure consisting of a 'zero' ditransitive verb, an unspecified subject, a direct object encoding the possessee, and an indirect object encoding the possessor. Such a hypothesis is not compatible with any of the source schemas of possession identified in chapter 2; ditransitive verbs, for example, are not found to provide cross-linguistically relevant sources for possession. Hence Lynch's claim is not very likely to reflect historical reality (cf. Pawley 1973:153ff.; Lichtenberk 1985:126–8). Thus, the findings made here can be of use in diachronic reconstruction when it comes to deciding whether a given hypothesis is more plausible than some alternative hypothesis.

The Oceanic group of languages provides yet another example of the uses that the observations made in this work may have. We saw in chapter 2 that one of the most popular structural templates employed for the creation of both predicative and attributive possession is provided by the Location Schema, whereby possessive concepts are expressed in terms of locative structures. With reference to historical reconstruction this means that, for example, if we find in a given language a morpheme that is used to denote both a locative and a possessive relation then we can reconstruct a situation according to which the locative sense is older than the possessive one. We may therefore argue that the locative uses of the German item *von* ('from'), or of the Romance item *de*, are older than the uses of these items in attributive possession ('of'). Similarly, the locative uses of the French preposition *à* must have predated its possessive uses. Now, in Oceanic languages like Babatana and Roviana there is an item *ta* used as a linker in constructions of attributive possession ('of'). This item is reconstructed as a Proto-Oceanic preposition **ta* marking spatial relations, location, or place of origin, while its possessive uses are postulated to be later innovations (see especially Pawley 1973:149). Such a reconstruction based on diachronic comparison could, in fact, have been predicted on the basis of the framework that has emerged in the course of the preceding chapters.

Finally, the observations made in this book explain why any attempt at setting up one single universal structure of predicative possession, to account for all the morphosyntactic variation to be found in the languages of the world, is doomed to failure. Such attempts have been made time and again in the history of linguistics; we dealt with a few examples in 5.1 above. The observations made here likewise show why a number of other generalizations proposed for 'have'-constructions are not tenable. For example, in his worldwide survey of 'have'-constructions, Ultan (1978:37) concludes that if we find a subject-marked possessor then this implies a comitative-marked possessee, which, if translated into our terminology, means that the Companion Schema would be the only source for possessors encoded as subjects. This claim can easily be falsified since, as we saw, there is a second schema that gives rise to possessors marked as sentence-subjects, namely the Action Schema. Predictably therefore, European languages like English, German, French, or Spanish, whose major source schema for 'have'-constructions is derived historically from the Action Schema, have subject-marked possessors but not comitative-marked possessive expressions.

Appendix: A world-wide survey of 'have'-constructions

(Sample: 100 languages. Only major schemas considered; for details, see section 2.1).

Language	Genetic affiliation	Reference	Source schema
Amharic	Semitic, Afro-Asiatic	Otten 1992	Location
Anywa	Nilotic, Nilo-Saharan	Reh 1994a	Genitive, Goal
Apalai	Carib	Stassen 1995	Topic
Palestinian Arabic	Semitic, Afro-Asiatic	Freeze 1992	Goal
Armenian	Indo-European	Seiler 1983	Genitive
Baagandji	Pama-Nyungan, Australian	Hercus 1982	Action
Bambara	Mande, Niger-Congo	Bird 1972	Location
Basque	Unaffiliated	Saltarelli et al. 1988	Opaque
Karo Batak	West Indonesian, Austronesian	Stassen 1995	Genitive
Beja	Cushitic, Afro-Asiatic	Otten 1992	Opaque
Belorussian	Slavic, Indo-European	Orr 1992	Action, Location
Moroccan Berber	Berber, Afro-Asiatic	Locker 1954	Location
Bisa	Gur, Niger-Congo	Naden 1982	Genitive
Breton	Celtic, Indo-European	Orr 1992	Goal
Buduma	Chadic, Afro-Asiatic	Otten 1992	Location
Cahuilla	Takic, Uto-Aztecan	Seiler 1983	Topic
Mandarin Chinese	Sinitic, Sino-Tibetan	Hengeveld 1992	Topic

Language	Genetic affiliation	Reference	Source schema
Comanche	Numic, Uto-Aztecan	Robinson et al. 1990	Opaque
Daza	Saharan, Nilo-Saharan	Otten 1992	Action
Deiga	Kordofanian, Niger-Kordofanian	Reh 1994b	Location
Djerma	Songhai, Nilo-Saharan	Otten 1992	Goal, Companion
Dullay	Cushitic, Afro-Asiatic	Amborn, Minker, and Sasse 1980	Action
Dutch	Germanic, Indo-European	Janssen 1993	Action
Efik	Benue-Congo, Niger-Congo	Otten 1992	Action
Egyptian, Late	Afro-Asiatic	Erman 1933	Location
Estonian	Finnic, Uralic-Yukaghir	Lehiste 1969	Location
Ewe	Kwa, Niger-Congo	Westermann 1907	Location, Goal
Finnish	Finnic, Uralic Yukaghir	Freeze 1992	Location
Fur	Fur, Nilo-Saharan	Otten 1992	Companion
Old Georgian	South Caucasian	Stolz 1995	Goal
Gola	West Atlantic, Niger-Congo	Otten 1992	Action
Hausa	Chadic, Afro-Asiatic	Wolff 1993	Companion
Hebrew, modern	Semitic, Afro-Asiatic	Glinert 1989	Goal
Hindi	Indic, Indo-European	Locker 1954	Location
Hittite	Indo-European	Benveniste 1960	Goal
Huailu	Oceanic, Austronesian	Locker 1954	Genitive
Hungarian	Uralic, Uralic-Yukaghir	Biermann 1985	Goal
Igbo	Kwa, Niger-Congo	Otten 1992	Action
Japanese	Korean-Japanese, Altaic	Makino 1968	Goal

Language	Genetic affiliation	Reference	Source schema
Kabiye	Gur, Niger-Congo	Otten 1992	Companion
Kafa	Omotic, Afro-Asiatic	Otten 1992	Action, Goal
Kanuri	Saharan, Nilo-Saharan	Hutchinson 1980; Cyffer (p.c.)	Genitive
Kashmiri	Indic, Indo-European	Kachru 1968	Goal
Kawaiisu	Numic, Uto-Aztecan	Munro 1990	Opaque
K'ekchi'	Mayan, Penutian	Freeze 1992	Genitive
Kobon	Papuan	Stassen 1995	Topic
Korean	Korean-Japanese, Altaic	Sohn 1994	Location
Kpelle	Mande, Niger-Congo	Otten 1992	Location
Krongo	Kordofanian, Niger-Kordofanian	Reh 1985	Opaque
Kurdish	Iranian, Indo-European	Benveniste 1960	Goal
Lezgian	Caucasian	Haspelmath 1993	Goal, Location
Limbu	Tibeto-Burman, Sino-Tibetan	van Driem 1987	Topic
Malay	Malayo-Polynesian, Austronesian	Locker 1954	Goal
Malayalam	Dravidian, Elamo-Dravidian	Asher 1968	Goal
Maltese	Semitic, Afro-Asiatic	Ultan 1978	Location
Mandarin, see Chinese			
Manja	Adamawa-Ubangi, Niger-Congo	Otten 1992	Location
Masalit	Maban, Nilo-Saharan	Otten 1992	Action
Mixtec	Zapotecan, Oto-Manguean	Stolz 1995	Companion
Mokilese	Oceanic, Austronesian	Stolz 1995	Companion
Mongolian	Altaic proper, Altaic	Locker 1954, Stolz 1995	Location
Mupun	Chadic, Afro-Asiatic	Frajzyngier 1993	Companion
Nama	Central Khoisan, Khoisan	Heinz Roberg, p.c.	Action

Language	Genetic affiliation	Reference	Source schema
Nasioi	Papuan	Hengeveld 1992	Goal, Genitive
Newari	Tibeto-Burman, Sino-Tibetan	Malla 1985	Location
Nupe	Kwa, Niger-Congo	Otten 1992	Opaque
Panjabi	Indic, Indo-European	Ultan 1978	Location
Pipil	Aztecan, Uto-Aztecan	Campbell 1985	Action
Polish	Slavic, Indo-European	Orr 1992	Action
Portuguese	Romance, Indo-European	Freeze 1992	Action
Qawasqar	Southern, Andean	Stolz 1995	Companion
Bolivian Quechua	Quechuan, Andean	Bills, Vallejo, and Troike 1969	Goal
Rengao	Mon-Khmer, Austroasiatic	Gregerson 1979	Goal
Rotuman	Central Pacific, Austronesian	Stassen 1995	Companion
Selkup	Samoyed, Uralic-Yukaghir	Erdélyi 1970	Action
Slave	Athabaskan, Na-Dene	Rice 1989	Source
So	Kuliak, Nilo-Saharan	Carlin 1993	Location
Tagalog	Meso-Philippine, Austronesian	Freeze 1992	Location
Tahitian	Oceanic, Austronesian	Locker 1954	Goal
Tamil	Dravidian, Elamo-Dravidian	Ultan 1978; Hengeveld 1992	Goal
Telugu	Dravidian, Elamo-Dravidian	Bhaskararao 1972	Goal
Thai (Siamese)	Austro-Tai, Austric	Locker 1954	Topic
Tolai	Oceanic, Austronesian	Mosel 1983	Genitive
Tondano	Philippine, Austronesian	Stassen 1995	Topic
Tongan	Oceanic, Austronesian	Freeze 1992	Genitive

244 *Appendix*

Language	*Genetic affiliation*	*Reference*	*Source schema*
Toradja	East Indonesian, Austronesian	Stassen 1995	Topic
Turkish	Turkic, Altaic	Lyons 1968a	Genitive
Tzutujil	Mayan, Penutian	Dayley 1985	Topic
Ukrainian	Slavic, Indo-European	Orr 1992	Action
Uradhi	Austronesian	Stolz 1995	Companion
Urubu-Kaapor	Tupi-Guarani	Stassen 1995	Genitive
Venda	Bantu, Niger-Congo	Poulos 1990	Companion
Welsh	Celtic, Indo-European	Orr 1992	Location
Yanomama	Chibchan, Chibchan-Paezan	Migliazza 1972	Genitive
Yaqui	Taracahitic, Uto-Aztecan	Jelinek and Escalante 1988	Opaque
Yimas	Papuan	Foley 1991	Companion
Yucatec	Mayan, Penutian	Freeze 1992	Location
Yurak	Samoyed, Uralic-Yukaghir	Collinder 1957	Genitive
Ixtlan Zapotec	Zapotecan, Oto-Manguean	Stassen 1995	Topic
//Ani	Central Khoisan, Khoisan	Claudi 1986	Companion

References

Abbott, Miriam 1991. Macushi. In: Derbyshire and Pullum (eds.) 1991. Pp. 23–160.
Agel, Vilmos 1993. *Valenzrealisierung, Finites Substantiv und Dependenz in der deutschen Nominalphrase.* (Kölner Linguistische Arbeiten – Germanistik, 29.) Hürth: Gabel.
Agheyisi, Rebecca Nogieru 1971. West African Pidgin English: Simplification and simplicity. Ph.D. Dissertation, Stanford University. Ann Arbor, Michigan: University Microfilms.
Allen, W. Sidney 1964. Transitivity and possession. *Language* 40,3:337–43.
Amborn, Hermann, Gunter Minker, and Hans-Jürgen Sasse 1980. *Das Dullay: Materialien zu einer ostkuschitischen Sprachgruppe.* (Kölner Beiträge zur Afrikanistik, 6.) Berlin: Dietrich Reimer.
Ameka, Felix K. 1991. Ewe: Its grammatical constructions and illocutionary devices. Ph.D. Dissertation, Canberra: Australian National University.
— 1996. Body parts in Ewe grammar. In: Chappell and McGregor (eds.) 1996a. Pp. 783–840.
Anderson, John M. 1971. *The grammar of case: Towards a localistic theory.* Cambridge University Press.
— 1973. *An essay concerning aspect: Some considerations of a general character arising from the Abbé Darrigol's analysis of the Basque verb.* (Janua Linguarum, Series Minor, 167.) The Hague, Paris: Mouton.
— 1979. Serialization, dependency, and the syntax of possessives in Moru. *Studia Linguistica* 33,1:1–25.
Anderson, Lloyd B. 1974. The part–whole squish, main vs. subsidiary predications. *Chicago Linguistic Society* 10:1–16.
— 1975. Grammar-meaning universals and proto-language reconstruction or, Proto-World NOW! *Chicago Linguistic Society* 11:15–36.
Anderson, R. C., R. J. Spiro, and W. E. Montague (eds.) 1977. *Schooling and the acquisition of knowledge.* Hillsdale, N.J.: Erlbaum.
Antal, L. 1964. The possessive form of the Hungarian noun. *Linguistics* 3:50–61.
Arends, Jaques 1982. Een typologie van bezitsaanduidende constructies. Doctoral Dissertation, Katholieke Universiteit Nijmegen.
Aristar, Anthony Rodrigues 1991. On diachronic sources and synchronic pattern: An investigation into the origin of linguistic universals. *Language* 67,1:1–33.
Asher, R. E. 1968. Existential, possessive, locative and copulative sentences in Malayalam. In: Verhaar (ed.) 1968a. Pp. 88–111.

References

Austin, Peter 1981. *A grammar of Diyari, South Australia.* (Cambridge Studies in Linguistics, 32.) Cambridge University Press.
Bach, Emmon 1967. *Have* and *be* in English syntax. *Language* 43,2:462–85.
Bach, Emmon and Robert T. Harms (eds.) 1968. *Universals in linguistic theory.* New York: Holt, Rinehart and Winston.
Bahr, Donald M. 1986. Pima-Papago *-ga*, 'alienability'. *International Journal of American Linguistics* 52,2:161–71.
Bally, Charles 1926. L'expression des idées de sphère personelle et de solidarité dans les langues indo-européennes. In: Fankhauser and Jud (eds.) 1926. Pp. 68–78.
Bargery, G. P. 1934. *A Hausa-English dictionary and English-Hausa vocabulary.* Oxford University Press.
Barshi, Immanuel & Doris Payne 1996. The interpretation of 'possessor raising' in a Maasai dialect. *AAP* (Afrikanistische Arbeitspapiere, Cologne) 45:207–26.
Bartlett, Frederic C. 1932. *Remembering: A study in experimental and social psychology.* Cambridge University Press.
Bavin, Edith 1996. Body parts in Acholi: Alienable and inalienable distinctions and extended uses. In: Chappell and McGregor (eds.) 1996a. Pp. 841–64.
Bendix, Edward Herman 1966. *Componential analysis of general vocabulary: The semantic structure of a set of verbs in English, Hindi, and Japanese.* Bloomington: Indiana University Press.
Benveniste, Emile 1960. 'Etre' et 'avoir' dans leurs fonctions linguistiques. *Bulletin de la Société de Linguistique de Paris* 55,1:113–34. Reprinted in *Problèmes de linguistique générale.* Paris: Gallimard, 1966.
Bhaskararao, Peri 1972. On the syntax of Telugu existential and copulative predications. In: Verhaar (ed.) 1972. Pp. 153–206.
Bickerton, Derek 1981. *Roots of language.* Ann Arbor: Karoma Publishers, Inc.
  1990. *Language & species.* University of Chicago Press.
Biermann, Anna 1985. *Possession und Zuschreibung im Ungarischen.* (Continuum – Schriftenreihe zur Linguistik, 4.) Tübingen: Gunter Narr.
Bierwisch, Manfred (ed.) 1965. *Syntaktische Studien.* (Studia Grammatica, 5.) Berlin: Akademie-Verlag.
Bills, Garland D., Bernardo Vallejo C., and Rudolph C. Troike 1969. *An introduction to spoken Bolivian Quechua.* Austin, London: University of Texas Press.
Bird, Charles S. 1972. *The syntax and semantics of possession in Bambara.* Paper presented at the Conference on Manding Studies, London 1972.
Blake, Barry J. 1984. Problems of possessor ascension: Some Australian examples. *Linguistics* 22:437–53.
  1990. *Relational grammar.* London: Routledge.
  1994. *Case.* Cambridge University Press.
Boeder, Winfried 1980. 'Haben' in den Kartwelsprachen. In: Lehmann and Brettschneider (eds.) 1980. Pp. 207–17.
Bolkestein, Machtelt 1983. Genitive and dative possessors in Latin. In: Dik (ed.) 1983. Pp. 55–91.
Bonneau, José and Pierre Pica 1995. *From 'appertainence' to possession: Predicative and internally-headed relative constructions in French nominals.* Paper presented

at the Annual Meeting of the Societas Linguistica Europaea, 31 August to 2 September, 1995, University of Leiden.

Borillo, Andrée 1996. La relation partie-tout et la structure [N1 à N2] en français. In: *La relation d'appartenance.* (Faits de langues, 7.) Paris: Ophrys. Pp. 111–20.

Bowe, Heather J. 1990. *Categories, constituents and constituent order in Pitjantjatjara.* London, New York: Routledge.

Bowers, J. S. 1975. Some adjectival nominalizations in English. *Lingua* 37:341–61.

Brauner, Siegmund 1993. *Einführung ins Schona.* (Afrikawissenschaftliche Lehrbücher, 5.) Cologne: Rüdiger Köppe.

Brinkmann, Hennig 1959. Die 'haben'-Perspektive im Deutschen. In: *Sprache – Schlüssel zur Welt: Festschrift für Leo Weisgerber.* Düsseldorf: Schwann. Pp. 176–94.

Brugman, Claudia Marlea 1988. *The syntax and semantics of HAVE and its complements.* Ph.D. Dissertation, University of California, Berkeley.

Buck, Carl Darling 1949. *A dictionary of selected synonyms in the principal Indo-European languages: A contribution to the history of ideas.* University of Chicago Press.

Bugenhagen, Robert D. 1986. Possession in Mangap-Mbula: Its syntax and semantics. *Oceanic Linguistics* 25,1/2:124–66.

Burridge, Kate 1990. Sentence datives and the grammaticization of the dative possessive: Evidence from Germanic. *La Trobe University Working Papers in Linguistics* 3:29–47.

Byarushengo, Ernest Rugwa Alessandro Duranti, and Larry M. Hyman (eds.) 1977. *Haya grammatical structure.* (Southern California Occasional Papers in Linguistics, 6.) June 1977. Los Angeles: University of Southern California.

Bybee, Joan L. 1985. *Morphology: A study of the relation between meaning and form.* (Typological Studies in Language, 9.) Amsterdam, Philadelphia: John Benjamins.

Bybee, Joan L. and Östen Dahl 1989. The creation of tense and aspect systems in the languages of the world. *Studies in Language* 13,1:51–103.

Bybee, Joan L. and William Pagliuca 1985. Cross linguistic comparison and the development of grammatical meaning. In: Fišiak, Jaček (ed.) 1985. Pp. 59–83.

Bybee, Joan L., William Pagliuca and Revere D. Perkins 1991. Back to the future. In: Traugott and Heine (eds.) 1991b. Pp. 17–58.

Bybee, Joan L., Revere D. Perkins and William Pagliuca 1994. *The evolution of grammar: Tense, aspect, and modality in the languages of the world.* University of Chicago Press.

Bynon, Theodora 1994. Syntactic reconstruction. *The encyclopaedia of language and linguistics.* Volume 2. Oxford, New York, Seoul, Tokyo: Pergamon Press. Pp. 4468–75.

Campbell, Lyle 1985. *The Pipil language of El Salvador.* (Mouton Grammar Library, 1.) Berlin, New York, Amsterdam: Mouton.

Capell, A. 1949. The concept of ownership in the languages of Australia and the Pacific. *Southwestern Journal of Anthropology* 5,3:169–89.

Carlin, Eithne 1993. *The So language.* (AMO, Afrikanistische Monographien, 2.) Cologne: Universität zu Köln.

References

Casagrande, J. B. and Kenneth L. Hale 1967. Semantic relations in Papago folk definitions. In: Hymes and Bittle (eds.) 1967. Pp. 165–96.

Chapin, Paul G. Easter Island: A characteristic VSO language. In: Lehmann (ed.) 1978. Pp. 139–68.

Chappell, Hilary 1996. Inalienability and the personal domain in Mandarin Chinese discourse. In: Chappell and McGregor (eds.) 1996a. Pp. 465–527.

Chappell, Hilary and William McGregor 1989. Alienability, inalienability and nominal classification. *Berkeley Linguistics Society* 15:24–36.

Chappell, Hilary and William McGregor (eds.) 1996a. *The grammar of inalienability: A typological perspective on body part terms and the part-whole relation.* Berlin, New York: Mouton de Gruyter.

Chappell, Hilary and William McGregor 1996b. Prolegomena to a theory of inalienability. In: Chappell and McGregor (eds.) 1996a. Pp. 3–30.

Chomsky, Noam 1965. *Aspects of the theory of syntax.* Cambridge, Mass.: MIT Press.

1972. Remarks on nominalization. *Studies on semantics in generative grammar.* The Hague: Mouton. Pp. 11–61.

Christie, J. 1970. Locative, possessive and existential in Swahili. *Foundations of Language* 6:166–77.

Cienki, Alan 1994. *The semantics of possessive and spatial constructions in Russian and Bulgarian: A comparative analysis in cognitive grammar.* Typescript, Department of Russian Studies, Emory University, Atlanta, Georgia.

Clark, Eve V. 1970. Locationals: A study of 'existential,' 'locative,' and 'possessive' sentences. *Stanford University Working Papers in Language Universals* 3:1–36.

1978. Locationals: Existential, locative, and possessive constructions. In Greenberg (ed.) 1978b. Pp. 85–126.

Clasen, Bernd 1981. Inhärenz und Etablierung. *AKUP* (Arbeiten des Kölner Universalien-Projekts) 41. Cologne: Universität zu Köln.

Claudi, Ulrike 1986. To have or not to have: on the conceptual base of predicative possession in some African languages. Typescript, University of Cologne.

1993. *Die Stellung von Verb und Objekt in Niger-Kongo-Sprachen: Ein Beitrag zur Rekonstruktion historischer Syntax.* (AMO, Afrikanistische Monographien, 1.) Cologne: Universität zu Köln, Institut für Afrikanistik.

1994. Word order change as category change: The Mande case. In: Pagliuca (ed.) 1994. Pp. 191–231.

1995. *Die Beziehung zwischen Relativsatz und Genitivattribut im Amharischen.* In: Sprachkulturelle und historische Forschungen in Afrika. Beiträge zum 11. Afrikanistentag Köln, 19.–21. Sept. 1994. Ed. by Axel Fleisch & Dirk Otten. Cologne: Köppe. Pp. 91–102.

Claudi, Ulrike and Bernd Heine 1985. From metaphor to grammar: some examples from Ewe. *AAP* (Afrikanistische Arbeitspapiere) 1:17–54.

1986. On the metaphorical base of grammar. *Studies in Language* 10,2:297–335.

1989. On the nominal morphology of 'alienability' in some African languages. In: Newman and Botne (eds.) 1989. Pp. 3–19.

Claudi, Ulrike and Fritz Serzisko 1985. Possession in Dizi: Inalienable or not? *Journal of African Languages and Linguistics* 7,2:131–54.

Colby, Benjamin N., James W. Fernandez, and David B. Kronenfeld 1981. Toward a convergence of cognitive and symbolic anthropology. *American Ethnologist* 8,3:422–50.
Cole, Desmond T. 1955. *An introduction to Tswana grammar.* Cape Town: Longman Penguin South Africa.
Cole, Peter (ed.) 1976. *Studies in modern Hebrew syntax and semantics: The transformational generative approach.* Amsterdam, New York, Oxford: North-Holland.
Collinder, Björn 1957. *Survey of the Uralic languages.* Stockholm: Almqvist and Wiksell.
Comrie, Bernard 1981. *Language universals and linguistic typology: Syntax and morphology.* Oxford: Basil Blackwell.
Corbett, Greville G. 1991. *Gender.* (Cambridge Textbooks in Linguistics.) Cambridge University Press.
Crazzolara, J. P. 1933. *Outlines of a Nuer grammar.* (Linguistische Anthropos-Bibliothek, XIII.) Vienna: Anthropos.
Creissels, D. 1979. Le comitatif, la coordination et les constructions dites 'possessives' dans quelques langues africaines. *Annales de l'Université d'Abidjan*, Série H. Linguistique, 12,1:125–44.
 1996. Remarques sur l'émergence de verbes *avoir* au cours de l'histoire des langues. In: *La relation d'appartenance.* (Faits de langues, 7.) Paris: Ophrys. Pp. 149–58.
Croft, William 1985. Indirect object 'lowering'. *Berkeley Linguistics Society* 11:39–51.
 1991. *Typology and universals.* Cambridge University Press.
Crowley, Terry 1996. Inalienable possession in Paamese. In: Chappell and McGregor (eds.) 1996a. Pp. 383–432.
Cyffer, Norbert 1991. *We learn Kanuri.* (Afrikawissenschaftliche Lehrbücher, 2.) Cologne: Rüdiger Köppe.
Dal, I. 1952. *Kurze deutsche Syntax.* Tübingen: Niemeyer.
Davies, William D. 1984. Inalienable possession and Choctaw referential coding. *International Journal of American Linguistics* 50,4:384–402.
Dayley, Jon P. 1985. *Tzutujil grammar.* (University of California Publications in Linguistics, 107.) Berkeley, Los Angeles, London: University of California Press.
Deane, Paul 1987. English possessives, topicality, and the Silverstein hierarchy. *Berkeley Linguistics Society* 13:65–76.
Deeters, Gerhard 1954. 'Haben' im Georgischen. In: *Sprachgeschichte* 1954. Pp. 109–19.
Demiraj, Shaban 1985. About the origin of the possessive perfect in Albanian and some other languages. (Sprachwissenschaftliche Forschungen: Festschrift für Johannes Knobloch.) *Innsbrucker Beiträge zur Kulturwissenschaft* 23:81–5.
Derbyshire, Desmond C. and Geoffrey K. Pullum (eds.) 1991. *Handbook of Amazonian languages.* Vol. 3. Berlin, New York: Mouton de Gruyter.
Devitt, Dan 1990. The diachronic development of semantics in copulas. *Berkeley Linguistics Society* 16:102–15.

Diem, Werner 1986. Alienable und inalienable Possession im Semitischen. *Zeitschrift der Deutschen Morgenländischen Gesellschaft* 136,2:227-91.
Dik, Simon C. (ed.) 1983. *Advances in functional grammar.* Dordrecht: Foris.
Dimmendaal, Gerrit Jan 1983. *The Turkana language.* Dordrecht, Cinnaminson: Foris Publications.
— 1993. *Conversational implicatures, metonymy, and attitude markers in Turkana speech acts.* Typescript, Leiden, The Netherlands.
Diver, William 1964. The system of agency of the Latin noun. *Word* 20:178–96.
Dixon, Robert M. W. 1980. *The languages of Australia.* Cambridge University Press.
Dixon, Robert M. W. and Barry Blake (eds.) 1979. *Handbook of Australian languages.* Vol. 1. Canberra: The Australian National University.
Doke, Clement M. 1930. *Textbook of Zulu grammar.* Cape Town: Maskew Miller.
Driem, George van 1987. *A grammar of Limbu.* Berlin, New York, Amsterdam: Mouton de Gruyter.
Duridanov, Ivan 1956. Kăm problemata za razvoja na bălgarskija ezik ot sintetizăm kăm analitizăm. Godišnik na Sofiskija Universitet, Filologičeski fakultet 51 (1955), Sofia.
Durie, Mark and Malcolm Ross (eds.) 1996. *The comparative method reviewed.* Oxford University Press.
Erdélyi, István 1970. *Selkupisches Wörterverzeichnis. Tas-Dialekt.* (Indiana University Publications, Uralic and Altaic Series, 103.) The Hague: Mouton.
Erman, Adolf 1933. *Neuaegyptische Grammatik.* Leipzig: Engelmann.
Fankhauser, F. and Jakob Jud (eds.) 1926. *Festschrift Louis Gauchat.* Aarau: Verlag Sauerländer and Co.
Ferguson, Charles A. 1978. Historical background of universals research. In: Greenberg, Ferguson and Moravcsik (eds.) 1978. Pp. 7–31.
Fillmore, Charles J. 1968. The case for case. In: Bach and Harms (eds.) 1968. Pp. 1–88.
Fišiak, Jaček (ed.) 1985. *Historical semantics, historical word formation.* Berlin: Mouton de Gruyter.
Fleischman, Suzanne 1982a. *The future in thought and language: Diachronic evidence from Romance.* (Cambridge Studies in Linguistics, 36.) Cambridge University Press.
— 1982b. The past and the future: Are they coming or going? *Berkeley Linguistics Society* 8:322–34.
Flier, Michael S. (ed.) 1974. *Slavic Forum: Essays in linguistics and literature.* (Slavistic Printings and Reprintings, 277.) The Hague/Paris: Mouton.
Foley, William A. 1991. *The Yimas language of New Guinea.* Stanford University Press.
Fortescue, Michael 1984. *West Greenlandic.* (Descriptive Grammars.) London, Sydney, Dover, New Hampshire: Croom Helm.
Fortune, G. 1968. Predication of 'being' in Shona. In: Verhaar (ed.) 1968b. Pp. 110–25.
Fox, Barbara 1981. Body part syntax: Towards a universal characterization. *Studies in Language* 5,3:323–42.
Frajzyngier, Zygmunt 1983. Marking syntactic relationship in Proto-Chadic. In: Wolff, E. and H. Meyer-Bahlburg (eds.) 1983. Pp. 115–38.

1987. Encoding locative in Chadic. *Journal of West African Languages* 17,1:81–97.

1993. *A grammar of Mupun*. (Sprache und Oralität in Afrika, 14.) Berlin: Dietrich Reimer.

Freeze, Ray 1992. Existentials and other locatives. *Language* 68,3:553–95.

Friedländer, Marianne 1992. *Lehrbuch des Malinke*. Leipzig, Berlin, München, Wien, Zürich, New York: Langenscheidt.

Fritze, Marie-Elisabeth 1976. Bezeichnungen für den Zugehörigkeits- und Herkunftsbereich beim substantivischen Attribut. In: Kettmann and Schildt (eds.) 1976. Pp. 417–76.

Fromm, Erich 1976. *To have or to be?* New York, Hagerstown, San Francisco, London: Harper and Row.

Geider, Thomas H. and Raimund Kastenholz (eds.) 1994. *Sprachen und Sprachzeugnisse in Afrika: Eine Sammlung philologischer Beiträge, Wilhelm J. G. Möhlig zum 60. Geburtstag zugeeignet*. Köln: Rüdiger Köppe Verlag.

Gentner, Derdre 1975. Evidence for the psychological reality of semantic components: The verbs of possession. In: Norman, Donald A. and David E. Rumelhart (eds.) 1975. Pp. 211–46.

Ginneken, Jacques van 1939. Avoir et être (du point de vue de la linguistique générale). In: *Mélanges de linguistique offerts à Charles Bally*. Geneva: Georg et Cie, SA. Pp. 83–92.

Givón, Talmy 1973. The time-axis phenomenon. *Language* 49:890–925.

1979. *On understanding grammar*. New York, San Francisco, London: Academic Press.

1984. *Syntax: A functional typological introduction*. Volume 1. Amsterdam: John Benjamins.

1993. *English grammar: A function-based introduction*. Two volumes. Amsterdam, Philadelphia: John Benjamins.

1995. *Functionalism and grammar*. Amsterdam, Philadelphia: John Benjamins.

Glinert, Lewis 1989. *The grammar of modern Hebrew*. Cambridge University Press.

Greenberg, Joseph H. 1963a. *The languages of Africa*. The Hague: Mouton.

1963b. *Universals of language*. Cambridge, Mass.: MIT Press.

1963c. Some universals of grammar with particular reference to the order of meaningful elements. In: Greenberg (ed.) 1963b. Pp. 58–90.

(ed.) 1978a. *Universals of human language*. Vol. 3: *Word structure*. Stanford University Press.

(ed.) 1978b. *Universals of human language*. Vol. 4: *Syntax*. Stanford University Press.

1978c. Generalizations about numeral systems. In: Greenberg (ed.) 1978a. Pp. 249–95.

Greenberg, Joseph H., Charles A. Ferguson, and Edith Moravcsik (eds.) 1978. *Universals of human language*. Vol. 1. Stanford University Press.

Greene, D. 1962. The development of the construction **is liom**. *Éigse* 10 (1962): 1:45–8.

1976. The preposition *in-* as subject marker. *Celtica* 11:61–7.

Gregerson, Kenneth 1979. *Predicate and argument structure in Rengao grammar*. (Summer Institute of Linguistics Publications in Linguistics, 61.) Arlington, Texas: Summer Institute of Linguistics and University of Texas at Arlington.

Groot, C. de 1983. On non-verbal predicates in Functional Grammar: The case of possessives in Hungarian. In: Dik (ed.) 1983. Pp. 93–122.

Guiraud-Weber, Marguerite 1996. L'appartenance: le cas du russe. In: *La relation d'appartenance*. (Faits de langues, 7.) Paris: Ophrys. Pp. 139–48.

Hagège, Claude 1993. *The language builder: An essay on the human signature in linguistic morphogenesis*. (Amsterdam Studies in the Theory and History of Linguistic Science, 94.) Amsterdam, Philadelphia: John Benjamins.

Haiman, John 1985a. *Natural syntax*. Cambridge University Press.

Haiman, John (ed.) 1985b. *Iconicity in syntax*. Amsterdam: John Benjamins.

Halim, Amran, Lois Carrington, and Stephen A. Wurm (eds.) 1982. *Papers from the Third International Conference on Austronesian Linguistics*. Vol. 1: *Currents in Oceanic*. Pacific Linguistics, Series C, 74. 1982.

Harris, Martin 1982. The 'Past simple' and the 'Present perfect' in Romance. In: Vincent and Harris (eds.) 1982. Pp. 42–70.

Harweg, R. 1968. Besitzanzeigende *haben*-Konstruktionen als Katalysator für die Doppeldeutigkeit der Gruppe 'Nomen+Possessivsuffix' im Türkischen. *Archiv Orientální* 36:407–28.

Haspelmath, Martin 1993. *A grammar of Lezgian*. (Mouton Grammar Library, 9.) Berlin, New York: Mouton de Gruyter.

Havers, Wilhelm 1911. *Untersuchungen zur Kasussyntax der indoeuropäischen Sprachen*. Straßburg: Trübner.

Haviland, John 1979. Guugu Yimidhirr. In: Dixon and Blake (eds.) 1979. Pp. 27–182.

Hawkins, Roger 1981. Towards an account of the possessive constructions: *NP's N* and *the N of NP*. *Journal of Linguistics* 17:247–69.

Hawkinson, Annie K. 1979. Homonymy versus unity of form: The particle -a in Swahili. *Studies in African Linguistics* 10,1:81–109.

Heath, Jeffrey 1978. Functional universals. *Berkeley Linguistics Society* 4:86–95.

Heilmann, Luigi (ed.) 1974. *Proceedings of the Eleventh International Congress of Linguists, Bologna–Florence, August 28 – September 2, 1972*. Vol. 2. Bologna: Società editrice il Mulino.

Heine, Bernd 1973. *Pidgin-Sprachen im Bantu-Bereich*. Berlin: Dietrich Reimer Verlag.

1982. *The Nubi language of Kibera – an Arabic creole: Grammatical sketch and vocabulary*. (Language and Dialect Atlas of Kenya, 3.) Berlin: Dietrich Reimer.

1983. *The Ik language*. Typescript, Cologne.

1991. The Hausa particle *naa*. In: Mendel, Daniela and Ulrike Claudi (eds.) 1991. Pp. 157–70.

1992. Grammaticalization chains. *Studies in Language* 16,2:335–68.

1993. *Auxiliaries: Cognitive forces and grammaticalization*. Oxford University Press.

1994a. Areal influence on grammaticalization. In: Pütz (ed.) 1994. Pp. 55–68.

1994b. On the nature of semantic change in grammaticalization. In: Negri and Poli (eds.) 1994. Pp. 11–28.

1994c. Grammaticalization as an explanatory parameter. In: Pagliuca (ed.) 1994. Pp. 255–87.

Heine, Bernd, Ulrike Claudi and Friederike Hünnemeyer 1991. *Grammaticalization: A conceptual framework.* University of Chicago Press.
Heine, Bernd, Tom Güldemann, Christa Kilian-Hatz, Donald A. Lessau, Heinz Roberg, Mathias Schladt, and Thomas Stolz 1993. Conceptual shift: A lexicon of grammaticalization processes in African Languages. *AAP* (Afrikanistische Arbeitspapiere, Cologne) 34/35:1–322.
Heine, Bernd and Christa Kilian-Hatz 1994. Polysemy in African languages: An example from Baka (Cameroon). In: Geider and Kastenholz (eds.) 1994. Pp. 177–87.
Heine, Bernd and Mechthild Reh 1984. *Grammaticalization and reanalysis in African languages.* Hamburg: Helmut Buske Verlag.
Hengeveld, Kees 1992. *Non-verbal predication: Theory, typology, diachrony.* (Functional Grammar Series, 15.) Berlin, New York: Mouton de Gruyter.
Hercus, L. A. 1982. *The Baagandji language.* (Pacific Linguistics, Series B, 67.) Canberra: The Australian National University.
Herslund, Michael 1996. Partitivité et possession inaliénable. In: *La relation d'appartenance.* (Faits de langues, 7.). Paris: Ophrys. Pp. 33–42.
Hester, Thomas R. 1976. A universal explanation for several syntactic shifts in Basque. *Chicago Linguistic Society, Papers from the Parasession on Diachronic Syntax, April 22, 1976.* Pp. 105–17.
Hetzron, Robert 1970. Nonverbal sentences and degrees of definiteness in Hungarian. *Language* 46,4:899–927.
Hinnebusch, Thomas J. and Robert S. Kirsner 1980. On the inference of 'inalienable possession' in Swahili. *Journal of African Languages and Linguistics* 2:1–16.
Hockett, Charles F. 1958. *A course of modern linguistics.* New York: Macmillan.
Hodge, Carleton T. 1947. *An outline of Hausa grammar.* (Language Dissertations, 41.) Baltimore: Linguistic Society of America.
  1963. Morpheme alternants and the noun phrase in Hausa. *Language* 21:87–91.
  1969. Hausa *naà*—: 'To be' or not 'to be'? *African Language Review* 8:156–62.
Holes, Clive 1990. *Gulf Arabic.* (Croom Helm Descriptive Grammars Series.) London, New York: Routledge.
Holm, John A. 1988. *Pidgins and creoles.* Vol. 1: *Theory and structure.* (Cambridge Language Surveys.) Cambridge University Press.
Hopper, Paul J. 1972. Verbless stative sentences in Indonesian. In: Verhaar (ed.) 1972. Pp. 115–52.
  1986. Discourse function and word order shift: A typological study of the VS/SV alternation. In: Lehmann, W. (ed.) 1986. Pp. 123–40.
  1991. On some principles of grammaticalization. In: Traugott & Heine (eds.) 1991a. Pp. 17–35.
Hopper, Paul J. and Sandra Thompson 1984. The discourse basis for lexical categories in universal grammar. *Language* 60:703–52.
Hopper, Paul J. and Elizabeth C. Traugott 1993. *Grammaticalization.* Cambridge University Press.
Hoskison, J. T. 1983. A grammar of the Gude language. Ph.D. Dissertation, Ohio State University.

Hutchison, John P. 1980. The Kanuri associative postposition: A case for subordination. *Studies in African Linguistics* 11,3:321–51.
Hyman, Larry M. 1977. The syntax of body parts. In: Byarushengo, Duranti, and Hyman (eds.) 1977. Pp. 99–117.
Hyman, Larry M., Danny Keith Alford, and Elizabeth Akpati 1970. Inalienable possession in Igbo. *Journal of West African Languages* 7,2:85–101.
Hymes, Dell and W. E. Bittle (eds.) 1967. *Studies in southwestern ethnolinguistics.* The Hague: Mouton.
Isačenko, Alexander V. 1965. Das syntaktische Verhältnis der Bezeichnungen von Körperteilen im Deutschen. In: Bierwisch (ed.) 1965. Pp. 7–27.
  1974a. On be-languages and have-languages. In: Heilmann (ed.) 1974. Pp. 71–2.
  1974b. On 'have' and 'be' languages. A typological sketch. In: Flier (ed.) 1974. Pp. 43–77.
Jackendoff, Ray S. 1977. X̄ syntax: A study of phrase structure. Cambridge, Mass.: MIT Press.
Janssen, Theo A. J. M. 1976. Hebben-konstrukties en indirekt-objektskonstrukties. Ph.D. Dissertation, Katholieke Universiteit Nijmegen. Utrecht: HES Publishers.
  1993. *'Possession:' expressed or culturally conceived?* Paper presented at the Third International Cognitive Linguistics Conference, July, 18–23, 1993, Leuven, Belgium.
Jelinek, Eloise and Fernando Escalante 1988. 'Verbless' possessive sentences in Yaqui. In: Shipley, William (ed.) 1988. Pp. 411–29.
Kachru, Yamuna 1968. The copula in Hindi. In: Verhaar (ed.) 1968a. Pp. 35–59.
Kahn, C. H. 1966. The Greek verb 'to be' and the concept of being. *Foundations of Language* 2:245–65.
Kastenholz, Raimund 1988. Note sur l'expression énonciative de la possession en bambara. *Mandenkan* 14–15:193–203.
  1989. *Grundkurs Bambara (Manding) mit Texten.* (Afrikawissenschaftliche Lehrbücher, 1.) Cologne: Rüdiger Köppe.
Kayne, R. 1993. Towards a modular theory of auxiliary selection. *Studia Linguistica* 47:3–31.
Kettmann, Gerhard and Joachim Schildt (eds.) 1976. *Zur Ausbildung der Norm der deutschen Literatursprache auf der syntaktischen Ebene (1470–1730). Der Einfachsatz.* (Bausteine zur Sprachgeschichte des Neuhochdeutschen, 56/I.) Berlin: Akademie.
Kiefer, Ferenc 1968. A transformational approach to the verb *van* 'to be' in Hungarian. In: Verhaar (ed.) 1968b. Pp. 53–85.
Kilian-Hatz, Christa 1992. Der Komitativ im Baka: Eine Fallstudie zur Grammatikalisierung. M.A. Thesis, University of Cologne.
  1994. Das Baka: Ein morphosyntaktischer Überblick aus der Grammatikalisierungsperspektive. Ph.D. Dissertation, University of Cologne.
Kilian-Hatz, Christa and Thomas Stolz 1992. Comitative, concomitance, and beyond: On the interdependence of grammaticalization and conceptualization. Paper presented at the Annual Conference of the Linguistic Society of Belgium, November 26–28, 1992, University of Antwerp.

1993. Grammatikalisierung und grammatische Kategorien: Ein Bericht aus der Pathologie. (Arbeitspapier 14.) *ProPrinS* 14. University of Essen.
Kimball, J. 1973. The grammar of existence. *Chicago Linguistic Society* 9 262–70.
Köhler, Oswin 1973. *Grundzüge der Grammatik der Kxoe-Sprache.* Typescript. Cologne: University of Cologne.
König, Ekkehard and Martin Haspelmath 1995. Les constructions à possesseur externe dans les langues de l'Europe. To appear in: Feuillet, J. (ed.), *Actance et valence dans les langues de l'Europe.* Berlin: Mouton de Gruyter.
Koptjevskaja-Tamm, Maria forthc.a. Possessive NPs in Maltese: Alienability, iconicity and grammaticalization. In: Borg, Albert and Frans Plank (eds.), The Maltese noun phrase meets typology. *Rivista di Linguistica*, special issue.
  forthc.b. Genitives and possessive NPs in the languages of Europe. In: Plank, Frans (ed.), *Noun phrase in the languages of Europe.* Berlin: Mouton de Gruyter.
Kraft, Charles H. 1963. *A study of Hausa syntax.* 3 volumes. Hartford: Hartford Seminary Foundation.
  1964a. A new study of Hausa syntax. *Journal of African Languages* 3:66–74.
  1964b. The morpheme *naà* in relation to a broader classification of Hausa verbals. *Journal of African Languages* 3:231–40.
Kraft, Charles H. and Salisu Abubakar 1965. *An introduction to spoken Hausa.* Preliminary edition. (African Language Monograph, 5.) East Lansing: Michigan State University, African Studies Center.
Kraft, Charles H. and A. H. M. Kirk-Greene 1973. *Hausa.* (Teach Yourself Books). London: St. Paul's House.
Kuno, Susumu 1971. The position of locatives in existential sentences. *Linguistic Inquiry* 2:333–78.
  1973. *The structure of the Japanese language.* Cambridge, Mass.: MIT Press.
Kwon, Joung-Mi 1995. *Possession im Swahili.* (AMO Afrikanistische Monographien, 7.) Cologne: Universität zu Köln, Institut für Afrikanistik.
Lakoff, George 1987. *Women, fire, and dangerous things: What categories reveal about the mind.* University of Chicago Press.
Lakoff, George and Mark Johnson 1980. *Metaphors we live by.* University of Chicago Press.
Langacker, Ronald W. 1968. Observations on French possessives. *Language* 44,1:51–75.
  1972. Possessives in Classical Nahuatl. *International Journal of American Linguistics* 38:173–86.
  1978. The form and meaning of the English auxiliary. *Language* 54, 4:853–84.
  1987. *Foundations of cognitive grammar.* Vol. 1: *Theoretical perspectives.* Stanford University Press.
  1993. Reference-point constructions. *Cognitive Linguistics* 4,1:1–38.
  1994. Culture, cognition, and grammar. In: Pütz (ed.) 1994. Pp. 25–53.
  1995. Possession and possessive constructions. In: Taylor and MacLaury (eds.) 1995. Pp. 51–79.
Lass, Roger 1980. *On explaining language change.* Cambridge University Press.

Lébikaza, Kézié K. 1991. Les constructions possessives prédicatives et nominales en kabiye. *Journal of West African Languages* 21,1:91–103.

Lehiste, Ilse 1969. 'Being' and 'having' in Estonian. *Foundations of Language* 5:324–41.

— 1972. 'Being' and 'having' in Estonian. In: Verhaar (ed.) 1972. Pp. 207–24.

Lehmann, Christian and Gunter Brettschneider (eds.) 1980. *Wege zur Universalienforschung.* (Tübinger Beiträge zur Linguistik, 145.) Tübingen: Gunter Narr.

Lehmann, Winfred P. (ed.) 1978. *Syntactic typology: Studies in the phenomenology of language.* Sussex: The Harvester Press.

— (ed.) 1986. *Language typology 1985: Papers from the Linguistic Typology Symposium, Moscow, 9 – 13 December, 1985.* (Current Issues in Linguistic Theory, 47.) Amsterdam, Philadelphia: John Benjamins.

Levine, James S. 1984. On the dative of possession in contemporary Russian. *Slavic and East European Journal* 28:493–501.

Lévy-Bruhl, Lucien 1914. L'expression de la possession dans les langues mélanésiennes. *Mémoires de la Société de Linguistique de Paris* 19,2:96–104.

Lichtenberk, Frantisek 1983. Relational classifiers. *Lingua* 60:147–76.

— 1985. Possessive constructions in Oceanic languages and in Proto-Oceanic. In: Pawley and Carrington (eds.) 1985. Pp. 93–140.

Locker, Ernst 1954. Etre et avoir. Leur expressions dans les langues. *Anthropos* 49:481–510.

Lockwood, W. B. 1968. *Historical German syntax.* Oxford: Clarendon Press.

Löfstedt, Bengt 1963. Zum lateinischen possessiven Dativ. *Zeitschrift für vergleichende Sprachforschung auf dem Gebiete der indogermanischen Sprachen* 78:64–83.

Lukas, Johannes 1970. *Studien zur Sprache der Gisiga (Nordkamerun).* (Afrikanistische Forschungen, 4.) Glückstadt: J. J. Augustin.

Lynch, John 1969. On Fijian possession. Unpublished paper.

— 1971. *Melanesian 'possession' and abstract verbs.* Paper delivered to the Fifth Annual Congress of the Linguistic Society of Papua New Guinea.

— 1973. Verbal aspects of possession in Melanesian languages. *Working Papers in Linguistics* (Honululu) 5,9:1–29. Also published in *Oceanic Linguistics* 12, 1/2 (1973):69–102.

— 1982. Towards a theory of the origin of the Oceanic possessive constructions. In: Halim, Carrington, and Wurm (eds.) 1982. Pp. 243–68.

— forthc. Possessive structures in Lenakel. *Linguistic Communications.* Melbourne: Monash University.

Lyons, John 1967. A note on possessive, existential and locative sentences. *Foundations of Language* 3:390–96.

— 1968a. *Introduction to theoretical linguistics.* Cambridge University Press.

— 1968b. Existence, location, possession and transitivity. In: van Rootselaar, B. and T. F. Staal (eds.) 1968. Pp. 495–509.

— 1977. *Semantics.* Two volumes. Cambridge University Press.

Makino, Seiichi 1968. Japanese 'be'. In: Verhaar (ed.) 1968b. Pp. 1–19.

Malla, Kamal P. 1985. *The Newari language: A working outline.* (Monumenta Serindica, 14.) Tokyo University of Foreign Studies.

Mallinson, Graham and Barry J. Blake 1981. *Language typology: Cross-linguistic studies in syntax*. Amsterdam, New York, Oxford: North-Holland Publishing Company.
Manoliu-Manea, Maria 1996. Inalienability and topicality in Romanian: Pragmasemantics of syntax. In: Chappell and McGregor (eds.) 1996a. Pp. 711–43.
Marcel, G. 1935. *Etre et avoir*. Paris: F. Aubier.
Martin, Jack 1993. 'Inalienable possession' in Creek (and its possible origin). *International Journal of American Linguistics* 59,4:442–521.
Matlin, Margaret W. 1989. *Cognition*. Second edition. New York: Holt, Rinehart and Winston.
McGregor, William 1990. *A functional grammar of Gooniyandi*. (Studies in Language Companion Series, 22.) Amsterdam, Philadelphia: Benjamins.
McKay, Graham R. 1996. Body parts, possession marking and nominal classes in Ndjébbana. In: Chappell and McGregor (eds.) 1996a. Pp. 293–326.
McLendon, Sally 1975. *A grammar of Eastern Pomo*. (University of California Publications in Linguistics, 74.) Berkeley, Ca.: University of California Press.
Meillet, Antoine 1923. Le développement du verbe 'avoir.' In: *Festschrift, Jacob Wackernagel zur Vollendung des 70. Lebensjahres*. Göttingen: Vandenhoeck and Ruprecht. Pp. 9–13.
1926. *Linguistique historique et linguistique générale*. Paris: Champion.
Mélanges de linguistique et de philologie offerts à Jacques van Ginneken à l'occasion du soixantième anniversaire de sa naissance (21 avril 1937). Paris: Librairie C. Klincksieck 1937.
Mendel, Daniela and Ulrike Claudi (eds.) 1991. *Ägypten im afro-orientalischen Kontext: Aufsätze zur Archäologie, Geschichte und Sprache eines unbegrenzten Raumes, Gedenkschrift Peter Behrens*. (Afrikanistische Arbeitspapiere, Special Issue). Cologne: Institut für Afrikanistik.
Migliazza, Ernest Cesar 1972. *Yanomama grammar and intelligibility*. Ph.D. Dissertation, Indiana University, 1972. Ann Arbor, Michigan: University Microfilms.
Miller, George A. and Philip N. Johnson-Laird 1976. *Language and perception*. Cambridge, Mass.: Harvard University Press.
Mithun Williams, Marianne 1976. *A grammar of Tuscarora*. New York, London: Garland Publishing.
1996. Multiple reflections of inalienability in Mohawk. In: Chappell and McGregor (eds.) 1996a. Pp. 633–49.
Mosel, Ulrike 1983. Adnominal and predicative possessive constructions in Melanesian languages. *AKUP* (Arbeiten des Kölner Universalien-Projekts) 50. Cologne.
Munro, Pamela (ed.) 1990. *Kawaiisu: A grammar and dictionary with texts*. (University of California Publications in Linguistics, 119.) Berkeley, Los Angeles: University of California Press.
Muslim, M. Umar 1995. *Malay possessive verbs: Where do they come from?* Paper prepared for the Linguistic Institute, Linguistic Society of America, University of New Mexico, Albuquerque, 25 June – 4 August, 1995.
Naden, Tony 1982. Existence and possession in Bisa. *Studies in African Linguistics* 13,2:211–14.

Negri, Mario and Diego Poli (eds.) 1994. *La semantica in prospettiva diacronica e sincronica: Atti del Convegno della Società Italiana di Glottologia, Macerata – Recanati, 22–24 ottobre, 1992*. Pisa: Giardini Editori e Stampatori.

Newman, Paul and Robert D. Botne (eds.) 1989. *Current approaches to African linguistics*. Vol. 5. Dordrecht: Foris.

Newman, Paul and Russell G. Schuh 1974. The Hausa aspect system. *Afroasiatic Linguistics* 1,1:1–39.

Nichols, Johanna 1988. On alienable and inalienable possession. In: Shipley (ed.) 1988. Pp. 557–609.

— 1992. *Linguistic diversity in space and time*. University of Chicago Press.

Nikiforidou, Kiki 1991. The meanings of the genitive: A case study in semantic structure and semantic change. *Cognitive Linguistics* 2,2:149–205.

Noonan, Michael 1992. *A grammar of Lango*. (Mouton Grammar Library, 7.) Berlin: Mouton de Gruyter.

Norman, Donald A. and David E. Rumelhart (eds.) 1975. *Explorations in cognition*. San Francisco: Freeman.

O'Connor, Mary Catherine 1992. *Topics in Northern Pomo grammar*. New York, London: Garland Publishing.

Orr, Robert 1984. An embryonic ergative construction in Irish? *General Linguistics* 24,1:38–45.

— 1991. More on embryonic ergativity. *General Linguistics* 31:163–75.

— 1992. Slavo-Celtica. *Canadian Slavonic Papers (Revue canadienne des slavistes)* 34,3:245–68.

Osumi, Midori 1996. Body parts in Tinrin. In: Chappell and McGregor (eds.) 1996a. Pp. 433–62.

Otten, Dirk 1992. *Strategien prädikativer Possession in afrikanischen Sprachen*. Hauptseminararbeit, Institut für Afrikanistik. Typescript, University of Cologne.

Pagliuca, William (ed.) 1994. *Perspectives on grammaticalization*. (Amsterdam Studies in the Theory and History of Linguistic Science, 109.) Amsterdam, Philadelphia: John Benjamins.

Palmer, Frank R. 1965. Bilin 'to be' and 'to have'. *African Language Studies* 6:101–11.

Parsons, F. W. 1960. The verbal system in Hausa. *Afrika und Übersee* 44,1:1–36.

Pasch, Helma 1985. Possession and possessive classifiers in 'Dongo-ko. *Afrika und Übersee* 68,1:69–85.

Pawley, Andrew 1973. Some problems in Proto-Oceanic grammar. *Oceanic Linguistics* 12, 1/2:103–88.

Pawley, Andrew and Lois Carrington (eds.) 1985. *Austronesian linguistics at the 15th Pacific Science Congress. Pacific Linguistics*, C-88, 1985.

Payne, Doris and Immanuel Barshi 1995. A holistic account of possessor raising in Maasai. Paper presented at the International Conference on Functional Approaches to Grammar, Albuquerque, University of New Mexico, 24 – 28 July, 1995.

Pit'ha, Petr 1973. On some meanings of the verb to have (on material from the Czech language). *Folia Linguistica* 6:301–4.

Plank, Frans (ed.) 1979. *Ergativity: Towards a theory of grammatical relations*. New York: Academic Press.
Plank, Frans 1984. The modals story retold. *Studies in Language* 8,3:305–64.
Postma, Gertjan 1995. On the syntactic encoding of possession. Paper presented at the Annual Meeting of the Societas Linguistica Europaea, 31 August – 2 September, 1995, University of Leiden.
Poulos, George 1990. *A linguistic analysis of Venda*. Pretoria: Via Afrika.
Pountain, Christopher J. 1985. Copulas, verbs of possession and auxiliaries in Old Spanish: The evidence for structurally interdependent changes. *Bulletin of the Hispanic Society* 62:337–55.
Pustet, Regina 1985. Possession im Dakota. *Arbeitspapier* 47. Institut für Sprachwissenschaft, University of Cologne.
Pütz, Martin (ed.) 1994. *Language contact and language conflict*. Amsterdam, Philadelphia: John Benjamins.
Quirk, Randolph, Sidney Greenbaum, Geoffrey Leech, and Jan Svartvik 1985. *A comprehensive grammar of the English language*. London, New York: Longman.
Qvonje, Jørn Ivar 1980. Die Grammatikalisierung der Präposition *na* im Bulgarischen. *Folia Linguistica Historica* 1,2:317–51.
Ramos, Teresita V. and Resty M. Ceña 1980. Existential, locative and possessive in Tagalog. *Philippine Journal of Linguistics* 11,2:15–26.
Raum, J. 1909. *Versuch einer Grammatik der Dschaggasprache (Moschi-Dialekt)*. Berlin. Reprint Ridgewood, New Jersey: The Gregg Press, 1964.
Ray, Sidney H. 1919. The Melanesian possessives and a study in method. *American Anthropologist* 21:347–60.
Reh, Mechthild 1985. *Die Krongo-Sprache (nìino mó-dì). Beschreibung, Texte, Wörterverzeichnis*. (Kölner Beiträge zur Afrikanistik, 12.) Berlin: Dietrich Reimer.
1994a. *Anywa language: Description and internal reconstructions*. Habilitationsschrift. Typescript, University of Bayreuth.
1994b. A grammatical sketch of Deiga. *Afrika und Übersee* 77:197–261.
Rice, Keren 1989. *A grammar of Slave*. (Mouton Grammar Library, 5.) Berlin, New York: Mouton de Gruyter.
Robinson, Lila Wistrand and James Armagost 1990. *Comanche dictionary and grammar*. (Summer Institute of Linguistics and The University of Texas at Arlington Publications in Linguistics, 92.) Dallas: Summer Institute of Linguistics.
Rootselaar, B. van and T. F. Staal (eds.) 1968. *Logic, methodology, and philosophy of science, III*. Amsterdam: North-Holland Publishing Co.
Rufa'i, Abba 1978. On the progressive aspect in Hausa. In: *Proceedings of the Conference for the Hausa Language and Literature*, vol. 1. Kano: Bayero University. Pp. 293–303.
Rumelhart, D. E. and Anthony Ortony 1977. The representation of knowledge in memory. In: Anderson, Spiro, and Montague (eds.) 1977.
Saltarelli, Mario, Miren Azkarate, David Farwell, Jon Ortiz de Urbina and Lourdes Oñderra 1988. *Basque*. London, New York, Sydney: Croom Helm.

Sanford, Anthony J. 1985. *Cognition and cognitive psychology*. New York: Basic Books.

Santandrea, Stefano 1965. *Languages of the Banda and Zande groups: A contribution to a comparative study*. Naples: Istituto Universitario Orientale.

Sapir, Edward 1921. *Language: An introduction to the study of speech*. San Diego, New York, London: Harcourt Brace Jovanovich.

Sasse, Hans-Jürgen 1982. *An etymological dictionary of Burji*. (Cushitic Language Studies, 1.) Hamburg: Buske.

Schneider, Gilbert Donald 1966. West African Pidgin English: A descriptive linguistic analysis with texts and glossary from the Cameroon area. Ph.D. Dissertation, Athens, Ohio.

Schuh, Russell G. 1976. The Chadic verbal system and its Afroasiatic nature. *Afroasiatic Linguistics* 3,1:1–14.

Sebeok, Thomas A. 1943. The equational sentence in Hungarian. *Language* 19:320–27.

Seiler, Hansjakob 1973. Zum Problem der sprachlichen Possessivität. *Folia Linguistica* 6,3/4:231–50.

— 1977a. *Sprache und Sprachen: Gesammelte Aufsätze*. (Struktura: Schriftenreihe zur Linguistik, 11.) Munich: Wilhelm Fink.

— 1977b. On the semanto-syntactic configuration 'Possessor of an Act'. In: Seiler 1977a. Pp. 169–86.

— 1977c. Universals of language. In: Seiler 1977a. Pp. 207–29.

— 1983. *Possession as an operational dimension of language*. (Language Universals Series, 2.) Tübingen: Gunter Narr.

— 1988. Die universalen Dimensionen der Sprache: Eine vorläufige Bilanz. *AKUP* (Arbeiten des Kölner Universalien-Projekts) 75. Cologne: University of Cologne.

Service, Elman R. 1963. *Profiles in ethnology*. New York: Harper and Row.

Serzisko, Fritz 1984. *Der Ausdruck der Possessivität im Somali*. (Continuum – Schriftenreihe zur Linguistik, 1.) Tübingen: Gunter Narr.

— 1992. Possession. Typescript, University of Cologne.

Shibatani, Masayoshi 1996. *Applicatives and benefactives: A cognitive account*. In: Shibatani and Thompson 1996.

Shibatani, Masayoshi and Sandra Thompson (eds.) 1996. *Grammatical constructions: Their form and meaning*. Oxford University Press.

Shipley, William (ed.) 1988. *In honor of Mary Haas: From the Haas festival conference on native American linguistics*. Berlin: Mouton de Gruyter.

Snare, F. 1972. The concept of property. *American Philosophical Quarterly* 9:200–206.

Sohn, Ho-min 1994. *Korean*. (Descriptive Grammars.) London, New York: Routledge.

Sprachgeschichte und Wortbedeutung: Festschrift Albert Debrunner 1954. Bern: Francke Verlag.

Spradley, James P. 1979. *The ethnographic interview*. New York: Holt, Rinehart and Winston.

Stafford, R. L. 1967. *An elementary Luo grammar. With vocabularies*. Nairobi: Oxford University Press.

Stassen, Leon 1995. *The typology of predicative possession*. Paper presented at the Annual Meeting of the Societas Linguistica Europaea, 31 August – 2 September, 1995, University of Leiden.

Steele, Susan 1977. On being possessed. *Berkeley Linguistics Society* 3:114–31.

Steere, E. 1933. *Swahili exercises (revised by Canon Hellier)*. London: Sheldon Press.

Stolz, Thomas 1991. *Von der Grammatikalisierbarkeit des Körpers*. Part I: *Vorbereitung*. (Prinzipien des Sprachwandels, 2.) University of Essen.

— 1993. *Wege zu einer Typologie des Komitativs*. Paper presented at the Philosophische Fakultät, University of Potsdam, 3 December, 1993.

— 1994. *Über Komitative: Natürlichkeit und Grammatikalisierung, Prädiktabilität von struktureller Organisation und Dynamik*. Typescript, University of Bochum.

— 1995. *'Besitz' und 'Begleitung': Universalien, Typologie und Areale*. Paper presented on 22 May, 1995, at the Free University, Berlin.

Svorou, Soteria 1993. *The grammar of space*. (Typological Studies in Language, 25.) Amsterdam, Philadelphia: John Benjamins.

Takizala, Alexis 1974. On the similarity between nominal adjectives and possessive forms in Kihungan. *Studies in African Linguistics*, Supplement 5. Pp. 291–305.

Tannen, Deborah 1993. *Framing in discourse*. Oxford University Press.

Taylor, F. W. 1923. *A practical Hausa grammar*. Oxford University Press.

— 1959. *A practical Hausa grammar*. Second edition. Oxford University Press.

Taylor, John R. 1989a. Possessive genitives in English. *Linguistics* 27, 4/6:663–86.

— 1989b. *Linguistic categorization: Prototypes in linguistic theory*. Oxford: Clarendon Press.

Taylor, John R. and Robert E. MacLaury (eds.) 1995. *Language and the cognitive construal of the world*. (Trends in Linguistics, Studies and Monographs, 82.) Berlin, New York: Mouton de Gruyter.

Teng, Shou-hsin 1974. Double nominatives in Chinese. *Language* 50,3:455–73.

Thompson, Chad 1996. On the grammar of body parts in Koyukon. In: Chappell and McGregor (eds.) 1996a. Pp. 651–76.

Trask, R. L. 1979. On the origins of ergativity. In: Plank (ed.) 1979. Pp. 385–404.

Traugott, Elizabeth C. and Bernd Heine (eds.) 1991a. *Approaches to grammaticalization*. Vol. 1. Amsterdam, Philadelphia: John Benjamins.

Traugott, Elizabeth C. and Bernd Heine (eds.) 1991b. *Approaches to grammaticalization*. Vol. 2. Amsterdam, Philadelphia: John Benjamins.

Traugott, Elizabeth C. and Ekkehard König 1991. The semantics-pragmatics of grammaticalization revisited. In: Traugott and Heine (eds.) 1991a. Pp. 189–218.

Tsunoda, Tasaku 1996. The possession cline in Japanese and other languages. In: Chappell and McGregor (eds.) 1996a. Pp. 565–630.

Tucker, A. N. and M. A. Bryan 1966. *Linguistic analyses*. (Handbook of African Languages.) Oxford University Press.

Ultan, Russell 1978. Toward a typology of substantival possession. In: Greenberg (ed.) 1978b. Pp. 11–49.

Vendryes, J. 1937. Sur l'emploi de l'auxiliaire 'avoir' pour marquer le passé. In: *Mélanges.* Pp. 85–92.
Verhaar, John W. M. (ed.) 1968a. *The verb 'be' and its synonyms.* Part 2. (Foundations of Language, Supplementary Series, 6.) Dordrecht: Reidel.
— (ed.) 1968b. *The verb 'be' and its synonyms.* Part 3. (Foundations of Language, Supplementary Series, 8.) Dordrecht: Reidel.
— (ed.) 1972. *The verb 'be' and its synonyms.* Part 5. (Foundations of Language, 14.) Dordrecht: Reidel.
Vet, C. 1983. Possessive constructions in French. In: Dik (ed.) 1983. Pp. 123–40.
Vincent, Nigel 1982. The development of the auxiliaries HABERE and ESSE in Romance. In: Vincent and Harris (eds.) 1982. Pp. 71–96.
Vincent, Nigel and Martin Harris (eds.) 1982. *Studies in the Romance verb.* London: Croom Helm.
Voeltz, Erhard F. K. 1976. Inalienable possession in Sotho. *Studies in African Linguistics,* Supplement 8. Pp. 255–66.
Watkins, Calvert 1967. Remarks on the genitive. In: *To honor Roman Jakobson: Essays on the occasion of his 70th birthday.* Vol. III. The Hague, Paris: Mouton. Pp. 2191–8.
Webb, Karen E. 1977. An evolutionary aspect of social structure and a verb 'have'. *American Anthropologist* 79,1:42–49.
Welmers, William E. 1968. *Jukun of Wukari and Jukun of Takum.* (Occasional Publication, 16.) Ibadan: Institute of African Studies.
— 1973. *African language structures.* Berkeley, Los Angeles: University of California Press.
Weninger, Stefan 1993. *Ge'ez (Classical Ethiopic).* (Languages of the World/Materials, 01.) Munich, Newcastle: LINCOM/EUROPA.
Westermann, Diedrich 1907. *Grammatik der Ewe-Sprache.* Berlin: Dietrich Reimer.
— 1924. *Die Kpelle-Sprache in Liberia: Grammatische Einführung, Texte und Wörterbuch.* (Zeitschrift für Eingeborenen-Sprachen, Beiheft 6.) Berlin: Dietrich Reimer.
White, Leslie A. 1959. *The evolution of culture: The development of civilization to the fall of Rome.* New York: McGraw-Hill.
Wilkins, David P. 1989. *Mparntwe Arrernte (Aranda): Studies in the structures and semantics of grammar.* Doctoral Dissertation, Australian National University, Canberra.
— 1996. Natural tendencies of semantic change and the search for cognates. In: Durie and Ross (eds.) 1996. Pp. 264–304.
Williams, Marianne Mithun, See Mithun
Wilson, Bob 1983. An examination of crosslinguistic constraints on the lexicalization of predications of ownership, possession, location and existence. *Working Papers in Linguistics* (University of Hawaii) 15,2:1–15.
Wolff, Ekkehard 1993. *Referenzgrammatik des Hausa zur Begleitung des Fremdsprachenunterrichts und zur Einführung in das Selbststudium.* (Hamburger Beiträge zur Afrikanistik, 2.) Münster, Hamburg: Lit Verlag.
Wolff, Ekkehard and Hilke Meyer-Bahlburg (eds.) 1983. *Studies in Chadic and Afroasiatic linguistics.* Hamburg: Buske Verlag.

Young, Robert W. and William Morgan 1980. *The Navajo language: A grammar and colloquial dictionary*. Albuquerque: University of New Mexico Press.

Zigmond, Maurice L., G. Booth Curtis, and Pamela Munro 1990. *Kawaiisu: A grammar and dictionary with texts*. Berkeley, Los Angeles, Oxford: University of California Press.

Ziv, Yael 1976. On the reanalysis of grammatical terms in Hebrew possessive constructions. In: Cole, Peter (ed.) 1976. Pp. 129–52.

Z'graggen, J. A. 1965. Possessor–possessed relationship in the Saker language, NE-New Guinea. *Oceanic Linguistics* 4, 1/2:119–26.

Index of authors

Adam, Hassan, xiv
Agel, Vilmos, 183
Allen, W. Sidney, 187, 209
Amborn, Hermann, 48, 241
Ameka, Felix, 69, 94, 125, 126, 127, 128, 129, 130, 131, 177, 181, 182
Anderson, John M., 192, 199, 205
Aristar, Anthony Rodrigues, 148
Asher, R. E., 60, 242
Austin, Peter, 31, 146

Bach, Emmon, 2, 4, 221, 229, 235
Bahr, Donald M., 181, 182
Barshi, Immanuel, 168
Bartlett, Frederic C., 45
Behrens, Leila, xiii
Bendix, Edward Herman, 18, 72–3, 215, 216
Benveniste, Emile 42, 43, 78, 90, 91, 187, 190, 210, 211, 236, 241, 242
Bhaskararao, Peri, 93, 243
Bickerton, Derek, 1, 3, 32, 48, 137, 138, 203, 204, 205, 208, 236
Biermann, Anna, 27, 31, 60, 93, 111, 113, 241
Bills, Garland D., 59, 243
Bird, Charles, 36, 117, 118, 119, 120, 240
Blake, Barry J., 6, 14, 163, 166
Boeder, Winfried, 23, 57
Bonneau, José, 151, 152
Borillo, Andrée, 151
Bowe, Heather J., 161, 177
Bowers, J. S., 21
Brauner, Siegmund, 95
Brinkmann, Hennig, 50
Broschart, Jürgen, xiii
Brugman, Claudia Marlea, xiii, 3, 37, 190, 191, 235
Bryan, M. A., 103
Buck, Carl Darling, 1
Bugenhagen, Robert D., 24, 26, 38
Burridge, Kate, 184
Bybee, Joan L., xiii, 6, 7, 8, 45, 46, 76, 187, 188, 192, 193, 197, 199
Bynon, Theodora, 97

Campbell, Lyle, 147, 148, 243
Capell, A., 23, 24
Carlin, Eithne, 52, 243
Casagrande, J. B., 223
Cato, 109
Ceña, Resty M., 214
Chapell, Hilary, xiv, 3, 6, 10, 11, 12, 14, 20, 22, 37, 44, 116, 155, 160, 162, 163, 172, 182
Chomsky, Noam, 2, 21
Christie, J., 203, 214
Cicero, 109
Clark, Eve V. 25, 41, 42, 43, 58, 66, 104, 134, 136, 203, 204, 208, 214, 217, 228, 229
Clasen, Bernd, 30, 224
Claudi, Ulrike, xiii, xiv, 6, 12, 41, 45, 46, 47, 48, 49, 50, 51, 52, 53, 54, 55, 74, 76, 77, 78, 81, 87, 94, 100, 102, 103, 107, 111, 114, 145, 149, 176, 177, 187, 194, 210, 212, 236, 244
Colby, Benjamin N., 224
Cole, Desmond T., 23, 24
Collinder, Björn, 244
Comrie, Bernard, 6, 8, 113, 114
Corbett, Greville, 15
Crazzolara, J. P., 56, 57
Creissels, D., 2, 48, 49, 55, 56, 84, 140, 234
Croft, William, 7
Crowley, Terry, 12, 182
Cyffer, Norbert, 100, 101, 242

Dahl, Östen, 187, 192, 193
Dal, I., 193
Davies, William D., 177
Dayley, Jon P., 180, 244
Demiraj, Shaban, 140, 192
Devitt, Dan, 72, 205
Diem, Werner, 16, 19, 20, 21, 149
Dimmendaal, Gerrit Jan, 27, 61, 147
Dixon, Robert M. W., 55, 159
Doke, Clement M., 24
Driem, George van, 242

264

Index of authors

Duridanov, Ivan, 152, 233

Ebert, Karen, xiii
Emanatian, Michele, xiii, 56
Erdélyi, István, 243
Erman, Adolf, 78, 100, 241
Escalante, Fernando, 189, 244

Fernandez, James W., 224
Fillmore, Charles J., 18, 86, 203, 215
Fleischman, Suzanne, xiii, 192, 207
Foley, William A., 56, 244
Fortescue, Michael, 25
Fox, Barbara, 20
Frajzyngier, Zygmunt, xiii, 242
Freeze, Ray, 47, 54, 58, 59, 68, 79, 82, 108, 206, 215, 217–21, 241, 243
Friedländer, Marianne, 145
Fritze, Marie-Elisabeth, 183
Fromm, Erich, 234

Gentner, Derdre, 3, 44
Ginneken, Jacques van, 196
Givón, T., xiii, 6, 47, 116
Glinert, Lewis, 241
Greenberg, Joseph H., 6, 117, 187
Gregerson, Kenneth, 243
Guiraud-Weber, Marguerite, 84
Güldemann, Tom, xiii

Hagège, Claude, 3, 78, 113, 117, 195
Haiman, John, 11, 180
Hale, Kenneth, 223
Harris, Martin, 193
Haspelmath, Martin, xiv, 107, 148, 150, 166, 167, 168, 170, 172, 242
Havers, Wilhelm, 167
Haviland, John, 54
Hawkins, Roger, 2, 21, 135, 150
Hawkinson, Annie K., 155
Heine, Bernd, xiii, 6, 8, 12, 45, 46–7, 48, 51, 55, 60, 67, 74, 75, 76, 77, 79, 82, 87, 88, 94, 97, 99, 104, 111, 114, 116, 137, 145, 176, 177, 187, 194, 198, 199, 200, 201, 202, 205, 222, 227, 232, 236, 237
Heine, Ingo, xiii, 6
Hengeveld, Kees, 55, 70, 71, 212, 213, 236, 240, 243
Hercus, L. A., 241
Herslund, Michael, 19
Holes, Clive, 56, 70
Hopper, Paul J., xiii, 6, 38, 45, 70, 76, 79, 130, 141, 151, 229
Hünnemeyer, Friederike, xiii, 6, 45, 47, 51, 55, 74, 76, 87, 94, 111, 114, 194, 236
Hutchison, John P., 100, 101, 242

Hyman, Larry, 13

Isačenko, Alexander V., 83, 84, 85, 107, 138, 139, 140, 141, 167, 187, 191, 211, 228, 232

Jackendoff, Ray S., 21
Janssen, Theo A. J. M., 241
Jelinek, Eloise, 189, 244
Johnson, Mark, 45, 156
Johnson-Laird, Philip N. 1, 5, 9, 26, 34, 38, 44, 94

Kachru, Yamuna, 59, 242
Kahn, C. H., 203
Kastenholz, Raimund, 36, 118, 119, 120–121
Kayne, R., 215, 222
Kiefer, Ferenc, 107, 108
Kilian-Hatz, Christa, xiii, 55, 57, 93, 108, 146, 206
Kimball, J., 18, 203
Kirk-Greene, A. H. M., 188
König, Christa, xiii
König, Ekkehard, 166, 167, 170, 172
Kouteva, Tania, xiv, 95, 152, 232, 233
Kraft, Charles H., 188
Kronenfeld, David B., 224
Kuno, Susumu, 62, 160, 203
Kwon, Joung-Mi, 169

Lakoff, George, xiii, 45, 156
Langacker, Ronald, 2, 33, 37, 46, 155, 215, 216, 225
Lass, Roger, 232
Lébikaza, Kézié, 20, 21, 134
Lehiste, Ilse, 51, 86–7, 241
Lévy-Bruhl, Lucien, 10
Lichtenberk, Frantisek, xiii, 14, 15, 16, 23, 145, 148, 159, 238
Locker, Ernst, 4, 43, 46, 47, 50, 59, 63, 71, 139, 198, 209, 210, 211, 212, 236, 241, 242, 243
Lockwood, W. B., 183
Löfstedt, Bengt, 4, 109, 110, 138, 140, 141
Lukas, Johannes, 52, 63
Lynch, John, 3, 12, 15, 16, 18, 19, 24, 29, 238
Lyons, John, 19, 25, 41, 43, 51, 58, 61, 65, 83, 84, 139–40, 203, 217, 222, 244

Makino, Seiichi, 59, 241
Malla, Kamal P., 243
Mallinson, Graham, 6
Martin, Jack, 176
Matlin, Margaret W., 46

Index of authors

McGregor, William, 3, 10, 11, 12, 14, 20, 22, 37, 44, 155, 162, 163, 172, 182
McLendon, Sally, 177
Meillet, Antoine, 139, 140, 143, 192, 234
Migliazza, Ernest Cesar, 58, 159, 244
Miller, George A., 1, 5, 9, 26, 34, 38, 44, 94
Minker, Gunter, 48, 241
Mosel, Ulrike, 51, 243
Munro, Pamela, 71, 242

Naden, Tony, 98, 99, 106, 240
Nichols, Johanna, 10, 11, 13, 16, 28, 143, 148, 172, 173, 175, 177, 178, 179, 180
Nikiforidou, Kiki, 41, 156
Noonan, Michael, 62

O'Connor, Mary Catherine 37, 153, 170, 171
Orr, Robert, 51, 60, 100, 107, 138, 140, 141, 197, 232, 233, 240, 243, 244
Otten, Dirk, xiv, 74, 80, 81, 138, 240, 241, 242, 243

Pagliuca, William, xiii, 6, 7, 8, 45, 46, 76, 187, 188, 197, 199, 201
Pasch, Helma, 25
Pawley, Andrew, 15, 16, 23, 33, 145, 238, 239
Payne, Doris, xiii, 168
Perkins, Revere D., xiii, 6, 7, 8, 45, 76, 187, 188, 197, 199, 201
Petöfi, Sándor, 111
Pica, Pierre, 151, 152
Plank, Frans, 193
Poulos, George, 55, 244
Pountain, Christopher J., 88

Qvonje, Jørn Ivar, 152

Ramos, Teresita V., 214
Raum, J., 49
Reh, Mechthild, xiii, 67, 79, 105, 116, 205, 240 241, 242
Rice, Keren, 64, 243
Roberg, Heinz, xiii, 30, 47, 91, 143, 242
Robinson, Lila Wistrand, 241

Saltarelli, Mario, 240
Sanford, Anthony J., 46
Santandrea, Stefano, 63
Sasse, Hans-Jürgen, xiii, 48, 241
Schladt, Mathias, xiii
Schneider, Gilbert Donald, 48, 146, 159
Seiler, Hansjakob, 4, 5, 10, 11, 20, 21, 23, 26, 30, 38, 42, 62, 63, 155, 192, 198, 228, 236, 240

Serzisko, Fritz, xiii, 54, 108
Shibatani, Masayoshi, 46
Snare, F., 5
Sohn, Ho-min, 242
Spradley, James P., 224
Stafford, R. L., 54, 81
Stassen, Leon, xiii, 57, 63, 64, 98, 114, 149, 184, 185, 213, 233, 240, 240, 242, 243, 244
Steele, Susan, 28, 62, 114–15, 116, 195, 196
Steere, E., 227
Stolz, Christel, xiii
Stolz, Thomas, xiii, xiv, 6, 45, 55, 57, 65, 71, 93, 101, 108, 147, 241, 242, 243, 244
Svorou, Soteria, 12
Sweetser, Eve, xiii

Takizala, Alexis, 155
Talmy, Leonard, xiii
Tannen, Deborah, 46
Taylor, John R., 3, 5, 26, 31, 32, 38, 40, 41, 226
Teng, Shou-hsin, 160
Thompson, Chad, 178
Tossou, Kossi, xiv
Touré, Mohamed, xiv, 36, 118, 119, 121, 122, 123
Trask, R. L., 117, 194
Traugott, Elizabeth C., xiii, 6, 45, 76, 83, 130
Troike, Rudolph C., 59, 243
Trudgill, Peter, xiii, 154
Tsunoda, Tasaku, 18, 21, 71, 159, 169
Tucker, A. N., 103

Ultan, Russell, 10, 27, 41, 42, 44, 53, 54, 59, 61, 143, 183, 211, 212, 229, 236, 239, 242, 243

Vallejo C., Bernardo, 59, 243
Vendryes, J., 141, 192
Vincent, Nigel, xiv, 83, 95, 110, 149, 193
Voeltz, Erhard F. K., 10, 19, 20, 38

Watkins, Calvert, 29, 30, 32–3, 65, 66, 183
Weise, Elisabeth, 154
Welmers, William E., 42, 52, 68, 69, 80, 81
Westermann, Diedrich, 52, 80, 241
Wierzbicka, Anna, 181
Wilkins, David P., 82, 147
Wilson, Bob, 204, 205, 236
Wolff, Ekkehard, 202, 241

Ziv, Yael, 112
Z'graggen, J. A., 12

Index of Languages

Acholi, 176
Acoma, 27
African languages, 56, 74
Afrikaans, 148
Akkadian, 149
Amele, 22
Amharic, 240
Anindilyakwa, 71
Anywa, 67, 240
Apalai, 240
Arabic, 20–21
Arabic, Egyptian, 212
Arabic, Gulf, 56, 70
Arabic, Palestinian, 59, 240
Arabic, Proto-, *see* Proto-Arabic
Aramaic, 149
Aranda, 147
Armenian, 141, 190, 192, 240
Armenian, Classical, 58, 190
Aroma, 12, 24, 29
Asiatic languages, 75
Athabaskan, Koyukon, 178
Athabaskan languages, 11
Australian languages, 11, 24

Baagandji, 240
Babatana, 145, 239
Baka, 146, 206
Baltic languages, 211
Bambara *see* Manding
Bantu languages, 55, 95, 138, 206
Bantu languages, South African, 24
Basque, 139, 240
Batak, Karo, 240
Bau, 16
Beja, 240
Belorussian, 107, 211, 240
Bengali, 58
Berber, Moroccan, 240
Bisa, 98–99, 106, 240
Breton, 60, 240
Buduma, 240
Bulgarian, 95, 143, 152, 193, 233

Bulgarian, Middle, 232
Bulgarian, Old, 152

Caddoan languages, 28
Cahuilla, 62, 240
Caucasian languages, 194
Celtic languages, 110, 139, 140, 229
Chadic languages, 150
Chaga, Mochi dialect, 48, 49
Chinese (including Mandarin, Shanghainese), 19, 65, 82, 160, 213, 219, 240
Choctaw, 177, 182
Chuvash, 58
Cocopa, 183
Comanche, 241
Coptic, 78, 98
Cornish, 78, 98, 114
Creek, 176, 177
creole languages, 48, 137
Czech, 211

Daza, 241
Deiga, 241
Diyari, 31, 146
Djaru, 71, 159
Djerma, 241
Dullay, 48, 241
Dutch, 241
Dyula, 117

Efik, 241
Egyptian, Ancient, 77, 190
Egyptian, Late, 78, 241
English, Old, 141
English-based creoles, 137
Eskimo, 25, 194
Estonian, 51, 86–7, 211, 241
European languages, 43, 75, 78, 88, 111, 138, 139, 143, 145, 189, 191, 195, 197, 211, 229, 239
Ewe, 8, 11, 27, 43, 52, 61, 66, 69, 70, 94, 123–133, 136, 189, 197, 200, 202, 204, 241

Index of languages

Fijian, 12, 23, 24, 29, 51, 71, 204, 206
Finnish, 206, 211, 218, 241
Finno-Ugric languages, 229
French, 32, 48, 61, 78, 95, 110, 140, 150, 151–2, 156, 171, 185, 190, 195, 206, 215, 216, 219, 239
French, Old, 150
Fur, 241

Gabu, 63
Gaelic, 219
Georgian, Old, 241
German, 15, 17, 19, 30, 50, 58, 74, 140, 146, 148, 155, 164–5, 168, 183–84, 190, 195, 219, 238, 239
German, Middle High, 193
German, Old High, 141
Germanic languages, 50, 139, 140, 141, 147, 194, 211, 229, 232
Gisiga, 52, 63
Gola, 241
Gooniyandi, 163
Gothic, 141
Greek, 139, 156, 211, 219, 232
Greek, Homeric, 90, 141
Guugu Yimidhirr, 54
Guyanese Creole, 137

Haitian Creole, 137
Hausa, 188, 200, 201, 202, 204, 241
Hawaiian Creole English, 48, 137
Haya, 13
Hebrew, 112–3, 219, 241
Hindi, 58, 68, 79, 215, 218, 241
Hittite, 90, 141, 241
Huailou, 15, 59, 241
Hungarian, 27, 31, 60, 93, 107, 108, 111–2, 143, 145, 211, 241

Igbo, 241
Ik, 60, 64–5, 67, 68, 104
Indic, 140
Indo-European, 33, 138, 139, 140, 141
Irish, Modern, 51, 197
Iroquoian languages, 28
Italian, 185

Japanese, 59, 63, 169, 175, 215, 241
Jukun, Takum dialect, 80
Jukun, Wukari dialect, 80, 81

Kabiye, 21, 134, 176, 182, 242
Kafa, 242
Kairiru, 148
Kanuri, 100–101, 242
Kashmiri, 59, 242

Kawaiisu, 71, 242
K'ekchi', 58
Khalkha, 54
Khmer, 63
Khoekhoe, see Nama
Kobon, 242
Korean, 242
Kpelle, 52, 68, 242
Krongo, 105–6, 242
Kurdish, 194, 242
Kxoe, 149

Lango, 62
Laotian, 71
Latin, 32, 61, 66, 67, 109, 139, 141, 150, 156, 185, 192, 193, 196–7
Latin, Late, 95
Latvian, 211
Lenakel, 12, 24, 29,
Lezgian, 107, 242
Limbu, 242
Lithuanian, 211
Lotuxo, 102–3
Luiseño, 28, 114–16, 195, 196
Luo, 54, 81

Maasai, 168–9
Maewo, 145
Maisin, 22
Makushi, 23
Malay, 70, 242
Malayalam, 60, 242
Malinke, see Maninka
Maltese, 113, 114, 149, 242
Manchu, 113
Mandarin, see Chinese
Mande languages, 55
Manding (Bambara dialect), 8, 35, 36, 53, 117–123, 132, 133, 134, 240
Mandinka, 55, 117
Mangap-Mbula, 24
Mangbetu, 56
Maninka (Malinke), 117, 145
Manja, 242
Maori, 23
Masalit, 242
Melanesian languages, 24
Melanesian Pidgin English, see Tok Pisin
Mixtec, 242
Mixtec, Yosondua, 219
Mochi, see Chaga
Mokilese, 242
Mongolian, 63, 242
Mota, 24
Motu, 159
Mupun, 242

Index of languages 269

Nama (Khoekhoe), 30–31, 91, 143, 175, 242
Nasioi, 213, 243
Navajo, 70, 178–9
Newari, 243
Ngalakan, 55
Niger-Congo languages, 55
Norwegian, 154
Nubi, 137, 138
Nubian, Mountain, 187
Nuer, 56, 57
Nupe, 243

Oceanic languages, 14, 15, 145, 238
Old Church Slavonic, 232, 233
Oromo, Waata dialect, 49

Paamese, 11, 12, 182
Panjabi, 58, 243
Papago, 181, 182, 223
Papiamentu, 137
Persian, 192
Persian, Old, 194
Pima-Papago, 181, 182
Pipil, 147, 148, 243
Pitjantjatjara, 161–2, 177, 182
Polish, 211, 243
Pomo, Eastern, 177, 178
Pomo, Northern, 37, 153, 170–71
Portuguese, 54, 108, 141, 243
Proto-Arabic, 114
Proto-Indo-European, 139, 143, 234
Proto-Oceanic, 33, 145, 238, 239

Qawasqar, 243
Quechua, 59, 187, 243
Quechua, Bolivian, 59, 243
Quileute, 71

Rengao, 243
Romance languages, 50, 61, 140, 141, 146, 184, 192, 193, 194, 207, 211, 232, 239
Rotuman, 243
Roviana, 145, 239
Rumanian, 110
Russian, 51, 65, 84, 85, 88, 211, 218, 232
Russian, northern dialects, 197

Saker, 11
São Tomense, 137
Selkup, 243
Serbo-Croatian, 211
Shanghainese, see Chinese
Shona, 95
Siamese, 50
Siouan languages, 19
Slave, 243

Slavic languages, 107, 140, 141, 211, 229
Slovak, 211
So, 52, 243
Somali, 108
Spanish, 65, 88, 95, 109, 141, 185, 207, 239
Suau, 24, 29
Swahili, 66, 71, 81, 95, 96, 155, 169, 188, 195, 200, 206
Swahili, Kenya Pidgin, 71
Swedish, 147

Tagalog, 82, 218, 243
Tahitian, 243
Tajik, Classical, 61
Takum, see Jukun
Tamil, 59, 71, 212, 243
Telugu, 93, 243
Thai, 243
Tibetan, 194
Tinrin, 11
Tok Pisin, 183
Tolai, 243
Tondano, 243
Tongan, 243
Toradja, 184, 244
Trukese, 219
Tswana, 23
Turkana, 27, 61, 147
Turkish, 51, 58, 148, 219, 244
Tzutujil, 179–80, 185, 244

Ukrainian, 211, 244
Uradhi, 244
Urubu-Kaapor, 185, 244

Vedic, 90
Venda, 55, 244

Waata, see Oromo
Warrungu, 71
Welsh, 244
West African Pidgin English, 48, 146
Wolof, 49
Wukari, see Jukun

Yanomama, 58, 159, 244
Yaqui, 189, 244
Yimas, 56, 244
Yoruba, 58
Yucatec Maya, 218, 219, 244
Yurak, 244

Zande, 81
Zapotec, 63, 64
Zapotec, Ixtlan, 244

//Ani, 54, 244

Index of Subjects

abnormal possession, 10, 180
abstract function, 226
abstract locative, 203
abstract possession, 9, 34–5, 39, 40, 88, 106, 109, 110, 133, 141, 155, 233, 234
abstract verb, 19, 29
abstractness, 88, 94
acceptability, grammatical, 157
Accompaniment, *see* Companion Schema
acquisition model, 47
Action Schema, 45, 47, 48, 52, 69, 72, 74, 75, 76, 78, 84, 88, 90–1, 92, 97, 102, 105, 108, 109, 111, 129, 130, 135, 136, 137, 138, 140, 141, 143, 191, 192, 194, 196, 202, 210, 212, 213, 222, 224, 229, 230, 231, 232, 234, 239
action verb, 48, 74
active voice, 91
Afterthought Schema, 149
agreement, case, 159
agreement, gender, 16
agreement in person, 60
agreement, morphosyntactic, 16
agreement, possessive, 107, 159
agreement, verbal, 113, 114, 149
alienation marker, 178
Alimentary classifier, 15, 16
alternative approach, 9
ambiguity, 71, 82, 115, 133, 237
anaphora, 112
anthropology, 46, 222–4
Anti-topic sub-schema, 148
antonymy, 223
applicative, 46
apposition, 22, 158, 159, 161, 162
archaic morphology, 174
archaism, 140
archetype, conceptual, 37, 46
areal forces, 6
areal influence, 84
areal innovation, 232
ascension, *see* possessor ascension
aspect, 7, 9, 187–208

attribute, 223
attributive possession, 11, 17, 36, 44, 58, 135, 143–186, 225, 226, 238, 239
auxiliary, 77, 88, 100, 188, 192
auxiliation, 198

B-language, 139, 211
backgrounding, 233
basic schema, 90
belief system, 2
belong-construction, 29–33, 57, 61, 65, 90–1, 92, 110, 117, 124, 225, 226
bio-cultural domain, 4
bleaching, 47
Bloomfieldian linguistics, 236
body-part syntax, 171
cardinal numeral, 187
case agreement, *see* agreement
case function, 31, 147
center of innovation, 140
chômeur, 171
Chomskyan linguistics, 236
circularity, 223
class inclusion, 223
classification, 22, 23, 162
classifier, *see* possessive classifier
clausal syntax, 112, 143
clause-initial position, 62, 79, 136, 160
clitic, 28, 115, 116
closed class, 10
clothing, 18
cognition, 7
cognitive anthropology, 222
cognitive options, 225
cognitive psychology, 45
Companion Schema, 45, 47, 53–7, 63, 66, 71, 72, 75, 76, 80, 81, 90–91, 92, 93, 95, 96, 97, 100, 101, 102 103, 106, 107, 108, 124, 134, 135, 136, 138, 144, 147, 174, 175, 194, 195, 202, 210, 211, 212, 213, 222, 228, 229, 237
comparative method, 96
complementary distribution, 85, 220

Index of subjects   271

complex schema, 202
conceptual shift, 65, 99, 201
conceptual transfer, 7, 198, 212, 236
conceptualization, universal ways of, 6
concrete locative, 203
concrete possession, 9
conditional protasis, 187
context extension, 77
context-induced reinterpretation, 76
context manipulation, 76
context model, 199
contextual constraint, 106, 119
contextual frame, 83, 84
contiguity, physical, 20
contiguity constraint, 204, 205
contingency, 223
contingent vs necessary distinction, 19
contrastive set, 17
control, 3, 19, 23, 26, 33, 34, 38, 118, 119
creolization, 137
cross-referencing, 63, 149, 159, 178

dativus sympathicus, 167
decategorialization, 52, 78, 231, 232
definiteness, 30, 35, 42, 110, 135, 136
definition, 4, 5, 15, 16, 33
deontic modality, 187, 193
dependent-marking, 143, 173, 174, 175, 177
deranking, 233
diachronic principle, 7
diachrony, 7
diathesis, 91
disambiguation, 162
discontinuous marker, 55, 231
discourse-pragmatic principles, 134, 136
double case marking, 171
double marking, 148, 173
double-subject construction, 116, 160
double subject marking, 114, 160
double-subject strategy, 62
Drink classifier, 15
dummy participant, 206

emphasis, 55
epistemic modality, 193
Equation Schema, 47, 58, 65–7, 73, 90–1, 92, 117, 124, 203, 213, 219
equative construction, 73
equative predication, 213
ergative structure, 116–17
ergative syntax, 194
erosion, 79, 80, 97, 124, 126
ethnology, 222
Euro-centric perspective, 6
event schema, 8, 9, 45, 46, 117, 134, 222–4, 228, 231, 237

everyone-type vs not everyone-type inalienable possession, 21
evolution of mankind, 234
evolutionary scale, 207
Existence Schema, 57, 63, 73, 76, 96, 219, 222
existential construction, 41, 42, 73, 136, 137, 138
existential predication, 213
existential verb, 72, 74, 106, 205, 206
expectation norm, 237
experiencer, 23, 156
experiential gestalt, 5
explanation, 6, 80, 171, 186, 221, 228–33
explanation, external, 7
explanatory framework, 212
'extended existence', 57, 58, 96
external possessor, 167
extra-linguistic forces, 7

folk definition, 223
Food classifier, 15
formal model, 215, 216, 217
fossilization, 116
frame, 46
frame extension, 84
frequency of use, 174
functional differentiation, 109

gender system, 15, 16
general construction, 216
generative grammar, 28
genitive, 2, 22, 26, 31, 37–8, 41
Genitive Schema, 47, 58–9, 63, 65, 67, 68, 69, 75, 76, 90–1, 92, 99, 101, 106, 135, 184, 185, 186, 190, 192, 194, 195, 210, 213
geo-linguistic profile, 75
gerundival morphology, 197
goal-orientation, 69
Goal Schema, 47, 59–61, 64, 66, 67, 69, 73, 75, 76, 79, 90–1, 92, 93, 98, 102, 104, 108, 109, 109–10, 112, 127, 128, 129, 130, 135, 136, 138, 139, 143, 144, 145, 146, 147, 152, 158, 161, 171, 174, 175, 176, 177, 190, 192, 194, 196, 210, 212, 213, 215, 228, 229, 232
grading, 223
grammatical concept, 43, 45, 88, 129
grammaticalization, 6, 7, 8, 76–89, 96, 101, 124, 130, 164, 171, 179, 183, 186, 188, 199, 205, 211, 216, 220, 222, 226, 228, 229, 231, 232, 235, 236, 237, 238
grammaticalization chain, 70, 208, 235
grammaticalization, degree of, 71
grammaticalization, initial stage, 133

272 *Index of subjects*

grammaticalization, principle of, 87
grammaticalization process, 214, 230

H-language, 139, 211
habeo-type, 210
head, 22, 23
head-marking, 11, 13, 143, 172–3, 174, 177, 179
historical linguistics, 7

identification, 42, 188
identity of inequality, 65
implicational hierarchy, 11
'implicational' preposition, 85
implicational universal, 227
implicature, 76
implicit possessor, 172
inanimate possession, 22, 25, 35, 37, 38, 40, 85, 87, 93, 121, 122, 133, 151, 169, 191, 232
inanimate subject, 220
inchoative possession, 130, 131
indefiniteness, 30, 31, 35
inferencing, 76, 199
inferential mechanism, 200
infinitival morphology, 197
inherent construction, 216
inherent relationship, 11
innate structure, 8
integral relationship, 11
internal reconstruction, 96
intonation peak, 158
intrinsic connection, 2
invariant semantic content, 174

juxtaposition, 22, 161, 174, 175, 177

kinship, ascending vs descending, 20, 21

language context, 84
layering, 130, 131, 151
lexical feature, 15, 17, 29
lexical predication, 213
linguistic geography, 142
literal meaning fallacy, 235
localism, 199, 200, 207, 214, 219
localist theory, localist paradigm, *see* localism
location, animate, 25
Location Schema, 47, 50–53, 57, 60, 63, 68, 69, 73, 74, 75, 76, 79, 80, 82, 83, 86–7, 88, 90–1, 92, 93, 94, 100, 102, 103, 104, 107, 108, 113, 117, 118, 123, 124, 128, 129, 135, 136, 143, 144, 145, 152, 158, 166, 174, 175, 176, 177, 192, 194, 195, 199, 201, 202, 203, 210, 211, 212, 213, 216, 218, 219, 220, 222, 224, 228, 229, 230, 231, 232, 238
locative class, 95
locative-designated predicate, 212
locative predication, 213
locative verb, 72, 74, 99, 106

major schema, 72, 75, 104–9, 132
metaphor, 43, 55, 76, 77, 156, 192, 194, 198, 199, 222
metaphor model, 198, 199
metaphorical vehicle, 77
metonymy, 76
mihi est-type, 210
minor schema, 104–9, 132, 147
modality, 194
modality, *see also* deontic, epistemic modality
modifier, 14
movement, 218
multi-purpose preposition, 57
multiple subject construction, 62

necessary relationship, 20
nominal classification, 16
nominalization, 10
nominalizing morphology, 183
normal possession, 10, 180
nuclear existence, 57, 58, 96, 99, 137, 138, 202, 207

object, indirect, 14
object-designated predicate, 211–2
oblique case, 42, 90, 96, 104, 153, 224
oblique participant, 112
opaque construction, 100, 105
open class, 10, 172
optional relationship, 20
Overlap Model, 82, 83, 85, 116, 133, 183–84
ownership, 3, 24, 32–3, 34, 37, 66, 141, 202, 204, 205, 208, 234

paradigmatic gap, 42, 228
parameter, linguistic, 5
paraphrase, 73, 74, 107, 216
part-whole, 11, 12, 19, 20, 33, 37, 121, 156, 162, 169
passive voice, 91
patient, 23
peripheral language, 140
permanent possession, 34, 35, 38–9, 40, 41, 67, 85, 87, 88, 89, 92, 95, 103, 110, 117, 119, 120, 123, 124, 125, 126, 129, 130, 131, 133, 136, 191, 220, 225
PERSON-TO-OBJECT metaphor, 88
Pertinenzdativ, 167

Index of subjects   273

phrasal syntax, 143
physical possession, 9, 34, 35, 39, 40, 88, 89, 92, 93, 94, 103, 108, 118, 119, 120, 122, 123, 124, 125, 126, 127, 129, 131, 133, 191, 220, 232, 233
polysemous category, 156
polysemous view of semantic change, 82
polysemy, 226, 235
possessee specification, 157, 161, 162
possession, abnormal, *see* abnormal possession
possession, accidental, 9, 10, 34
possession, acquired, 10
possession cline, 169
possession, communal vs individual, 23
possession, concrete, *see* concrete possession
possession, direct vs descriptive, 24
possession, former vs present, 23
possession, inanimate, *see* inanimate possession
possession, inchoative, *see* inchoative possession
possession, inherent, 9, 10, 38
possession, inseparable, 10
possession, intimate, 10
possession, intrinsic vs non-intrinsic, 20
possession, momentary, 34
possession, necessary vs optional, 21
possession, normal, *see* normal possession
possession, optional, *see* possession, necessary vs optional
possession, passive, 23
possession, qualitative, *see* qualitative possession
possession, social, *see* social possession
possession, subordinate, *see* subordinate possession
possession, transferable, 10
possessive classifier, 14, 15, 16, 22, 25
possessive specification, 170
Possessor as Experiencer, 213
Possessor as Restrictor, 213
Possessor as Theme, 213
possessor ascension (promotion, raising), 13, 14, 17, 38, 163–172, 186
possessor deletion, 13, 162, 171, 172
possessor, non-human, 9
possessor-designated predicate, 212
Possessor-of-an-act configuration, 4, 198
possessor promotion, *see* possessor ascension
possessor raising, *see* possessor ascension
possessor specification, 157, 158, 159, 161, 162, 166, 167, 170, 171
possessor topicalization, *see* topicalization

pragmatic strategy, 171
predication type, 46, 214
predicative quantifier predication type, 70
prediction, 232
presupposed information, 143
presupposition, 26
productive pattern, 130, 151
proposition, 46
propositional concept, 144
proprietive/privative predication, 55, 213
proto-language, 138
prototype, 31, 32, 33, 37, 39, 40, 46, 85, 132
provenience, 223
proximity, spatial, 5, 38, 39
pseudo-transitive, 78, 98

qualitative possession, 155

radial network, 156
raising, *see* possessor ascension, subject raising
reanalysis, 113
reconstruction, 216, 217
recursive renewal process, 133
referentiality, 93
regularities, cross-linguistic, 3, 7
reinterpretation, 184, 192, 198
relation of consequence, 49
relational concept, 10, 38, 176, 182
relational noun, 12
relative clause marker, 149
relative clause morphology, 183
resultative possession, 130

Saussurean dogma, 173
schema choice, 109, 137, 152
schema of interest, 3
script, 46
secondary possession, 178
semantic relationship, 223–4
semantic space, 204
semantics of context selection, 87
semanto-syntactic configuration, 4, 5
similarity, 220, 230
social anthropology, 46
social possession, 9
source concept, 6
Source Schema, 47, 64, 65, 70, 144, 145, 146, 150, 151, 158, 166, 174, 175, 178 184
spatial orientation, 12, 88
specialization, 79,
specification, 23, 156–63, 165, 185, 186
specifier, 14
specifying possession, 190–95, 198
sphere of influence, 3

split patterns, 173
standard of comparison, 156
stative-active language, 13
subject property, 111, 112, 160, 196
subject raising, 113
subordinate possession, 23
substrate influence, 110
synchronic variation, 98, 99, 150
synonymy, 107, 223
syntacticization, 116

target schema, 8
temporary possession, 34, 35, 39, 40, 66, 89, 92, 103, 108, 119, 122, 133, 225, 232, 233
thematic argument LOCATION, 217
thematic argument THEME, 217
theme, 218
three-stage model, 48, 49
time, 38
topic, 29, 30
Topic Schema, 50, 61–4, 67, 75, 81, 92, 101, 114, 135, 144, 148, 149, 150, 153, 160, 162, 178, 179, 186, 196, 210, 213, 230, 233
topic-comment structure, 84, 224
topicalization, possessor, 79
transitional stage, 211
transitive vs intransitive action, 23
transitive verb in abolute use, 192
transitivity, 209
transitivization, 78, 110, 111

'true' possession, 32
type-token relation, 22
typological consistency, 96
typological regularity, 110
typological universal grammar, 6, 7

underlying structure, 19, 215, 216, 221, 237
unidirectionality, 87, 94, 96, 208
universal concept, 234
universal grammar, 218
universal hierarchy, 11
universal, implicational, *see* implicational universal
universal properties of possession, 227–8
universal underlying structure, 221
universality, notions of, 22

valence, 4
Valued Possession classifier, 15
verb of existence, 50, 62, 185
verb of possession, 31
verb-final language, 175
verb-final syntax, 55
verb-initial language, 68
verb-medial language, 68
verbal property, 78, 229
voice, 30

word order, 12, 27, 30, 42, 102, 104, 135, 136, 153, 160, 161, 162, 175

zero expression, 227

Printed in the United States
43956LVS00007B/136-141